HOLLIS FRAMPTON
RECOLLECTIONS·RECREATIONS

COMPRISING MUCH OF THE OTHER WORK
⬢ OF HOLLIS FRAMPTON ⬢
DURING THE YEARS
1958–1984

ESPECIALLY CELEBRATING
THREE GRAND COOPERATIONS
WITH
⬢ MARION FALLER ⬢
NAMELY

SIXTEEN STUDIES FROM VEGETABLE LOCOMOTION (1975)
FALSE IMPRESSIONS (1979)
RITES OF PASSAGE (1983–1984)

AND

⬢ INCLUDING BUT NOT LIMITED TO ⬢
NUMEROUS COLLABORATIONS
GIFTS TO OTHERS
BOTH ACCEPTED AND REJECTED
SEVERAL FINDINGS AND OUTRIGHT THEFTS
ALL BROUGHT TOGETHER WITH SUNDRY
ORIGINAL WORKS OF THAT TIME
LARGELY AND SURREPTITIOUSLY
RECREATED OR RECOLLECTED FOR THE
PRESENT OCCASION
⬢

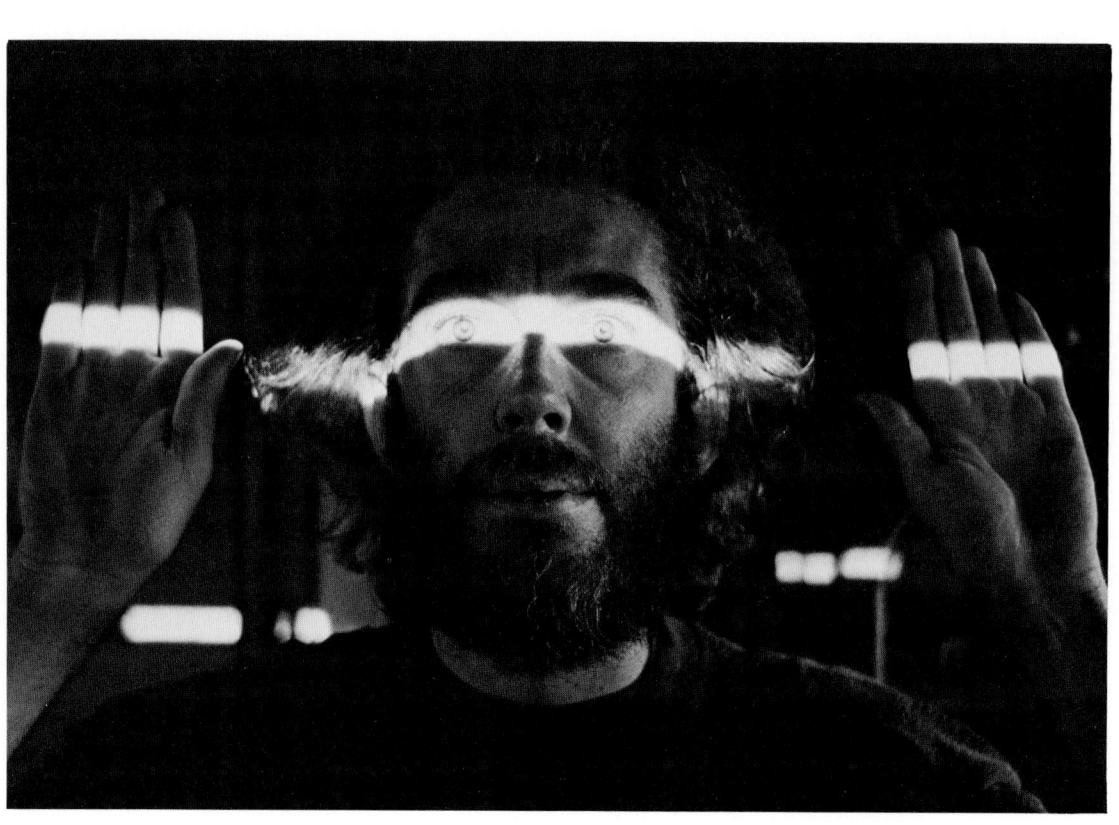

HOLLIS FRAMPTON
RECOLLECTIONS·RECREATIONS

BRUCE JENKINS
SUSAN KRANE

ALBRIGHT-KNOX ART GALLERY
BUFFALO, NEW YORK

THE MIT PRESS
CAMBRIDGE, MASSACHUSETTS
AND LONDON, ENGLAND

This publication was prepared in conjunction with the exhibition, *HOLLIS FRAMPTON: Recollections/Recreations,* organized by Susan Krane, curator, Albright-Knox Art Gallery. The exhibition was made possible by grants from the National Endowment for the Arts, a federal agency, and the New York State Council on the Arts.

September 29–November 25, 1984
Albright-Knox Art Gallery
Buffalo, New York

February 10–March 24, 1985
Long Beach Museum of Art
Long Beach, California

April 14–June 10, 1985
Neuberger Museum
State University of New York at Purchase
Purchase, New York

August 2–September 27, 1985
Laguna Gloria Art Museum
Austin, Texas

Cover: Computer portrait of the artist, c. 1975, made at a state or county fair in central New York state. Private collection.

Half-title page: Text and concept by Hollis Frampton.

Frontispiece: Marion Faller, portrait of Hollis Frampton (directed by H.F.), 1975, black and white photograph, 6⅜ x 9⁹⁄₁₆". Private collection.

REPRODUCTION CREDITS

Reproductions courtesy Estate of the Artist, except p. 108 courtesy Arthur Kres and Barbara Kres Beach, and p. 110 courtesy Walter Darby Bannard and Carl Andre.

Thomas Brown	p. 46
Marion Faller	pp. 2, 117
Hollis Frampton	pp. 14, 33, 54, 55, 67, 71, 72
Faller and Frampton	pp. 77-85
Biff Henrich	cover, 17, 24, 34-45, 47-53, 56-66, 68, 73-75, 86, 87, 89-91, 93-106, 108, 110-112, 116, 119

All rights reserved. No part of this book may be reproduced or utilized in any form or by any means, electronic or mechanical, including photocopying, recording, or by any information storage and retrieval system, without permission in writing from the publisher.
First edition
Editor: Georgette M. Hasiotis
Designer: Christine Narum-Eberle
© 1984 The Buffalo Fine Arts Academy
All works by Hollis Frampton © Estate of the Artist

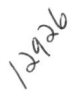

Library of Congress Cataloging in Publication Data

Jenkins, Bruce.
  Hollis Frampton, Recollections/Recreations
  Especially celebrating three grand cooperations with Marion Faller—Half T.P.

  Bibliography: p.
  1. Photography, Artistic–Exhibitions. 2. Frampton, Hollis, 1936-1984. I. Frampton, Hollis, 1936-1984. II. Krane, Susan. III. Faller, Marion. IV. Albright-Knox Art Gallery. V. Title. VI. Title: Recollections/Recreations.
TR647.F73 1984   779'.092'4   84-12563
ISBN 0-262-10030-4

CONTENTS

Foreword
Douglas G. Schultz   6

Introduction
Susan Krane   8

The "Other Work" of Hollis Frampton: A Tour   14
Bruce Jenkins

Plates   33

Illustrations   41

Chronology
Susan Krane   106

Selected Exhibitions   121

Selected Bibliography   122

Catalogue of the Exhibition   124

Acknowledgments
Susan Krane   128

FOREWORD

Hollis Frampton was a special, dynamic presence in the artistic and university community of Buffalo for nearly a decade. He encouraged the growth of photographic and later digital arts through his revolutionary role at the Center for Media Study, State University of New York at Buffalo, and through his involvement with Media Study/Buffalo. As a teacher, thinker and author, he fostered a philosophical approach and nurtured dialogue and debate, qualities seldom found in contemporary times. In his art and in his writings, the breadth and depth of his visionary intelligence are outstanding. Frampton's amazing, encyclopedic knowledge was enriched by a gentle humor, humanism and modesty: as his work provokes and delights us visually and conceptually, so it does emotionally.

In retrospect, the art historical importance of Frampton's photographic work is indisputable, and his distanced, satirical view of the sometimes strange goings-on of contemporary life is both keen and funny. The pure visual beauty and technical expertise of the work clearly speaks for itself.

First and foremost, I would like to extend my gratitude to Marion Faller for her invaluable assistance with this project. It is primarily through Marion, and the friendship and dialogue we have shared over the past three years, that I have come to know Hollis' work and developed a deep appreciation for it.

I wish to extend my gratitude to Bruce Jenkins, for the definitive scholarship in his essay, which makes this volume a valuable reference on Frampton's overall oeuvre. Susan Krane, curator, has skillfully organized all aspects of the exhibition, which includes an exceedingly diverse body of material, and has contributed a stimulating introduction as well as a chronology on the artist to this publication. I sincerely appreciate her devotion and perseverance in organizing the exhibition even during difficult circumstances.

It is with great pleasure that the Albright-Knox Art Gallery organized this tribute to Hollis Frampton's art. We thank the National Endowment for the Arts for their substantial support of the project. The New York State Council on the Arts provided additional funding.

Douglas G. Schultz
Director
Albright-Knox Art Gallery

INTRODUCTION

Susan Krane

Hollis Frampton is widely known as a theorist and filmmaker, a pioneer of the avant-garde cinema whose pivotal works have, since the late 1960s, helped define the course of film and narrative art. His explorations into the territories of meaning, perception and composition are contemporary legend. Yet before he began seriously experimenting with film some twenty years ago, Frampton was an accomplished still photographer and also made a variety of occasional pieces, such as sculptures, collages and modified found objects. He continued this "other work," as he called it, throughout his career: in recent years he had come to recognize it more clearly as an integral part of his oeuvre. When considered in an overall perspective, his non-filmic work gains further importance. Not only does it span his artistic life, but it was as well a formative occupation throughout his youth and an area of growing activity as of late. In contrast, the locus of his principal film work falls between the late sixties and mid-seventies, a consequence in part of time and logistics, since he perpetually had films underway. As making films became more expensive and as his adventuresome computer and digital arts projects more of a preoccupation, Frampton's voluminous ideas took shape with increasing frequency in tangible photographic form. Although these works remained for the most part private enterprises, they were for Frampton hardly contingent or peripheral. They are usually modest, often collaborative, and sometimes quite idiosyncratic. These works evince, however, the development of his aesthetics and intellectual vision with particular intimacy and freshness. As art objects, Frampton's photographic pieces moreover prove to be milestones in both technique and concept.

Many of Frampton's earliest photographs have survived only in the form of high quality proof prints; others were badly damaged, still others existed in various states of incompletion. Before his death in March of 1984, Frampton had discussed his ideas and many of the particulars for making exhibition prints, refabrications and realizations of several pieces he had conceived of earlier. Subsequently these guidelines were followed closely: in all cases vintage works are distinguished from recent prints. Crucial in this regard has been the advice and judgement of photographer Marion Faller, who worked closely with Hollis since 1971 and several of whose major collaborations with Frampton are included in this exhibition. In cases where information from discussion, the artist's notes, archival material or transcripts was insufficient, we excluded pieces rather than assume undue license. In his essay "Meditation Around Paul Strand," Frampton criticized a retrospective of Strand's photographs for including a disproportionate number of new prints and astutely wrote, with mockery: "What Strand has actually made, during 53 years, is a large number of negatives."[1] Such is not the case with his own work. What Frampton "made" during his prolific career was a multitude of ideas. Some were realized immediately, and others gestated over the course of years to emerge eventually as art works. The prospect of this exhibition was impetus for many works-in-progress to be brought to fruition. The abilities to ascertain with some surety the "photographer's nuance"—the specific eloquence of the print itself—and to uphold fundamental details have been the criteria governing this selection.

Frampton brought to his art, in whatever form it happened to take, an extrinsic, often anthropological view, perhaps because he approached his various media from the outside, so to speak. He came to photography via painting and poetry; to film via photography; and to his critical writings from all of the above, and still then more. His inquisitiveness was, it seems, boundless: he had a brilliance awe-inspiring for most of us yet was, at the same time, quite down-to-earth. This expansiveness freed his artwork from existing stylizations, definitions and internal constraints endemic to any one artistic genre.

The metamorphoses and the shifts in location of Frampton's art are in no sense linear. He worked on numerous ideas simultaneously, whether in thought or deed, often over long periods of time. Each realm of his work reverberated constantly with his activity in the others. For instance, many of his major films, like *Zorns Lemma,* 1970, and *nostalgia,* 1971, are based on earlier still photographs. Others, such as *Carrots and Peas,* 1969, and *Lemon,* 1969, overtly refer to painterly traditions. Conversely, the roots of the still works (themselves rarely discrete single images) can be discovered in his criticism, as is the case with *A Visitation of Insomnia,* 1970–1973 (cat. 23, p. 71).[2] Indeed, many of his theoretical writings deal with photographic history and issues that he approached variously in artwork. Specific subjects of his essays, such as Eadweard Muybridge, are too the subjects of his photographs (for example, the ironic *Sixteen Studies from VEGETABLE LOCOMOTION,* 1975, cat. 28, pp. 77-85). Like a spider's web, his work crosses back and forth on itself, interweaving previous structures and strands of thought, all the while spreading to new points of contact.

Understanding Hollis Frampton's photographic art is perhaps a keystone to seeing the span of meaning and the mechanics of his entire oeuvre. (To call him prolific would be trivial.) The development of his concept of photography is multifaceted and, typically, complex. As a student at Phillips Academy, he painted, made photographs, and pursued the study of languages and literature. Through his association with students and teachers there, he was already, as a teenager, vigorously involved in a dynamic and contemporary artistic milieu. His youthful canvases were, in fact, quite accomplished expressionistic abstractions. By the time he abandoned painting for good in the late fifties, he had absorbed a thorough knowledge of art history and the spatial tenets of modernism. He had also developed an enduring love of working with the physicality of materials. This carried through to his still work (seen in extreme in *The Temptation of St. Anthony,* 1962, cat. 7, pp. 50-51) and later to his radical, structural manipulations of film footage. His early photographs from the late fifties and sixties were thus made not only under the shadows of the ponderous giants of photography, especially Edward Weston, but also under the forceful, living tutelage of the Abstract Expressionists.

Frampton's linguistic accomplishments and literary penchants gave him a visual sensibility that was already what has, lately, been dubbed post-modern. He intuitively "read" images for their structure as much as for their beauty, keenly aware of their iconographic components and cognitive functions. Fascinated with concepts of science, encyclopedic thought and classification, Frampton approached the visual world-at-large in the same way—as a pretext of a vast vocabulary of images.[3] Photographs such as those in the series *The Secret World of Frank Stella,* 1958–1962, (cat. 1, pp. 46-49) and *Ways to Purity,* 1959, (cat. 3, pp. 41-45) are not so much influenced by the masters of painting and photography to which they nakedly refer as they are visual parodies, cathartics of weighty artistic traditions. In many cases, they are not images "taken" in the sense of photographic authorship, but rather, for instance, a Barnett Newman painting "found;" Leonardo da Vinci's Vitruvian man re-discovered on the streets of lower Manhattan; or a photographic allusion to a Robert Motherwell work claimed from a wall of worn graffiti. Typically, during the early sixties, Frampton used 2¼ x 2¼ inch negatives and heavily cropped his photographs. They are images that have been excavated from the environs, then codified further in the processes of cropping and printing.

At this time, Frampton's artistic milieu included, among others, Frank Stella and Carl Andre (both close friends from Phillips), Walter Darby Bannard, John Chamberlain, Larry Poons, James Rosenquist, and Richard Meier. His portraits of friends, done in casual series, ended up documenting a virtual pantheon of modernism. As a photographer at a time when the medium was still quite *outré,* his concerns were in some ways on the fringe: "All my friends were painters and sculptors, and the painters were, of course, in the throes of a grand final attack on illusionism. And there I was, in fact, a committed illusionist."[4] Yet, despite Frampton's overt divergencies, the objective order and stringency of minimal art are clearly paralleled in his serial and modular formats and the purported objectivity of his photographs, as well as by his use of a priori formulae and numerical systems in his films.

Integral to Frampton's photographic works, too, however, is the blatant outrage of the sixties, Pop Art. It is a factor overlooked, perhaps as a result of Pop's immediate accessibility, rampant commercial success and the concomitant denegration of its supposed intellectual vacuity. Yet for all the vagrancies for which Pop Art could then be blamed, it was one realm in the sixties which harbored illusionism, language, explorations of visual syntax and humor—aspects integral to Frampton's thinking. (Earlier works by Rauschenberg and Johns were, by comparison, still painterly and expressive.) Pop's artifice was upfront, its fascination with the world clear, and its renegade stance in relation to ethereal abstraction quite obvious. As a photographer, Frampton no doubt held such positions in empathy, even more so as he worked in commercial photo labs, routinely processing (literally and figuratively) masses of quotidian images. He later wrote of his alienation from the ideas of the high art establishment of the period:

> ...in the 1950's and '60's, one often heard the epithet "literary" applied as a pejorative to work that retained vestiges of recognizable (and thereby nameable) pretext sufficient to the identification of an imbedding deep space —although the presence of the word as a graphic sign (in Robert Motherwell's *Je t'aime* paintings, for instance, or Frank Stella's *Mary Lou* series) was accepted with routine serenity. One heard Barnett Newman admonish Larry Poons when the younger painter had published, as a show poster, a photograph incorporating an assertive pun on his own name; saw Carl Andre in ardent moral outrage at the very mention of Magritte; witnessed the monolithic public silence of the generation of Abstract Expressionists.
>
> The terms of the indictment were clear: language was suspect as the defender of illusion, and both must be purged together, in the interest of a rematerialization of a tradition besieged by the superior illusions of photography. Only the poetics of the title escaped inquisition, for a time....[5]

Given a climate generally hostile to the natural inclinations of Frampton's thinking, Pop was an ally, even if its venues into understanding the illusions with which we perceive images and the assault of the mass media were perhaps surreptitious then. Rosenquist's glossy faces and quips of gargantuan signs, or even Wesselmann's assemblage kitchen reliefs —Mondrian à la Pop—were, granted, raucous and flamboyant in sensibility compared to the studied, systematic control with which Frampton worked. Nonetheless, Frampton shared with Pop artists many interests and a philosophical bent. In his critical writings, he repeatedly urged a certain anti-elitist, catholic approach to the history of art and fostered what he later called the "metahistory" of painting, film and photography. All images, high or low in intent, even circumstantial in origin, had validity and were inextricable elements in the history of our images— and thus the history of art. In defending Rosenquist's work to Carl Andre, Frampton elucidated his posture:

> I suspect that Rosenquist's paintings irritate you, as you remarked you had noticed Flaubert's *Dictionnaire* annoying you, because they contain something of what you hadn't previously noticed yourself believing. Carl Andre, old friend, I here accuse you of believing that art, first and foremost, should be elevating. I suggest instead that we elevate *ourselves.*[6]

And later, more elaborately and with astute cynicism:

> How clean our hands are, and how pure our minds! The dollar that bought the film and paper that went into the best works I've done, the photograph of James Rosenquist I made on Palm Sunday last, and the taxi fare that took me to his studio and the dollar that kept me alive to do it, . . . all were money earned in an establishment that brings out of latency the images that plague us both. I work in a color laboratory, and nightly expend my skill and knowledge towards perfecting "commercial" photography: nylons, frozen orange juice, leaded gasoline, bread with calcium propionate and so forth. You run out to Jersey every afternoon and assist in the transport into and out of America's largest urban area of poisons for mind and body so filthy and unspeakable that I hesitate to remind you of them. The dollar you earned on the Jersey boondocks kept you alive to sit at this typewriter. Why rail against the billboard when you bring tons of Coca-Cola syrup in, to meet the desire the billboard pretends to promote? How can I clean my hands? Carl, we are not outside it. There is no crisis in art nor ever has been. The only natural activity, and all the natural activity of man, is art. The crisis is in and among us. . . .
>
> To use an image is to make another. I do it myself. I have only what is in me and before me, and can only examine the honesty of the effort by which I have come by the scraps I conserve. James Rosenquist is "in" the same thing . . . not a culture, a set of predicates, an informed and trenchant article on the latest trend, but the only human activity: art. I contend that he bears a tool; you, that he bears a weapon.[7]

Throughout his career, Frampton continually embraced a vast array of images found, altered or re-claimed (in truth, appropriated). He was among the first to experiment with Xerox art, and his xerographic series *Reasonable Facsimiles,* 1971, (cat. 25, pp. 34, 73-75) or *By Any Other Name,* 1979–1983, (cat. 29, pp. 40, 89, 90 and cat. 33, pp. 40, 91) use images culled mostly from consumer culture, arranged and fortified in a fashion that points a finger (and raises a smirk) at existing ironies, puns, and quizzical cultural habitudes. Others are mimetic references to works of art historical importance (such as *A Visitation of Insomnia,* 1970–1973, cat. 23, p. 71, is to the late nineteenth-century chronophotographs of E. J. Marey). Not surprisingly, his films, too, made use of found footage. Incorporated in *Maxwell's Demon,* 1968, is a film of Canadian Air Force exercises purchased on Canal Street for a dollar. *Works & Days,* 1969, again assisted by a Canal Street find, is an old "how-to" film on planting Victory Gardens, from which Frampton removed the sound track and then gave his signature to create what became for him a "great dance film" with allusions to the choreography of friend Yvonne Rainer.[8] His ties are obvious here with the Dada spirit and the traditions of assemblage and collage, as well as collage films such as Joseph Cornell's *Rose Hobart,* a refabrication of Columbia Picture's *East of Borneo.*[9]

The delight in intellectual humor and critical socio-cultural observations behind these works echoes of Marcel Duchamp, whom Frampton long admired and to whom he often paid homage.[10] Whether Frampton actually met or corresponded with Duchamp is to date unconfirmed. Duchamp was, however, certainly a spiritual forebearer. Frampton was fond of quoting Duchamp's definition of himself as a "sentimental scientist"—an aside of obvious interest to one also fascinated by precept and classification, although he denied sharing the sensibility outright. There are illustrative junctures in their thinking, most lucid when Frampton discusses the role of the artist as radically altered by the activities of contemporary photographers:

The received postures of Spirit Medium and Maker nearly disappear. On the deliberate level, the artist becomes a researcher, a gatherer of facts, like Confucius' ancients, who, desiring Wisdom, "sought first to extend their knowledge of particularities to the uttermost." And on the axiomatic level, where the real work is now to be done, the artist is an epistemologist.[11]

Like Duchamp, Frampton conceived of the artist as one who is involved with selecting, focusing experience, and conceptual issues. Thus we find many of his photographic works fall under the Duchampian appellation "assisted ready-made," and often deliberately present quixotical ambiguities. The title of this exhibition (designated by Frampton) even carries Duchampian inflection: "re-collections/re-creations" or pointedly "re: collections/re: creations." Such affinities stem, too, from their shared fascination with language, most jovially mirrored by a love of puns, the double entendre and the paradox. In 1972, Frampton delineated his inheritance from Duchamp:

> The rumour (anyway) that my mother's name was Rose Sélavy is substantially correct, and I think she has something to teach us all about the intimacy of the ties between language and perception.[12]

Language provided for Frampton a construct, as well as a foil, for understanding our faculties of perception. Indeed, it seems he placed word and image on opposite sides of the fulcrum on which consciousness—and his art—pivoted. The relationship of language and image is fundamental to many of his films, where soundtrack and projected vision are correlated in complex relationships. Similarly, text, explicative titles, and the appearance of words discovered by serendipity obviously play critical roles throughout the photographic work, from the *Word Pictures,* 1962–1963, (cat. 8, p. 52) to the pseudo-encyclopedic captions of *ADSVMVS ABSVMVS,* 1983, (cat. 31, pp. 93-99) which in fact are photographs of collected specimens. According to Frampton, the didactic power of the word has long dominated Western culture; the photograph, often scaled similarly to the written page and indeed "read," now rivals it for certitude as well. In his preface to Les Krims' *Fictcryptokrimsographs,* 1975, Frampton created a scenario that demonstrates the potency of photography's claim to veracity: "... in an age without refrigeration, the photograph was a kind of formaldehyde, superior even to words, serving to immobilize Reality until Culture should inexorably metabolize it into Knowledge."[13] There is here a humorous yet melancholic recognition of a situation in which the individual is passive, helplessly bombarded with multitudes of photographs that feign reality; a situation in which imitation—the souvenir—predominates.

Endemic to Frampton's works since the mid-sixties has been this cultural concept of photographic syntax. As he wrote in his essay on Weston:

> Thus the photograph is made to resemble the word, whose perpetuation is guaranteed by the mind of a whole culture, safe from moth and rust; and the photographer's art becomes the exercise of a *logos,* bringing into the world, by fiat, things that never escape....[14]

He had a strong sense that photography is ever a paltry substitute for experience—a propagator of fictions and cliches and a creator of immortal images depleted of vitality. His photographic works, elegant and beautiful as they are, are therefore not ends in themselves but instead serve as catalysts to recognition and to awareness. Their effects derive from the artist's careful manipulations of context and pretext. As such, the tenor of Frampton's photography is suspiciously akin to the aesthetic inquiries and cultural cynicisms of post-modernism and to the work of photographers heavily reliant on appropriation or the set-up, for instance Richard Prince, Barbara Kruger or Sherrie Levine. Their provocative questioning of traditional notions of authorship, an attitude intimated earlier by Pop Art, is similarly related. Recent artistic investigations of mass media imagery (typically viewed simultaneously as mute artifacts and powerful political manipulatives) were elucidated previously with brilliant humor by Frampton. In an essay of 1972, he dramatically recounts the fictive discovery of the lost Atlantis: its long sought-after archaeological remains turn out to be no more or less than a vast horde of documentary photographs, the making and staging of which were the sole purpose of the vanished civilization.[15]

Hollis Frampton's photographic work prefigured current mainstream artworld and critical interest in structuralism and appropriation. It is interesting to note that by the late sixties, Frampton and his associates, (artists in various media such as Ken Jacobs, Yvonne Rainer, Michael Snow and Twyla Tharp) had assimilated the reductivism of minimal art with integral concerns for illusionism, historic reference, autobiography and the use of vernacular forms. All were relentlessly aware of the prejudicial aspects of their respective artforms—of construct, disjuncture, and narrative. During the stasis left in the wake of minimalism and conceptualism, movement was underway in arenas outside the primary focus of the world of visual arts, ones that had never, by virtue of inherent characteristics, abandoned illusionism completely. As such, Frampton's photographic work occupies a unique place in the recent history of photography. It is an embodiment of concerns that have randomly traversed the last twenty-five years of contemporary art and have converged at the forefront today.

Frampton's "other art" is laced with intricacies and colored by the complex of his experience. The works are available to us for delectation, both visual and intellectual, on at least one immediate level, often one generously speckled with humor. Yet, in addition, each piece is frequently a rebus that with study and contemplation reveals strata of meanings, literary allusions and labyrinthine relationships with other of his projects. The conceptual rigor of Frampton's work, however, should not be mistaken for cool objectivity. Autobiographical references and his astute, sensitive observations constantly infuse his art with a warmth and a truly humanistic depth. Always on the wings, safely out of immediate view, is the presence of the artist as a man. His works are invigorated by his sheer pleasure in intellectual discovery and in knowledge: it is an enjoyment passed on in the puzzles of the oeuvre. Ultimately then, as Frampton said of his films, it is the viewer who is made the protagonist and therefore entrusted with certain responsibilities and requirements. He put it aptly: ". . . I feel the spectator is best served by laying out a dish that really requires chewing."[16] As such, an "epicurean delight" is afforded by the long-sequestered other work of Hollis Frampton.

NOTES

1. Hollis Frampton, "Meditations Around Paul Strand," *Artforum* (New York), vol. 10, no. 6, Feb. 1972, p. 52.
2. See Hollis Frampton, "For a Metahistory of Film: Commonplace Notes and Hypotheses," *Artforum* (New York), vol. 10, no. 1, Sept. 1971, p. 35 ["Film has finally attracted its own muse. Her name is Insomnia."].
3. See Hollis Frampton, "Impromptus on Edward Weston: Everything in its Place," *October* (Cambridge, Massachusetts), no. 5, summer 1978, pp. 51-52.
4. Lucy Fischer, "Frampton and the Magellan Metaphor," *American Film* (Washington, D.C.), vol. 4, no. 7, May 1979, p. 60.
5. Hollis Frampton, "Film in the House of Word," *October* (Cambridge, Massachusetts), no. 17, summer 1981, p. 61. Newman's reference was presumably to Frampton's *Larry Poons,* 1963, cat. 17, dubbed "Poons and Spoons," made for the poster for Poons' exhibition at the Green Gallery, Nov. 1963, see p. 112.
6. Hollis Frampton, "On James Rosenquist and Other Inquisitions, September 22, 1963," in *Carl Andre/Hollis Frampton: 12 Dialogues, 1962-1963* (Halifax: The Press of the Nova Scotia College of Art and Design and New York: New York University Press, 1981), p. 87.
7. Ibid. p. 92.
8. Scott MacDonald, "Interview with Hollis Frampton: The Early Years," *October* (Cambridge, Massachusetts), no. 12, spring 1980, p. 115.
9. Frampton probably knew Cornell's film early on through his friendships with Stan Brakhage and Ken Jacobs, both of whom had worked for Cornell. Listed in Frampton's resumé is also the film *Monsieur Phot: A film by Joseph Cornell* (16 mm, color, sound, uncompleted), initiated in 1973. The reference to Cornell is telling for he and Frampton shared interests in the juncture of the conscious and unconscious.
10. See Hollis Frampton, "On a Journey to Philadelphia and Consecutive Matters, October 28, 1962" in *Carl Andre/Hollis Frampton: 12 Dialogues, 1962-1963* for his discussion of an excursion with Andre to the Philadelphia Museum of Art to view works by Duchamp in the Dreier bequest as well as other works. See also Michael Snow, "Hollis Frampton Interviewed by Michael Snow," *Film Culture* (New York), nos. 48-49, winter-spring 1970, p. 7. Homages to Duchamp abound in his work: one clear example is the photograph *Larry Poons,* 1963, cat. 16, p. 55, which refers to Duchamp's *Tu m' (You-me)* (1918).
11. Hollis Frampton, "Meditations Around Paul Strand," p. 57.
12. Hollis Frampton, "Letter from Hollis Frampton to Peter Gidal on *Zorns Lemma* [25 August 1972]," *Structural Film Anthology,* Peter Gidal, ed. (London: British Film Institute), p. 75. Rose (Rrose) Sélavy was Duchamp's pseudonym and alter ego. It is a pun on the French "Eros, c'est la vie."
13. Hollis Frampton, "Fictcryptokrimsographology," in Les Krims, *Fictcryptokrimsographs* (Buffalo: Humpy Press, Inc., 1975), n.p. See also Frampton, "Impromptus on Edward Weston," *October,* p. 56, 65.
14. Hollis Frampton, "Impromptus on Edward Weston," *October,* p. 67.
15. Hollis Frampton, "Digressions on the Photographic Agony," *Artforum* (New York), vol. 2, no. 3, Nov. 1972, pp. 43-51. See also Hollis Frampton, "Incisions in History/Segments of Eternity," *Artforum* (New York), vol. 13, no. 2, Oct. 1974, pp. 39-40 and Carl Andre and Hollis Frampton, "On Forty Photographs and Consecutive Matters, Part II: February 24, 1963," in *Carl Andre/Hollis Frampton: 12 Dialogues, 1962-1963,* p. 69.
16. Fischer, "Frampton and the Magellan Metaphor," p. 62.

THE "OTHER WORK" OF HOLLIS FRAMPTON: A TOUR

Bruce Jenkins

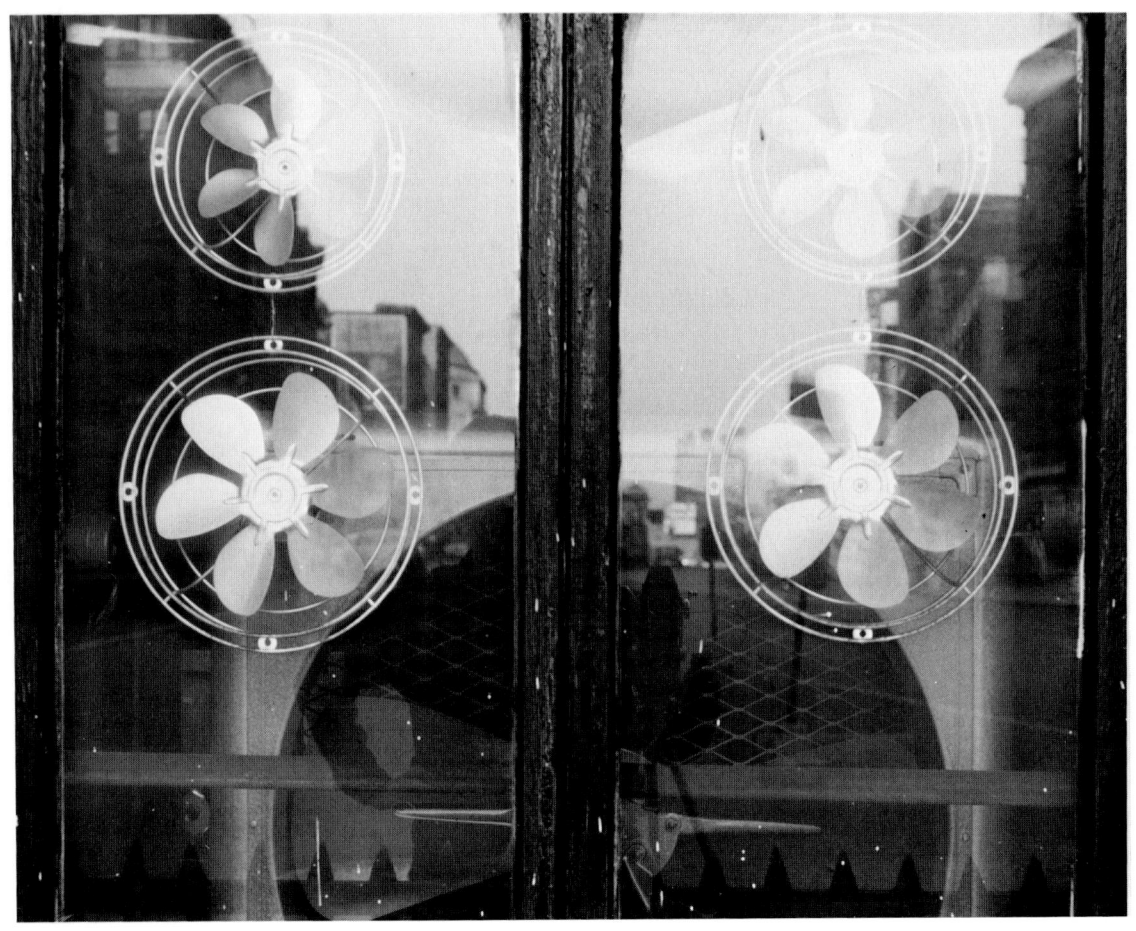

4. Untitled, 1961–1962, black and white photograph, 7½ x 9⅞

Hollis Frampton's work in other media—photography, xerography, assemblage, collage, and sculpture—is relatively unknown, tending to cluster at the limits of his more celebrated film work. Much of the photographic activity and various sculptural researches predate his "first fumblings with cinema" which began in late 1962. His subsequent photography, the xerography, and his work with found objects and materials come intermittently, at points of relative inactivity in film. So, for example, in 1973, Frampton's least productive year as a filmmaker (he completed and released only a single work, the one-second, silent, looped film *Less*), he ended a seven-year photographic hiatus by producing the series *A Visitation of Insomnia* (cat. 23, p. 71) and the sequential self-portrait *Stopping Down* (cat. 27, p. 116). Similarly, his burst of activity in color photography in the early eighties coincided with a lull in the work on his monumental film-cycle *Magellan*. Most of this still work in various media—the "flat stuff," as he called it—has been overshadowed by his cinematic output, thereby removing it from the field of active inquiry. Yet in any effort to fully grasp the substance of Frampton's oeuvre, this "other work" becomes privileged.

To some extent, it was Frampton himself who enforced this division of his artistic labors. He frequently portrayed his work in still photography as an apprenticeship for his eventual work in film: the severest phase of this self-critique coinciding, not surprisingly, with the first wave of critical attention paid to his films in the late sixties and early seventies.[1] The xerographic work, begun in 1971 during the most renowned period of his filmmaking and resumed only in the late seventies, remains virtually unseen. Although this "flat stuff" has been largely unknown, the films—Frampton's prime vehicle for artistic speculation for nearly twenty years—bear the marks of its existence. The degree to which the still photographs insinuate themselves whole or in various "assisted" forms into the films testifies to the aesthetic centrality of the photographic work. Correlatively, what are now considered central features of post-modern practice—concerns with language and illusionism, with textuality and the narrative—emerge within the films in an inchoate form that is later elaborated and formalized in the xerographic work. The films, then, informed by his photographic apprenticeship and in turn informing the xerography, can (on a viewing admittedly directed toward this end) serve to recover the "other work" and, in so doing, link the photographic and proto-cinematic aspirations of Frampton's art of the sixties with his later achievements. As an instrument of investigation, the films act as a lens to illuminate these nearly lost texts, but in focusing light they can also generate heat.

THE EARLY PHOTOGRAPHIC WORKS

In 1971, Hollis Frampton, with the assistance of Canadian artist, fellow filmmaker, and friend Michael Snow, burned a dozen of Frampton's photographs on a hotplate in his apartment in lower Manhattan. The act was recorded in a film aptly entitled *nostalgia* and afforded Frampton an occasion on which to reflect upon his first decade or so as a visual artist and to humanely dispose of a representative selection of works from this period. This disposition was for Frampton an aesthetic rite of passage, not unlike that of John Baldessari, who in 1969 burned all of his paintings and sealed them into a wall of the Jewish Museum in New York.[2] Frampton selected a more dynamic vessel to contain his burnt offerings: one that was not only repeatable, but even *reversible.* By inscribing his act of destruction onto film, he succeeded as well in transferring the content of one medium into another, recapitulating, of course, his own evolution as an artist.

With the exception of the first photograph, the images in *nostalgia* are destroyed in precisely the same order in which they had been created. That initial image is a Polaroid of Frampton's darkroom at his Walker Street apartment (cat. 24a., p. 56) and presumably portrays the site in which this and all the other photographs were produced. In a now celebrated "structural" maneuver, Frampton staggers the reading of the voice-over narration so that the burning of this first darkroom image is accompanied on the soundtrack not by a commentary on what we see, but rather by a text which describes the next image in the film, a portrait of artist Carl Andre. This dislocation of image and sound throughout the film achieves (by means of an anticipatory structure) an elegant linkage of the disparate array of images, whose ordering might otherwise lack motivation. More significant, though, is the way in which the staggering device allows the viewer to experience the film in a mnemonic manner so that, for example, when the image of Andre appears on the screen/burner, we necessarily identify it as an index of the past (albeit for us the immediate past experience of hearing the descriptive commentary) and therefore make of the appearance an occasion for recollection.

What appears on the burner in *nostalgia* is an anthology of the early photographic work, whose complexity and formal beauty often belie Frampton's critical assessment of this apprenticeship period. It is with *nostalgia* (now released as a separate photographic portfolio as well) that an examination of Frampton's early career in still photography logically begins. The individual images and the texts written to accompany their (dis)appearance in the film constitute a virtual "authorized tour" of his photographic output, standing in as they do for a vast body of other work. They serve here as a guide to particular styles, series, or genres of Frampton's early photographic activity and provide a ready-made outline for a discussion of that work. In reading back through these images, texts, and recollections, it is possible as well to note points of omission, acts of condensation, and modes of revision—all marks of Frampton's complex re-working of his past and of his art. This pathway back through the condemned images of *nostalgia* to the hundreds of others that have survived them has been "authorized" by the artist, who in describing the selection of a dozen images out of thousands of photographs, admitted to "leaving the rest for later investigators who would be doubly fortunate: first in their sentiment for their antagonist, and again in their intimacy with his work."[3]

PORTRAITURE: 1958–1966

> The mirror looks at them. They collect themselves. Carefully, as if tying a cravat, they compose their features. Insolent, serious and conscious of their looks they turn around to face the world.[4]
>
> —Rrose Sélavy

Portraits, especially of contemporary New York artists, were a major subset of Frampton's early photographic output. Of the images slated for destruction in *nostalgia,* nearly half belong to this genre, including a self-portrait, images of Carl Andre, Larry Poons, James Rosenquist, Michael Snow, and Frank Stella. Frampton had come to photography, having abandoned painting and set aside for the most part his poetic aspirations, at a time when the medium along with "its chief enforcer, language," were under severe attack:

> The terms of the indictment were clear: language was suspect as the defender of illusion, and both must be purged together, in the interest of a rematerialization of a tradition besieged by the superior illusions of photography.[5]

Frampton was in fact doubly susceptible to this indictment, maintaining as he then did an interest in merging photography and poetry. By the early sixties he had begun experimenting with methods of combining the two in photographic and film work ranging from the *Word Pictures* series, 1962–1963 (cat. 8, p. 52) to early films like *Clouds Like White Sheep,* 1962, in which he superimposed poetic phrases over images of clouds (toned "Mallarmé azure").[6]

One of Frampton's creative solutions to the issue of illusionism was to (en)counter it directly. As Man Ray had done in the twenties, he turned his camera, in a typically ironic gesture, onto the art world itself, appropriating for his task the medium's traditional repository of illusion—portraiture. The portrait of his friend and roommate, sculptor Carl Andre, which appears in *nostalgia* (cat. 24b., p. 57), was "the first photograph I ever made with the direct intention of making art." Taken in January of 1959, the shot concluded a session in which Frampton documented some of Andre's drawings. The artist is framed in closeup between a white shelf in the foreground and a bamboo shade in the rear. On the shelf rests a small picture frame through which Andre peers and a metronome, the arm of which he restrains. The effect of the composition is slightly surreal, with the small frame serving to suggest (after the manner of Magritte) a rendered space that is paradoxically congruent with itself, the metronome evoking a reflection on temporality that is

---

Fig. 1. Untitled, 1959, black and white photograph, collage; 10 x 8

doubly portrayed as restrained by and within the photograph. The image burned in *nostalgia* stands in for a number of others from the period in which Andre served as subject, and Frampton seems to have continued documenting all of the sculptor's work through 1963.

Two months after this initial portrait session, on the occasion of his twenty-third birthday, Frampton posed for a self-portrait (cat. 24c., p. 58). In all, twelve exposures were made that day, the one included in *nostalgia* being the penultimate. It shows in three-quarter view a wistful Frampton dressed in suit jacket and tie, framed simply against a white backdrop, looking off past the camera. Of the other self-portraits the narration states, "Some of them exhibit my features in more sensitive or imposing moods." Notable among these is one in which, turned partially toward the right, he offers a slight leer to the camera. According to the text (delivered during the destruction of the Andre portrait and in advance of the appearance of the other self-portrait), Frampton had "sent that one to a very pretty and sensible girl on the occasion of the vernal equinox." Despite the personal regret sounded in the narration ("I never heard from her again"), the photograph, as inscribed to his friend, constitutes one of the earliest extant examples of Frampton's experiments with textual and graphic materials (fig. 1). Executed in a manner reminiscent of constructivist photo-montage, the piece consists of the Frampton self-portrait set into a card mock-up dated with the headline 21 MARZO and inscribed with a text forming a right-angle adjacent to Frampton's right eye. The introduction of language here is characteristically comic, turning as it does on a charming pun that conflates a greeting (or greeting card) with Frampton's own visage: "On such an occasion, we consider it proper to offer Miss Ballantine our regards."

Within the same studio setup, Frampton later that year conducted a series of *Official Portraits,* 1959 (of which his own seems to have been the prototype) that again included Andre, as well as architect Richard Meier and painters Walter Darby Bannard and Frank Stella (cat. 2, p.53). Shot against white roll paper, these are full-figure portraits of the artists in jacket and tie, shown in an array of stock poses. Each artist is run through a virtual manual of arms designed to obtain the traditional expressions, poses, gestures, and actions of portraiture.

In contrast to these *Official Portraits,* the sixth image of *nostalgia* (5 of the portfolio) presents an example of a less formal variation on the theme. This image, an unposed shot of Frank Stella blowing smoke rings in his loft (cat. 24f., p. 61) seems to be the final one Frampton made of his most photographed subject. The *nostalgia* portrait serves to recall the extensive role that Stella played in Frampton's early photography, most importantly as the subject of and collaborator on *The Secret World of Frank Stella,* 1958–1962 (cat. 1, pp. 46-49). This elaborate exercise in portraiture consists of fifty-two images designed to be exhibited in what Frampton called "4 suits of 13," with top and bottom rows consisting of vertical prints and two center rows of horizontals.[7]

The series title refers to the then just-published photographic study by David Douglas Duncan, *The Private World of Pablo Picasso.*[8] In spite of the obvious level of parody —Picasso internationally venerated and living in his villa in France; Stella, then unknown and living down-and-out in lower Manhattan— Frampton does fulfill many of the conditions of such an assignment and even seems to have appropriated a few of Duncan's methods. In the Duncan study, for example, the first image presents Picasso in his bathtub. Conversely, *The Secret World of Frank Stella* concludes with a shot of Stella, seen from the back, bathing in a metal washtub (cat. 1h., p. 49). (Frampton labeled the image "Marat," owing to the

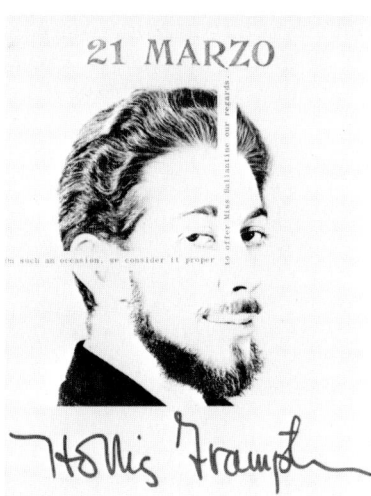

obvious historical reference evoked in the rather ghostly presence of Stella caused by Frampton's long exposure, and partly as an homage to Carl Andre's *A Marat,* an assisted ready-made of a telephone in a bowl of water.) There are shots of the artists at work (Picasso painting plates and doing etchings, Stella at work on *Getty Tomb,* cat. 1a., p. 46), as well as poses next to completed paintings (Picasso with his *Portrait of Jacqueline,* Stella with *Lake City*).

The subtexts of the Stella series range from a variety of photographic citations to a host of painterly homages. As Frampton described the series to Carl Andre, "There is no photograph in this Stella series that is not a 'gem.' There is not one shot that hasn't been made before by a photographer of reputation."[9] While an oversimplification, Frampton's work does make reference to such major figures of American photography as Edward Weston and Walker Evans and to photographic genres such as portraiture, landscape, photojournalism, and even the amateur forms of snapshot and tourist photos. Frampton often simply inserts the figure of Stella into a characteristic scene as, for example, when the artist reclines inside a thoroughly Westonic arrangement of bent girders and broken stone, stands before a typically Walker Evans frontal view of a shop (cat. 1c., p. 47), or poses full-figure in a corner formed by two of his canvases placed at right angles, creating the same compositional strategy used by photographer Irving Penn for his celebrated late-forties portraits of Duchamp and Stravinsky. The series' imagery of rubble is frequently evocative of various painterly and sculptural practices, as well, embracing a broad group of artists and ranging from classical homages to Leonardo and Mantegna to references to the work of more contemporary figures. In the final image of the second suit, for example, Stella is seen in silhouette within the interior of a half-demolished building, dramatically framed by broad-angled girders and a column that forms a stark environment reminiscent of the work of Franz Kline.

Like *nostalgia* itself, *The Secret World of Frank Stella* attempted to portray the history of the arts as if it were the daily life of a single man. In so doing, Frampton mapped out the passage of the arts onto the landscapes of New York much as in the early sixties he pierced the aesthetic facades of lower Manhattan and encountered their artistic inhabitants. If the shot of Stella blowing a smoke ring represented one of Frampton's final images of the artist, it simultaneously marked the beginning of a series of commissioned loft visits in which Frampton was hired to make portraits of artists at work. *Nostalgia* encapsulates this subgenre of Frampton's portraiture in the image of painter James Rosenquist in his studio (cat. 24g., p. 62). The shot was the last of ninety-six exposures made on Palm Sunday in 1963 and, according to the film's narration, was "unrelated to the others." Rosenquist is seated in the foreground, holding a map of the United States showing the distribution of songbirds. In the background is the usual clutter of such a workspace, with three of his paintings partially visible. Miming the working procedure of the artist, Frampton has reappropriated Rosenquist's own appropriated imagery to frame this portrait—casting the figure of the artist as but one image competing with others.

The Rosenquist session was followed by five other loft visits, all conducted in April of 1963. Metal sculptor John Chamberlain is seen at various points of labor in his studio. Of particular interest are several exposures of Chamberlain seated sideways to the camera, reading the inside of the *Daily News,* the cover of which reads MARILYN DEAD in a banner headline printed above a large portrait of the actress waving farewell (cat. 10, p. 54). Other studio visits produced environmental portraits by Frampton of Lee Bontecou in the distance working at the far end of her loft under a large pair of arched windows; of painter Friedel Dzubas similarly distant, in casual social situations; of Larry Poons at rest and at work (cat. 16, p. 55); and of Robert Morris within the environment of two of his pieces, alternately seated within the frame of *Barrier,* 1962 or on the crosspiece of *Wheels,* 1963.

Like the portrait of Rosenquist, the photograph of Michael Snow (cat. 24k., p. 66) included in *nostalgia* represents a continued movement away from traditional portraiture toward a more complex environmental posture. Frampton placed his camera behind the free-standing plexiglass and masonite partition that framed (and was part of) *Sleeve,* 1965, a sizeable *Walking Woman* installation piece by Snow. From this perspective, the glass is both a frame for the space at the far end of Snow's studio, and reflects the ten or so

Walking Woman pieces seen in the studio itself. In addition, the large view camera and the blurred image of Frampton's arm making the exposure are also included. The works from *Sleeve* (including photographs, prints, wood constructions, drawings, paintings) are seen in Frampton's image in reverse form and superimposed upon other *Walking Woman* works in the adjoining space. The resulting image is replete with lateral movement in all directions. What Frampton achieves in his rendition of the *Walking Woman* series is a restatement in photographic terms of those aspects of replication and reversibility that preoccupied Snow in canvases, cutouts, drawings, constructions, and even photographs and films.

Nostalgia's tour of Frampton's experiments with portraiture concludes with a portrait of Larry Poons reclining on a mattress (cat. 24l., p. 67). The image was taken in 1965 on a commission from *Vogue* magazine and is simultaneously one of the last such photographs Frampton would make and one of the first to be published. As with the informal portrait of Stella smoking, the image of Poons reclining in *nostalgia* signals the end of Frampton's photographic encounters with the artist. There had been at least two previous sessions: the loft visit in the spring of 1963 and an exterior shot later that fall. The latter produced a portrait which, like the image of Snow, was incorporated (quite possibly by Frampton) into an exhibition poster for the artist (p. 112). A helmeted Poons in paint-stained jumpsuit peers through what at first appear to be goggles but are, on closer inspection, two teaspoons—"Poons Spoons." A helmeted female with oversized goggles stands behind him, heroically holding a Poons canvas bearing his typical arrangement of dots. The aggressiveness of Frampton's visual "spoonerism" here captures the enchantment with visual punning, with the possibility of a linguistic reading of images, that pervades so much of his filmic and "other" work.[10]

These images from *nostalgia* and the many others that they summarize recall Frampton's somewhat unlikely origins as a portrait photographer. Edward Weston began his career with portraiture as well, renouncing this genre in the teens when an encounter with advanced forms of painting and sculpture reshaped his vision of the possibilities of the photographic image. Frampton's encounter with the advanced art of his generation led to the early experiments with portraiture, experiments which he later renounced and publicly destroyed—but not, however, before he had expropriated a number of valuable lessons which came to inform much of his later work. By surveying a range of visual artists he was able to compile a series of photographic interpretations of movements in painting and sculpture of the time, and to derive analogues for a distinctly modernist agenda for the camera arts that could inflect the traditions of that medium with the visual lessons and broader artistic lexicon of sixties' art making. In addition, these early portraits mark the initial deployment by Frampton of a number of devices and global strategies that reoccur consistently throughout the films and in other media: interpolation of textual and graphic materials (as in the Miss Ballantine self-portrait), parody (most obvious in the *Official Portraits* and *The Secret World of Frank Stella*), allusion and homage, metaphor, and visual language play.

STREET SCENES: 1959–1963

> [Should not] the street be thought of as one of the fine arts?[11]
>
> —*Fernand Léger*

Another direction in which Frampton's early photographic work went was into the streets—in some ways a logical outgrowth of the increasing distance that he maintained from his portrait subjects as environmental factors began to supplant traditional aspects of portraiture. This movement toward the streets is signaled in the image of the cabinetmaker's window in *nostalgia* (cat. 24d., p. 59), a photograph with a rather ancient look suggestive perhaps of Atget's inventory of such subjects.

Frampton's narration for this image describes a series of photographs made over a period of years of the same window. The others, as the commentary notes, were destroyed, but remaining from roughly the same period is an entire series, *Ways to Purity,* 1959 (cat. 3, pp. 41-45), which consists of images taken on the streets of lower Manhattan. In one version, the cabinetmaker's window was to have become the thirteenth and final image in the series. The twelve images that now comprise the work seem to have been made principally in the fall of 1959

19

and taken during Frampton's almost daily commute from his apartment on Mulberry Street to Frank Stella's at West Broadway and Broome Street above the Purity restaurant. In capturing points of his various pathways to Stella, the peripatetic Frampton attempts to encapsulate certain trajectories of style within the contemporary art world, commenting playfully on their "purity."

Frampton's twelve images, all titled according to their pretextual sites, contain visual homages (or perhaps, at times, parodies), as he photographs surfaces in a manner that mimes the output of painterly practice. The penultimate photograph of the series, *450 Broome Street* (cat. 3k., p. 45), for example, consists of decorative architectural details from a building with colonnades symmetrically rendered with twin floral-patterned friezes. This stonework is depicted in a brilliant tone that makes the image (already suggestive of the classical symmetry of Louise Nevelson's sculptural assemblages) point rather precisely to her "White Show" presented as part of the Museum of Modern Art exhibition *16 Americans* in 1959. Similarly, *137 Prince Street* (cat. 3h., p. 44), with its iconographic "found" image and piece of graffiti text, simultaneously calls forth Robert Motherwell's quasi-figurative *Fishes with Red Stripe,* 1954, and mimes the central conceit of his *Je t'aime* series, 1955–1957, which interpolates the handwritten phrase into abstract compositions. Other homages within the series include a comic swipe at photographer Minor White in *"40" Crosby Street* (cat. 3c., p. 42), an evocative nod to the work of Alberto Burri in *154 Spring Street* (cat. 3d., p. 42), and a rather striking example of constructivist design (particularly the drawings, posters, and prints of El Lissitzky and Moholy-Nagy) in *49 Prince Street* (cat. 3f., p. 43).

The first and last shots serve to anchor the notion of Frampton's own aesthetic journey and to buttress the series' ironic punning title. The opening image, *488 Broadway* (cat. 3a., p. 41), is a cut-out of thirty-four hexagonal glass tiles vertically mounted and juxtaposed with six vertically stacked rectangles which illustrate the gray scale. The hexagons are less relevant for their location than for the function they will serve in later work as a signature for the artist. The final image, labeled a "terminal hoax" by Frampton in his notes, consists of two shots. The main portion depicts an old tenement building that is rather abruptly capped by an imaginary frieze (obviously appropriated from another building, another image) which incorporates the word PURITY in block letters and a circular advertising image bearing the inscription: DRINK Coca-Cola. This message engenders a simple, rebus-like critique of what might be termed the commercialization of "PURITY" and serves to comically inflect and partially politicize the reading of homage within the work.

The other example of Frampton's street imagery in *nostalgia* is, like the earlier image of the cabinetmaker's shop, of a window (cat. 24h., p. 63). Frampton refers to the image in his notes as "New Name," principally because the window, which opens onto the interior of a rather ornate bank lobby, has been inscribed "with a forefinger, on the dusty pane" with the caption *"I like my new name."* The apparent impulse behind the image has to do with an interest in the work of the French photographer Jacques-Henri Lartigue: ". . . and I wanted to make photographs as mysterious as his, without, however, attempting to comprehend his wit." A more compelling citation, however, might be Duchamp's *The Bride Stripped Bare by Her Bachelors, Even (the Large Glass),* 1915–1923, which, like Frampton's pretextual subject, was renamed. *The Large Glass* is composed of a double casement of which the lower panel frames an apparatus *(The Chocolate Grinder)* suspended in a manner not unlike the bank's veiled chandelier. For Frampton, Duchamp emblematized a complex modernist practice that seemed to encompass all of the arts (even the "anemic" cinema) and that was (as with Frampton) strongly inflected by a concern with language and humor. Frampton's glass highlights these shared aspirations in an homage inscribed with the signature of its maker (the Frampton persona indicated by hexagonal forms in the upper panel) and the aleatory presence of a found text. It is this last feature, the appearance of words within an actuality, that had now begun to fascinate Frampton.

Beginning in the fall of 1962, around the same time that he began experimenting with film, Frampton started to collect still images in which words appear. The *Word Pictures* (cat. 8, p. 52) were eventually to form the core of material for one of Frampton's most celebrated films, *Zorns Lemma,* 1970, and were based largely on his fascination with the spatial paradoxes that these images pose for the viewer. As he explained:

> . . . looking at a photograph of a world situated in an illusionist space, be it deep or shallow, involves the perceiver, paradoxically, in two simultaneous activities which seem to be at odds with each other.[12]

The illusionist cues of the photographic image engage the viewer in recreating the depth and palpability of the profilmic space, while the inclusion of words immediately stops the eye and collapses the image into a flat, book-like space of reading.

Frampton made hundreds of *Word Pictures* in black and white over the period of a year or so, photographing shop windows, awnings, billboards, posters, neon signs, subway signs, graffiti—any form of legible text one might encounter within an urban area. He continued to expand the series until late 1963, when having already decided to shift the work onto film, he attempted to animate the still photographs, only to discover that rephotography transformed the entire photograph (text and spatial depth) into a flat object: "This meant that my treasured spatial paradox was lost entirely."[13] Frampton abandoned the photographic series and initiated what was to become a seven-year project of filming (in color) his set of word pictures. Few of the images from the photographic series remain (although about twenty of these black and white photographs were interpolated into the array of nearly 1,300 word images that appear finally in *Zorns Lemma).*

ART DOCUMENTS/STILL LIFE: 1961–1965

> Wit is really never purposeless even if the thought contained therein shows no tendency and merely serves a theoretical, intellectual interest.[14]
>
> *–Sigmund Freud*

While Frampton photographed the work of a number of painters and sculptors throughout the early sixties, he also on occasion created still life documents of his own work in other media. *Nostalgia* intimates the other artistic forms in which he engaged at various points in his early career, as for example, in a photographic document of one of his sculptural pieces, *A Cast of Thousands,* 1961 (cat. 24e., p. 60). The cast itself consists of two plates for molding the numerals 1000, but in printing the photograph, Frampton reversed the numerals to "enhance their intelligibility."

A Cast of Thousands is perhaps the most notable work from his limited range of sculptural endeavors which had begun a year earlier in Ohio when he completed a wood sculpture carved from a railroad tie. In discussion with Carl Andre, however, he disclaimed such work as mere research, not "sculpture activity."[15] Much the same could probably be said of other lost pieces from that period, including a pair of geometric reliefs constructed from empty cans and a tinker-toy assemblage. Perhaps the only work comparable to *A Cast of Thousands* in its punning assault on art making was the unexecuted companion piece *Years in the Making,* a design Frampton sketched involving the eventual fabrication of the titled phrase itself as a wood relief. The carving of the individual block letters would bear the marks of a gradual lessening of craft to a point where the letters would degenerate into either sawdust or an uncarved block.

While *A Cast of Thousands* delivers a humorous assault on contemporary sculptural activity, another photograph from *nostalgia* suggests an analogous critique of painterly practice. Frampton's image of decaying canned spaghetti (cat. 24j., p. 65) comes from a photographic series he undertook in August of 1964 for his friend James Rosenquist, who needed an image of "a suitably random arrangement of pasta strands." Frampton complied: "I set up my camera above an empty darkroom tray, opened a Number 2 can of Franco-American Spaghetti, and poured it out." According to the commentary, the image of freshly poured spaghetti was delivered to Rosenquist, but Frampton persisted with the piece by documenting daily its decomposition into desiccated, mold-encrusted pasta.

Frampton's photograph seems to have been used by Rosenquist in a number of paintings and lithographs, most notably *Spaghetti and Grass,* 1965, where the strands from Frampton's image form the upper half of the lithograph. Frampton later contrasted this initial image and a subsequent one of the decomposed product in a pair of color photographs (cat. 21, p. 33). Of particular interest in these images is the double temporal reading implied by their painterly pretexts: not only do they portray, in condensed form, the passage of time, but they also present a rather humorous reversal of a then-recent development within the history of the New York School of painting. From this perspective, the first image serves to invoke and characterize, literally and figuratively, the emergence of Pop Art while the later photograph bears uncanny resemblance to a generalized Abstract Expressionist mode of composition. From the poured effects in the upper right corner to the modeled and veiled compositions against black, it is quite simply a painterly pasta.

ANOMALIES/HERMENEUTICS: 1964–1967

> Never did the Greeks reach a more significant consummation to their culture, and it [the toilet in his photograph *Excusado*] somehow reminded me, in the glory of its chaste convolutions and in its swelling, sweeping, forward movement of finely progressing contours, of the Victory of Samothrace.[16]
>
> —Edward Weston

The humor that inflects Frampton's meditation on contemporary sculpture and painting, evidenced respectively in *A Cast of Thousands* and the spaghetti images, shifts focus in subsequent work from the making of art to the reception of art. While not in the generic sense hermeneutic images, these photographs are invested by their texts with other, deeper meanings so that, in a literal sense, the images become the site for interpretation. They represent an aesthetic integration of image and text in which the commentary serves no longer as exegesis, but as a formal component of a verbal conceptualist work.

In the first of these images (cat 24i., p. 64), Frampton juxtaposes a view camera portrait of two decrepit-looking pull-chain toilets with an elegant art-historical analysis of the image "as an imitation of a painted renaissance crucifixion." In phrases seemingly culled from textbook descriptions, Frampton constructs a hilarious iconographic reading of such banal details as a toilet with a closed bowl (the Blessed Virgin), the left one with a raised lid (St. Mary Magdalene), and the roll of toilet paper lying on the floor (the skull of Adam). This elaborate reading concludes with speculation about the iconography of two bare light bulbs hanging in front of each stall. It is tempting to seek the identity of these luminous details not from among the Christian saints, but rather from among the more secular forces behind Frampton's own art making. The photograph is thoroughly Westonic: while the text parodies Weston's surprising invocation of the Victory of Samothrace in reference to his own image of a toilet in *Excusado,* 1925, the image parodies the actual look of a later rendition of the motif in *Golden Circle Mine,* 1939. The re-contextualization of Frampton's subject, on the other hand, bears the mark of that "sentimental scientist," Marcel Duchamp, and refers, of course, to one of Duchamp's inaugural acts, the exhibition of a urinal.

An analogous incongruity of image and interpretation occurs with the final photograph from *nostalgia,* an appropriated news photo taken from the pages of the *Daily News* of September 22, 1967 (cat. 24m., p. 68). The subject, a Texas fruit-grower crouching in his flooded citrus grove, holding remnants of a lost grapefruit crop, is rendered with stock gestures in the anonymous style of the natural disaster genre of photojournalism. Frampton inflects this overdetermined photograph by offering a description of the image recast in the rhetoric of formalist art criticism. Under the sway of this analysis, details are described in formal terms without recourse to the customary assumptions employed in realist readings of the photographic image. The fruit-grower, for example, is not seen to be squatting in his flooded grove, but is caught "in the midst of a display of spheres, each about the size of a grapefruit, and of some nondescript light color." The effect of such a reading is humorous, given the banality of the subject and the defamiliarization attendant upon the fine arts context provided. As with the image of toilets, Frampton's wit acts out a double-edged aggression toward both photography and art-historical/critical methods while attempting to reconcile these two seemingly unassimilable discourses.

While these final images from *nostalgia* appear anomalous in relation to Frampton's total output, they in fact reflect the overall ambition of his first period of photography, and foreshadow his later xerographic studies. The underpinnings for much of the work involved a desire to make of photography a modernist art comparable to painting and sculpture. The means to such an end were diverse, offering Frampton an open set of artistic options that far exceeded those that his photographic heritage alone could afford. In attempting to harmonize his photographic work with the contemporary plastic and visual arts, Frampton began by training his camera upon the artists themselves, upon their working procedures, and then upon the artwork itself. His ability to visualize with the camera these new forms within painting and sculpture soon alerted him to the presence of aesthetic forms discoverable or recoverable in the world at large. In a final stage of development, he simply expanded the range of suitable materials to include not only his own experiments in the medium, but also the work of others. As the workings of the film *nostalgia* amply demonstrated, art could proceed just as readily from appropriation as from creation. In this expanded arena, it was no longer necessary to employ a camera in order to "take" an image.

XEROGRAPHY

> A certain appetite of the mind can, then, find more nourishment in the label on the can than in its contents: a poetic, if wayward, feast.
>
> If that appetite came with photography, and grew in film, it has not found its limit; rather it seeks it in a *metapraxis* of observation, analysis, production.[17]
>
> —Hollis Frampton

In 1971, amidst work on his long serial film *Hapax Legomena,* Frampton undertook his first efforts in xerography and worked discontinuously in that medium for twelve years. The work emerged partially out of the process of reappropriation begun in *nostalgia* and can be further traced to Frampton's linguistically-inflected sculpture and even to some of the photographic series. A stronger basis, however, stems from Frampton's major encounter with the confluence of text and image, of names and spaces, that inflect his 1970 feature film *Zorns Lemma,* a key transitional work that serves both as a summary of his early still photography and films and as a precursor of the later xerographic studies.

Zorns Lemma represented a major departure from the purely photographic character of the earlier films and marked the incorporation of methods from the other visual arts. In interpolating photographs from his *Word Pictures* into the film, for example, Frampton opted not merely to rephotograph them, but to place them into mixed-media assemblages in which the black and white photographs from the early sixties enter into a series of surreal encounters with an array of banal or outrageous found objects. These rectified ready-mades include a photograph of shop windows (the word picture for "Depot" with a glass eyeball atop it), graffiti ("May" with a gold watch and chain laid upon it), and carved stone inscriptions ("Angel" with a pair of red dice on top).

In a series of collages in the film, Frampton demonstrated his willingness to take his imagery in hand as a physical material.[18] Both the process and the subjects are culled from the field of contemporary painting. The work of Rauschenberg, for example, is evoked in a series of collages that Frampton assembled from news photos that are often inverted, printed in negative, and/or tinted. These images achieve a dematerialization of the photographic material that mimes both the inventory of standard imagery and the material processes of Rauschenberg's work from the late fifties and early sixties. Perhaps more striking are the careful citations to the work of James Rosenquist, from whom Frampton seems to borrow not only iconography and technique, but an apperceptive determination toward visual recognition and decoding. In the word picture collage of "Own," for example, Frampton invokes Rosenquist's appropriation of advertising imagery and his interpolation of textual material drawn from commercials. This image of an inverted advertising photo of a shiny red and chrome automobile with the word "own" affixed to a fender clearly recalls in its composition Rosenquist's *I Love You With My Ford,* 1961, and *Lanai,* 1964. In another group of collages (fig. 2), Frampton refers to the work of abstract painters: in the image for "Fort" miming Noland's chevron series, in "Dildoe" cartooning Poons's dotted gridwork.

Zorns Lemma's playful cataloguing of the principal aesthetic practices of late fifties-early sixties art making required Frampton to apply materials and methods that exceeded the purely photographic conventions of the camera arts. On this level, then, the film became the testing ground for experiments in collage, with rectified ready-mades, with found material, and with the complex relationships that bind text to image—all of which emerge again in the

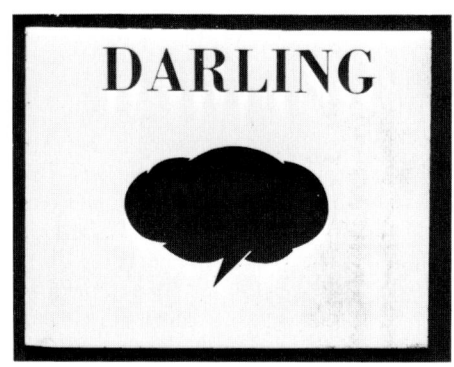
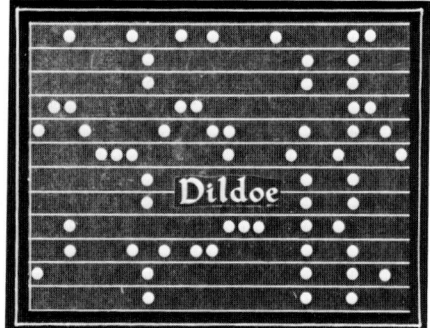
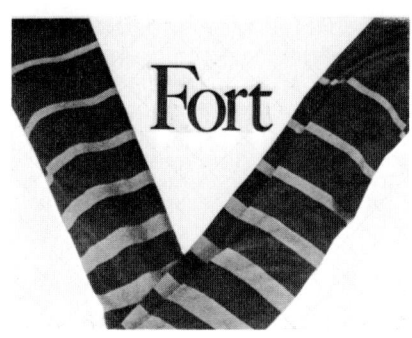
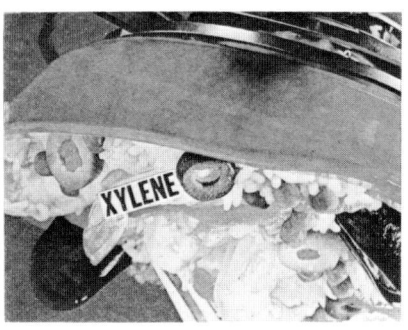

seventies, not in the film work, but in the xerographic studies.

REASONABLE FACSIMILES: 1971

The first of Frampton's three xerographic series, *Reasonable Facsimiles* employs a set of appropriational strategies that transforms a group of documents into seven rectified ready-mades. Five of these laminated pieces involve texts by the artist (lists, artistic aphorisms, sketches for abandoned projects); two derive from other sources (a found letter, an advertising illustration appropriated from a historical painting). Except for the final reappropriated image, these are primarily textual pieces in which, nonetheless, the reproduction of the original work is often invested with graphic and even pictorial qualities.

Means and Ends Belong to Different Sets (cat. 25c., p. 34) presents an aphoristic text which reflexively opens onto several of the aesthetic issues explored within the series. The title may well have engendered the complex word matrices of *Zorns Lemma* or the seven-part structure of the serial *Hapax Legomena*. Here, it seems to generate a piece in which both the original text and the xerographic means of production clearly differ from the finished work. The facsimile, in fact, bears the marks of several forms of revision that may well challenge reason. The blue lines of the original legal pad scrap, for example, emerge as "applied" red lines in the facsimile. More puzzling, perhaps, is the manner in which the copy appears more complete than the original, which exhibits a semi-circular gap at the top. The writing, too, seems to differ. While verifiably the same, the facsimile hand seems more kinetic, squigglier than in the original. Even the signs of the aesthetic appropriation are transposed—the artist's stamp appearing on the original and a typed version of the aphorism, now in the mode of a title, underscoring the facsimile.

Other original texts recycled by Frampton into *Reasonable Facsimiles* stem from particular projects rather than general speculation. *Notes for a Project Abandoned in 1963* (cat. 25d., p. 73), for example, combines three separate

---

Fig. 2. Four undated cells for the film *Zorns Lemma,* 1970. Top to bottom: black and white collage, 3½ x 4¼ ; black and white collage, 3½ x 4⅝ ; color collage, 3⁷⁄₁₆ x 4½ ; color collage, 3¼ x 4¼

lists handwritten by the artist on memo slips and assembled (collaged) onto a single sheet of xerography. The list on the upper left consists of ten items that simultaneously recall a shopping list for a trip to the hardware store and a checklist of Duchampian ready-mades, including at least two items that fit into both: a comb and a ruler. Opposite is a facsimile of a straight grocery shopping list detailing staples, condiments, and treats. The bottom list seems dialectically related to the others in its elaboration of the refuse and rejected by-products of daily domestic consumption: "shit," "butts," "coffee grounds and eggshells (garbage)." In its concreteness, the *Notes* mimes Duchamp's often ambiguous inventory of such materials, as in his *Receipt,* 1918. Frampton limits the means of "rectifying" these lists to a simple typed subtitling.

A similar procedure is employed in *Authentication* (cat. 25a., p. 73), the text of which consists of a facsimile of a "Dear John" letter evidently discarded or lost. *Authentication* derives from that rare genre of "unhappy ready-mades" and could well be classified as a doubled case of the form. Like Duchamp's output of such work, the physical materials of the piece were at a crucial point in their history unfelicitously handled—left wet, torn, and crumbled for the artist to discover.[19] In a more conventional sense, as well, *Authentication* partakes of unhappiness, since the content of its text bespeaks the traditional sorrows of a romantic triangle. Frampton has authenticated this latter aspect by typing out the contents of the letter and omitting all the proper names, including God, to (according to the *Dragnet* credo) "protect the innocent."

Matching Accessories (cat. 25b., p. 34) twice recycles the same painterly scene that Courvoisier ("The Cognac of Napoleon") had previously appropriated for its more direct commerce of image and text. In one variation, a grainy, muddy Xerox, Frampton has poorly reproduced this courtly scene and outlines the figure of Napoleon with "applied" red. In the other, a black and white schematic copy of the painting in which only the figure of Napoleon is rectified, his boots and the hat in his hand have been filled in red. The title of the piece derives from this last gesture, which comically reduces the complex iconography of the historical painting and the complicit codes of advertising imagery into a single domestic register of explanation.

FALSE IMPRESSIONS: 1979

Frampton's comic appropriation of advertising imagery in *Matching Accessories* prefigures the emergence of such material in his collaborative series with photographer Marion Faller, *False Impressions* (cat. 30, pp. 35, 86, 87). In the twenty-one works of the series, Frampton and Faller humorously assail the seriousness of semiotic attempts to unmask signifying systems within the mass visual culture of advertising, the cinema, and photojournalism. In *False Impressions,* the artists set their sights upon the same terrain, producing an analytical art that reveals and exploits the material falsifications, camera fictions, reappropriations, and cultural iconography that characterize the commerce of signs within contemporary social practice.

A dominant concern of the series is the literal inventory of falsifications perpetrated in the materials and processes of advertising imagery. In *Two exemplary applications of applied color,* Frampton and Faller juxtapose two simple ads in which black and white photographs of products (a scarlet maple tree and a kidney-shaped swimming pool) are enhanced by applied color. Enhancements based on scale are comically captured in *Your eyes are bigger than your stomach,* a complete rendering of a Post Raisin Bran ad which features a massive spoonful of the product subtended by a miniscule disclaimer that Frampton and Faller enlarge in their one rectifying maneuver: "Photo enlarged to show texture." A similar fiction is laid bare within *Still life with living room,* which comments upon a hyperbolic scene of an elaborate feast of American-style cuisine crammed into the traditional confines of an American living room.

A parallel area of interest is the confluence of art (and art-historical matter) with the design and content of commercial images. *If Muybridge were alive today, he'd turn over in his grave* (cat. 30d., p. 86) recycles an ad from the *New York Times* that features a sequential photographic display of shoes against a grid backdrop (reminiscent of Muybridge's "Human Locomotion" studies). Frampton and Faller annotate the facsimile of the ad with ten frames from one of Muybridge's studies, three frames from their own humorous homage to

Muybridge, *Sixteen Studies from VEGETABLE LOCOMOTION,* and a humor magazine's recreation full of tripping and toe-stubbing. A similar strategy is applied to the dynamic image of a golfer in action used in a J.C. Penney sweater ad that is juxtaposed with Harold E. Edgerton's mid-thirties stroboscopic photograph of the same subject (cat. 30e., p. 87). In still another exposé of blatant expropriation, Frampton and Faller encircle a boot ad from a fashion magazine with four images from Eleanor Antin's *100 Boots* series.

A related source of material emerges from the photographic profession itself, with its attendant fictions, coincidences, and absurdities. In *Somehow it loses something in translation,* Frampton and Faller reproduce a two-page prospectus for a series by French photographer Lucien Clergue that raises mistranslation into a comic art. In *More than we needed to know,* a graphic image of a nude woman being ogled by a group of gallery-goers is appended with the standard data on the camera and lens used, the film type, shutter speed, etc. *Out, damned spot! out, I say!* is a collage of three pages from *Photo-Lab-Index* elaborating no less than fifteen forms of streaking, blotching, and blurring, and offering rather bleak prognoses under the rubric, "Remedy." Finally, in *The conquest of culture and nature* (cat. 30g., p. 35), the xerographers straightforwardly juxtapose covers from *Filmmakers Newsletter* and *Sports Afield* bearing identical images.

The conflation of history and biography that had figured in earlier works like *nostalgia* and *The Secret World of Frank Stella* resurfaces as a theme in *False Impressions* as well. Frampton and Faller include in the series a collection of assembled photographic curios, as if to suggest that the history of camera fictions and oddities were but the photo album of a single family. *From the Virgin Mary's family album* consists of a copy of a small classified ad for a "camera snapshot of the snow in the trees and it turns out to be a rare photo of Christ Our Lord" and the collector's item itself—a suggestive abstract composition that bears no small resemblance to the Son of God. *Uncle Rudy at the fourth cervical vertebra* (cat 30b., p. 86) reproduces Arthur Mole's famous portrait of Woodrow Wilson composed of 21,000 light and dark attired "officers and enlisted men," with a small arrow affixed by Frampton and Faller indicating one soldier's head as the purported relative. In *Toad Tower* the xerographers insert an award-winning snapshot of a pyramid composed of five toads into an ornate picture frame; this in turn is inserted into a Xeroxed background of a mushroom-spiced forest floor—the likely site for this different species of family to display its framed portrait.

BY ANY OTHER NAME: 1979–1983

Concurrent with the production and collection of material for *False Impressions,* Frampton initiated an open-ended series consisting of unmodified color Xeroxes of can labels, product boxes, labels from bottles, printed product wraps, and crate labels. Like *Zorns Lemma* and the series of *Word Pictures,* the seventy pieces that comprise *By Any Other Name* (cat. 29, pp. 40, 89-90 and cat. 33, pp. 40, 91) present a configurational spectrum in which the spaces and discourses of text and image daily convene on the shelves of our pantry. In contrast to *False Impressions,* Frampton here presents the labels, boxes, wrappings, etc. in "unassisted" form, leaving his mode of critique and commentary to the original process of selection and to the titles he concocts for each. These two interpretive modes are closely aligned by one of the few rules governing the series—that brand name and product be as unrelated as "Bumblebees" are to tuna and that the label display words and illustrations for both terms. The experience of *Zorns Lemma* had demonstrated the truly arbitrary nature of naming; *By Any Other Name* presents some of the more outrageous case studies of the phenomenon. The titles that Frampton provides in turn play upon the unmotivated forms of nomination that link objects, people, places, a vast range of physical phenomena, and even history with items of consumption. He simply unanchors the referents and then reverses their relationship to create equally unmotivated, but radically different products for the marketplace.

Frampton's singular focus upon the process of naming embraces linguistic and visual metaphors. The "contradictory images" obtained by nomination must ultimately cohabitate within the same space—the flattened field of the printed label. Almost invariably, the balance between these items, the product and its iconographic double, results in comic inversions of scale (a phenomenon of commercial practice that was bared by *Your eyes are bigger than your stomach* from the *False Impressions* series). In *Blue Fruit Brand Pines for Salad,* for example, each piece of fruit in its still-life posture equals the size of the pine tree. *Bamboo Shoot Brand Globes* represents an even more ambitious inversion of scale in which the shoots on a plate emerge as larger than the world itself (portrayed on a globe featuring Asia and the Pacific). Equally odd are the comparisons with forces of nature, as in the inversion enacted between large but banal lemons and the spectacle of an iridescent meteor (cat 33e., p. 40) or between huge Magritte-like tomatoes and a schooner besieged by a hurricane.

Even the fictive figures that endorse many of these articles of consumption suffer from this diminution. Neither the Blue Boy nor the Blue Goose (cat. 33b., p. 91) compare in mass to the beans and fruit they respectively adorn. Even such venerable figures as Grandma Brown, Ole Skipper, the Quaker, Cristofo Colombo, and Chef Boy-ar-dee seem dwarfed by their products. (The last is another exemplary case of "applied color," being virtually the same hue as his pasta and tomato sauce.) Only the Green Giant is allowed to tower over the product he endorses.

The lessons to be gleaned from *By Any Other Name* exceed the seventy examples placed under its rubric. Like the Duchampian readymade, the works exert their force simultaneously against the practices of the world at large and against that smaller domain known as art. A cultural morphology emerges that is based upon an archive that, as Frampton recalled, was not always fit for human consumption. The *metapraxis* exercised within this work, however, is the result not only of a lifetime spent at the supermarket, but of one devoted to satisfying a "certain appetite of the mind."[20]

SERIAL PHOTOGRAPHY—THE RETURN OF THE MUSE

> This instrument, usually constructed for the amusement of children, generally represents grotesque or fantastic figures moving in a ridiculous manner. But it has occurred to us that, by depicting on the apparatus figures constructed with care, and representing faithfully the successive attitudes of the body during walking, running, etc., we might reproduce the appearance of different kinds of progression employed by man.[21]
>
> —E. J. Marey

In 1972, Frampton formally embarked upon his most ambitious project, the film cycle *Magellan.* This leviathan serial work would consume some thirty-six hours of film and was designed to be seen over a period of one year and four days. But beyond the sheer size of it, the magnitude of complexity informing the global strategies that shaped the work as a whole and the immense range of materials and devices that would be interpolated within each section were without precedent in the history of cinema. Frampton signaled the magnitude of his project in the figure of the eponymous Magellan. "During his 5-year voyage," Frampton noted, "Magellan trespasses (alive and dead) upon every psycholinguistic 'time-zone,' circumambulating the whole of human experience as a kind of somnambulist."[22] Magellan served, then, as the figurative center of this vast film series which attempted a complete tour of the imaginative world.

Magellan represented Frampton's supreme metahistorical contribution to the understanding of film and its complex social, cultural, and aesthetic underpinnings. Through its year-long cycle of screenings, the serial work would chart the development of the medium against the backdrop of the rise of modernism in the visual arts and the evolution of human consciousness. These intertwined trajectories could be seen at work in the earliest portions of the film in which Frampton returned to the origins of cinema in the actualities of the Lumière Brothers and the one-shot comedies and trick films that spawned the mainstream cinema. This enterprise fulfilled a promise Frampton had made years before that his work in film would reconstruct "the history of cinema as it 'should have been.'"[23]

It is in the context of Frampton's massive metahistorical labors upon *Magellan* that his return to still photography must be gauged. His working interests in photography during this second period of activity resided, as he put it, in "perceptual areas analogous to film."[24] Not surprisingly, then, Frampton quickly gravitated to the ontological and historical boundary point of the two media, the proto-cinematic practice of serial photography.

A VISITATION OF INSOMNIA: 1970–1973

A Visitation of Insomnia (cat. 23, p. 71) bears a close relationship to the work on *Magellan*. It was made at the same time that Frampton shot the original footage for one of the major celebratory sections of the film, *Vernal Equinox,* 1975, and features the same subject, a female nude performing a series of simple exercises and movements. The photographic series is also divided into twenty-four sections, a basic unit of Frampton's filmmaking being the number of frames contained in one second of film. Finally, the series title itself is taken from the concluding line of Frampton's first major essay, "For a Metahistory of Film—Commonplace Notes and Hypotheses," in which the author writes: "Film has finally attracted its own Muse. Her name is Insomnia."[25]

The series is a sequential work that exhibits a simple, symmetrical notion of narrative development. In this sense, *A Visitation of Insomnia* is quite literally a visitation, opening with an image of the nude's arrival and concluding with one of her departure. In between these two acts, Frampton's Muse enacts a series of movements that trace out a variety of graphic patterns. The resulting images made by long exposure on Frampton's view camera evoke the ghostly figures and waveform "géométrique" of motion traced out in the 1890s on the fixed plates of E. J. Marey's photochronographic apparatus. While the imagery conforms to the look of Marey (especially the pitch-black field, suggestive as well of Insomnia's nocturnal pursuits), the array of activity contained therein derives more directly from Muybridge's catalogue of human studies in *Animal Locomotion.* Like Muybridge before him, Frampton has his subject toss a ball, jump, lie down, throw a scarf over her shoulder, and even sit down to light a cigarette.

SIXTEEN STUDIES FROM VEGETABLE LOCOMOTION: 1975

The connection to Muybridge's work is deepened (albeit in a thoroughly humorous vein) in another of Frampton's collaborations with Marion Faller, *Sixteen Studies from VEGETABLE LOCOMOTION* (cat. 28, pp. 77-85). The title makes direct reference to Muybridge's famed 1887 portfolio of animal locomotion that included 781 plates. Frampton and Faller outdo their progenitor, claiming for their study (according to the numerical notation) 782 plates. Their work suggests the breadth and ambition of the original studies (displaced, however, onto less likely subjects for motion) while presenting caricatures of a number of minor sub-genres within the Muybridge canon. The more typical Muybridgean motion studies are represented by *484. Winter squash vacillating [var. "True Hubbard"]* (cat. 28i., p. 81) in which the circular squash slowly traverses the frame laterally and by *519. Tomatoes descending a ramp [var. "Roma"]* (cat. 28j., p. 82) in which a bucketful of the small circular subjects rolls down a ramp, with occasional alternate views of free-falling tomatoes.

Two of the more arcane (and erotic) forms of the earlier studies are comically cited in *481. Mature radishes bathing [var. "Black Spanish"]* (cat. 28g., p. 80) in which a stream of water is poured on top of a group of these sedentary bathers and in *601. Sweet corn disrobing [var. "Early Sunglow"]* (cat. 28l., p. 83) in which Faller sits against the grid backdrop shucking the husks from ears of corn. Frampton and Faller extend the sexual aspects of Muybridge and proceed into the novel realm of violence, serially enacted upon vegetable subjects. These include a gruesome operation performed upon a summer squash replete with ketchup blood (cat. 28f., p. 80), slightly more humane surgery upon a pumpkin (cat. 28h., p. 81), and a fatal fall suffered by a watermelon (cat. 28k., p. 82).

The series concludes with a striking frontal movement toward the camera that seems to represent a form of violence inflicted by the subject upon the recording apparatus itself. In *782. Apple advancing [var. "Northern Spy"]* (cat. 28p., p. 85) Frampton and Faller chart the path of the advancing fruit, maintaining a faithfulness to one of Muybridge's standard angles while strongly evoking comparison with Magritte's depiction of an apartment-dwelling apple in *La chambre d'écoute I,* 1953. The final step in the apple's advance obscures the picture plane and provides an elegant form of narrative closure to the series.

Sixteen Studies from VEGETABLE LOCOMOTION represents a humorous response to the emerging interests in "primitive cinema," in the technological and material underpinnings of the apparatus, as well as to Frampton's own metahistorical musings on the ontology of film. The cartooning of these concerns in the series, combined with the subtle suggestions of narrative sequence in *A Visitation of Insomnia,* serve to prefigure and inflect Frampton's serial photographic work *Protective Coloration,* the first color series of the period, in which Frampton again presses at the limits between the photographic and the filmic.

PROTECTIVE COLORATION: 1984

Protective Coloration (cat. 36., pp. 36-37) begins with the image of a focus chart and concludes with a signature stamp, as do all his early films. Between these images, Frampton's merging of the photographic frame with the display area of the t-shirt provides for a progression of imagery consonant not only with the vast repository of mass cultural iconography characteristic of the polyester medium, but also with the private array of signs and images that can on occasion inhabit that space. As in his most complex film work, the proto-narrative of *Protective Coloration* merges a personal journey with an exploration of the contours of the medium. The autobiographic aspects range from the inclusion of such ancestral mentors as the Vienna/Cambridge philosopher Wittgenstein, the Soviet filmmaker Vertov, and the archetypal French chef Escoffier, to a tour of personally significant sites (including the Digital Arts Lab and the Edinburgh Film Festival). His complex concerns with cinema and perception are cartooned in a magic lantern illustration and two versions of the human eye. These in turn become embedded within a larger fictive journey that moves from Atlantic City to Hollywood, from Puerto Rico to Canada, and after the fashion of *By Any Other Name,* ranges over the world of consumption of products like Volkswagens and Coors.

The title of the series is suggestive of an anthropological aspect of Frampton's photographic work which he describes in his semi-serious probing of such activity "as a form of human behavior." He asks in the manner of the neo-Darwinian ". . . what there may be in all this photographic behavior that is 'adaptive'; that is, in what way does it promote, actively or passively, the survival of the organism and of the species."[26] *Protective Coloration* provides an overdeterminedly Darwinian rejoinder to that query in its cataloguing of that doubly adaptive arena of t-shirt illustration—that clothing of oneself in images that seems annually to coincide with the summer solstice.

ADSVMVS ABSVMVS: 1982

Within the same series of speculations on photography as an adaptive activity, Frampton conducts a discussion of the work of an early practitioner, William Henry Fox Talbot, from which emerges an analysis of what he terms "two different sorts of perceptual time": the historic and the ecstatic.[27] Both derive from consequences of the photographic image and act out ontological claims made on behalf of that medium. The former reflects the factual/scientific aspects of the image, historic time being "composed of sequential, artificial, isometric modules which are related to one another, in language, by the connective phrase: 'and then.'"[28] The latter conception of temporal perception harks to the founding visions of Talbot's pursuit of "natural images," in which, "for an ecstatic moment, time is not."[29] It is from these two temporal faces of the photographic medium that Frampton generated his final two studies in the sequential mode.

ADSVMVS ABSVMVS (cat. 31, pp. 38, 39, 93-99) partakes of the ecstatic possibilities first glimpsed by Talbot. In their look, the fourteen images of the series are readily traceable to the photogenic drawings of botanical specimens made by Talbot in the 1830s by a process in which "Natural Objects May Be Made to Delineate Themselves without the Aid of the Artist's Pencil."[30] The subjects of Frampton's still lifes—vacated winter skins of snakes, skeletal remains of a bird, dehydrated jellyfish—seem in themselves to redouble the medium's capacity to fix these segments of eternity. These pinned specimens offer themselves as natural emblems for the photographic process: "desiccations, fossils, memories, mummies, traces indistinguishable from residues." They are, like the photographs in which they appear, indexical signs of life now absented—an aspect of the imagery recapitulated in the series title, literally, "We are here/We are not here."

As in *nostalgia,* Frampton has appended descriptions to each of the images providing circumstantial data about the acquisition of their subjects. As in the earlier work, one of the significant features of these texts is their inability to capture fully or to explain the force of the photographic work they describe. The texts do suggest a narrative, detailing Frampton's delight in acquiring the odd mixture of plants and animals, fish and frogs, charms and totems over a seven-year period of travels and home-life. On occasion, the texts indirectly confirm aspects of the "ecstatic" form of the imagery. In the gloriously dark, iridescent, thoroughly Westonic study of dried peppers (cat. 31j., p. 97), the text conceives a sense of the ecstatic within the register of the diaristic: "For an afternoon, I parched and flayed, she stuffed with three farces, we sauced and baked. Ah!"

While it is a series, *ADSVMVS ABSVMVS* seems, at afar, removed from such sequential photographic studies as *A Visitation of Insomnia* or *Protective Coloration.* It is as if the "ecstatic" temporal mode of each image, suspended within a timeless space, has precluded the designs of the linear narrative. And yet there is, even beyond the alternation of animal and vegetable or the increasing complexity of both phylum and image within the series, a sense of some teleology, of a movement toward something. This narrative subtext seems to turn upon the sequence of fourteen, miming after a fashion the Stations of the Cross, a "tour" (as Frampton would say) in which the greatest degradation—as in the thirteenth, the depilated *Brown Rat (Rattus rattus)* (cat. 31m., p. 99)—can be followed by absolute grace in the figure of the *Rose (Rosa damascena)* (cat. 31n., p. 99), "a keepsake from a funeral wreath."

RITES OF PASSAGE: 1983-1984

A similar movement, though informed by an overdeterminedly public symbology, is to be found in the final photographic series, *Rites of Passage* (cat. 35, pp. 100-105), made with Marion Faller. The twenty sequential images present the momentous events of a lifetime through a changing array of caketop iconography. As in Frampton's analysis of "historic time," the series proceeds in "isometric modules which are related to one another, in language, by the connective phrase: 'and then.'" There is birth, "and then" school, "and then" confirmation, "and then" the first car, "and then" graduation, "and then" marriage, "and then". . . .

An elegantly comic work, *Rites of Passage* reflexively derives its force from the efficiency of its inscription. While Frampton and Faller seem to cartoon the absolute ease of narrative construction, the comedic aspect of the series issues from the confluence of the mechanistic mode of the photographic and of life lived according to these public signs. Reduced to the hollow figures of ceremony and celebration, life devolves into a piece of artificial cake. The camera arts, too, have witnessed a like devolution in the wake of the promise held forth by narrativity—a loss emblematized in the figure of the empty cake that opens and closes this final work.

EPILOGUE: FRAMPTON AND *THE TEMPTATION OF ST. ANTHONY*

In 1962, Frampton produced a series of a dozen complex photograms under the title *The Temptation of St. Anthony* (cat. 7, p. 50-51). Made without the agency of the camera, these images were composed directly, built up in stages, through the application of inks and through chemical encounters with the surface of negative materials. Out of this process emerged sets of complex images that balance suggestions of spatial depth with graphic gestures erupting upon the surface. Ambiguous figures and oneiric forms briefly delineate themselves out of the biomorphic patterns, only to retreat into a shallow play of contrastive tones and senseless shapes. The profiles, hands, eyes, or alternately the landscapes, forests, boulders, and craters that reside within these prints map out an impossible continuum of artistic undertakings that Frampton embraced most thoroughly in his "other work." They bear the marks of the dual inscription of painting and the camera arts: "They are completely abstract except insofar as in all pictures of St. Anthony that I know, one sees the saint on all the picture planes." They bespeak of literary yearnings, having been influenced "not by painting (as one might expect) but by the problematic drama by Flaubert."[31] And finally, they present themselves as scientific probings of religious experience, satellite maps of privation and passion.

Here, as in all his "other work," Frampton eloquently weds an ancestral aesthetics with the practices of contemporaries, much as he merges the achievements of the camera arts with the metahistory of the fine arts. His portraits of Frank Stella had cartooned the entire history of representational art upon the streets of New York. *Ways to Purity* discovered even the contemporary canon upon his doorsteps. The collaborations with Rosenquist made explicit the photographic underpinnings of Pop Art. That his interest in dead or ancient languages proleptically anticipated a complex semiological engagement is not surprising. Frampton managed to live historically and to embrace thoroughly in his work what Eliot had termed "tradition." In sentiments that even Duchamp would echo, Eliot specified in 1919 the terms of the Framptonian enterprise:

> . . . we shall often find that not only the best, but the most individual parts of [an artist's] work may be those in which the dead poets, his ancestors, assert their immortality most vigorously.[32]

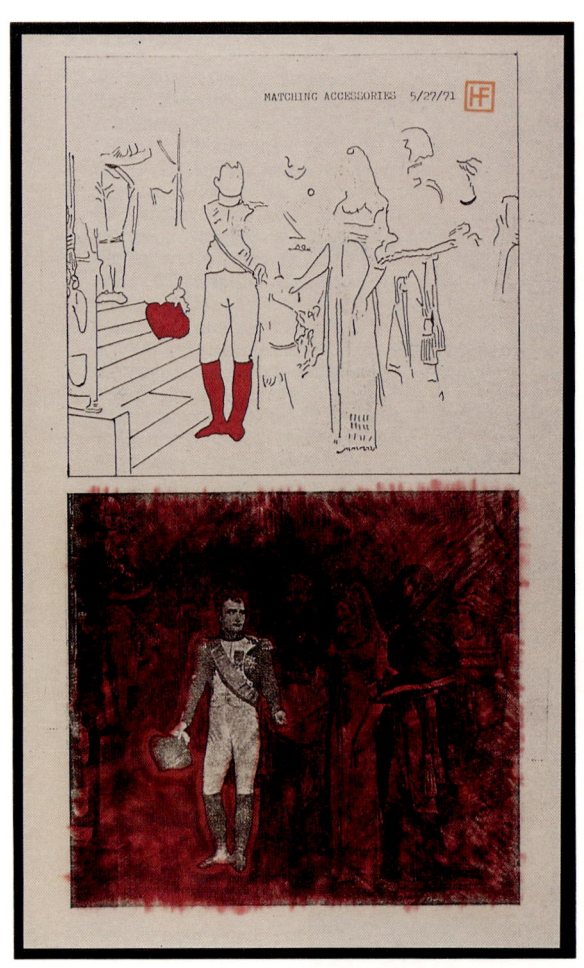
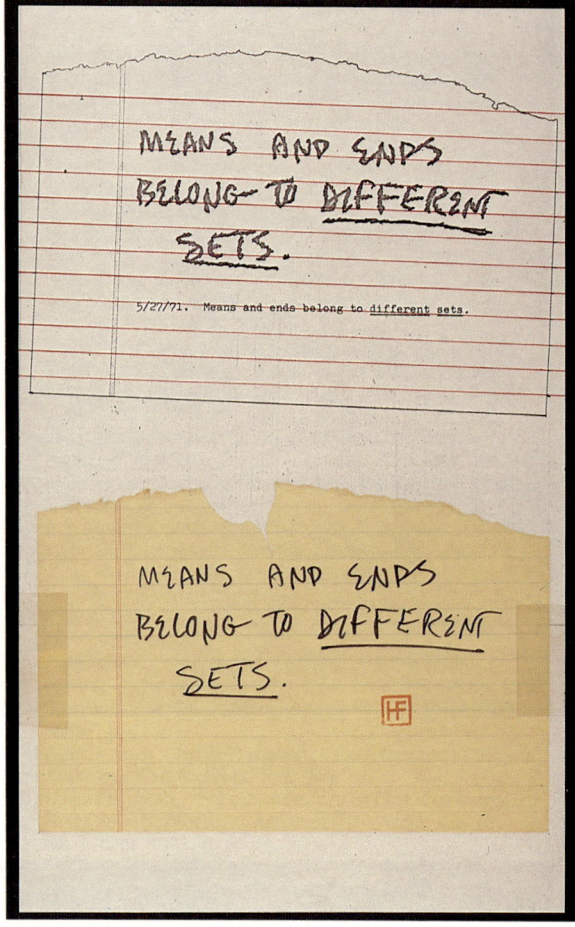

25b. *Matching Accessories*, from *Reasonable Facsimiles*, 1971
applied color on xerograph
13¾ x 8⅜

25c. *Means and Ends Belong to Different Sets*, from *Reasonable Facsimiles*, 1971
applied color on xerograph, collage
13⅝ x 8⁷⁄₁₆

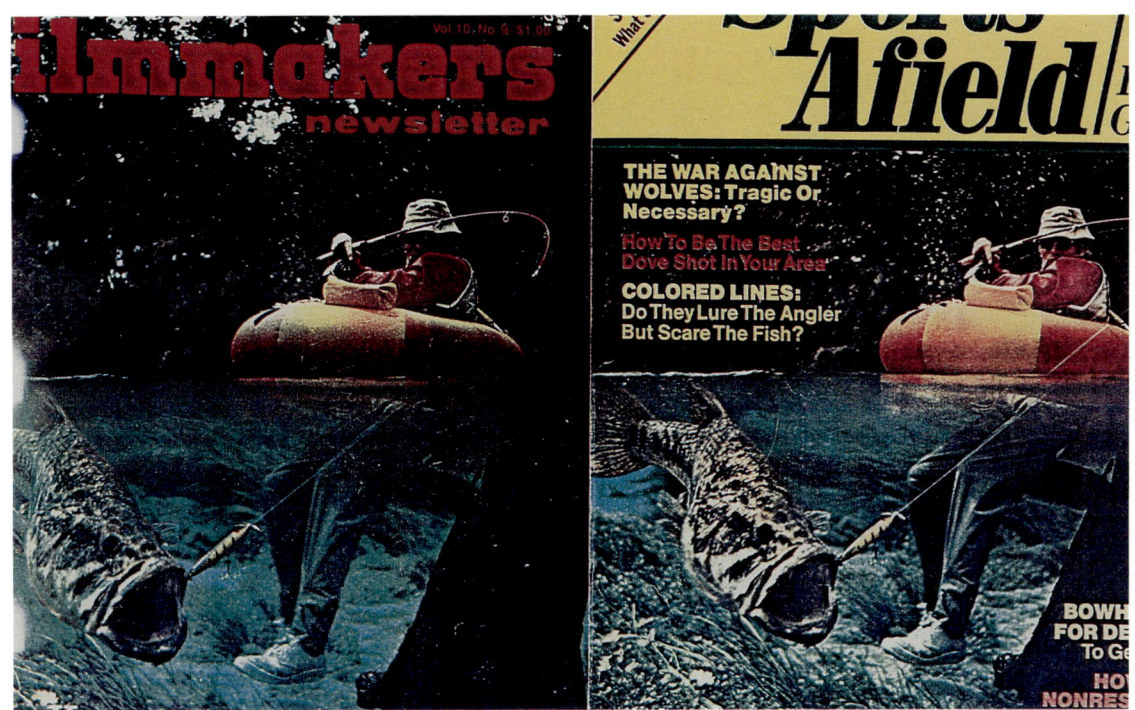

30g. *The conquest of culture and nature,* from *False Impressions,* 1979
color xerograph, 8¼ x 13½, 6/14

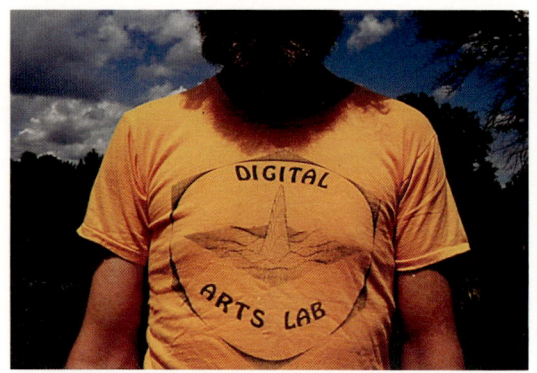
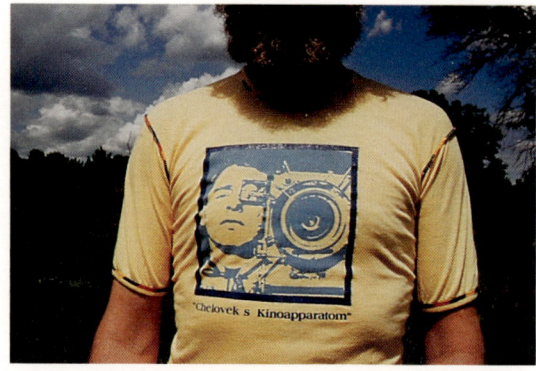
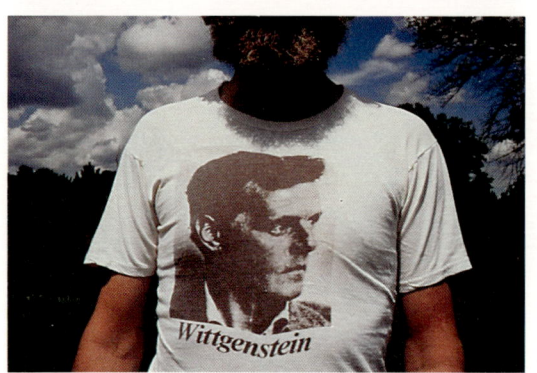
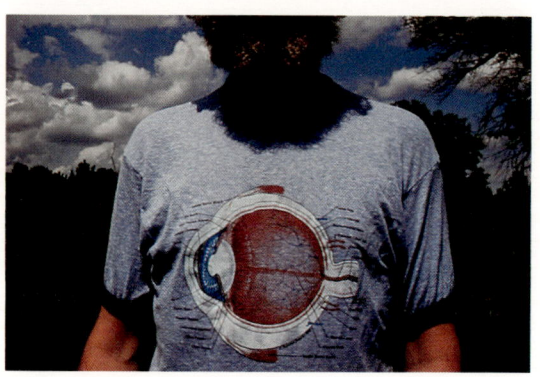

36. *Protective Coloration,* 1984
    Two details from a series of thirty-six Ektacolor photographs, each 4 x 6, assembled and matted to 44 x 54

    This series documents Frampton wearing prime examples from his prized t-shirt collection. The arrangement of the images is vaguely filmic: the first shows a focus chart from a film leader, the last is the emblem of his initials (set like a Chinese chop) which he used to sign the final frame of his films and some of his photographs.

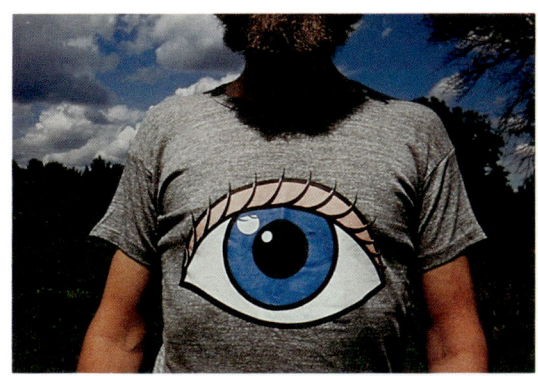
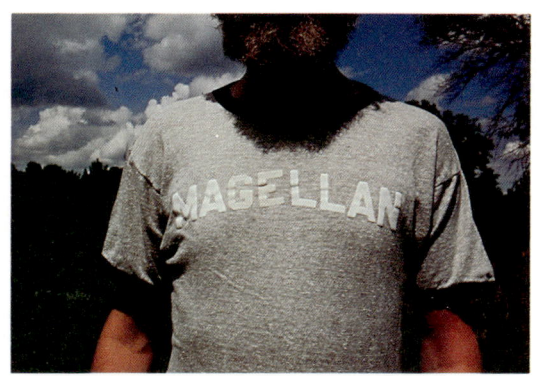
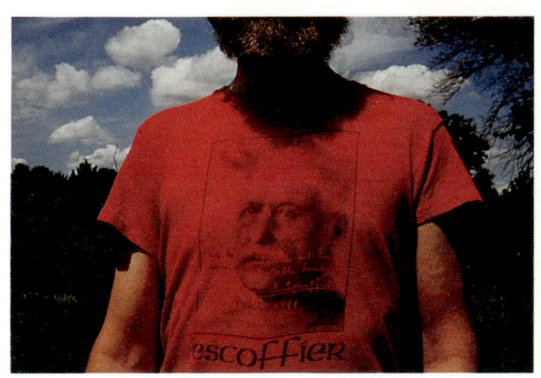
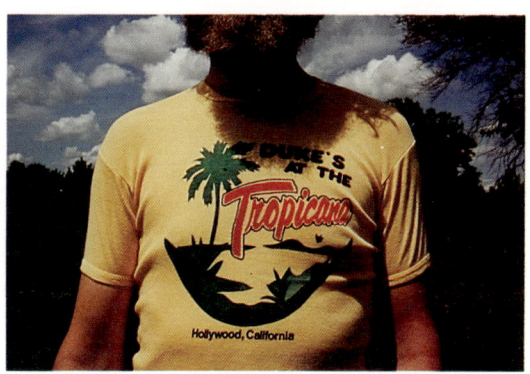

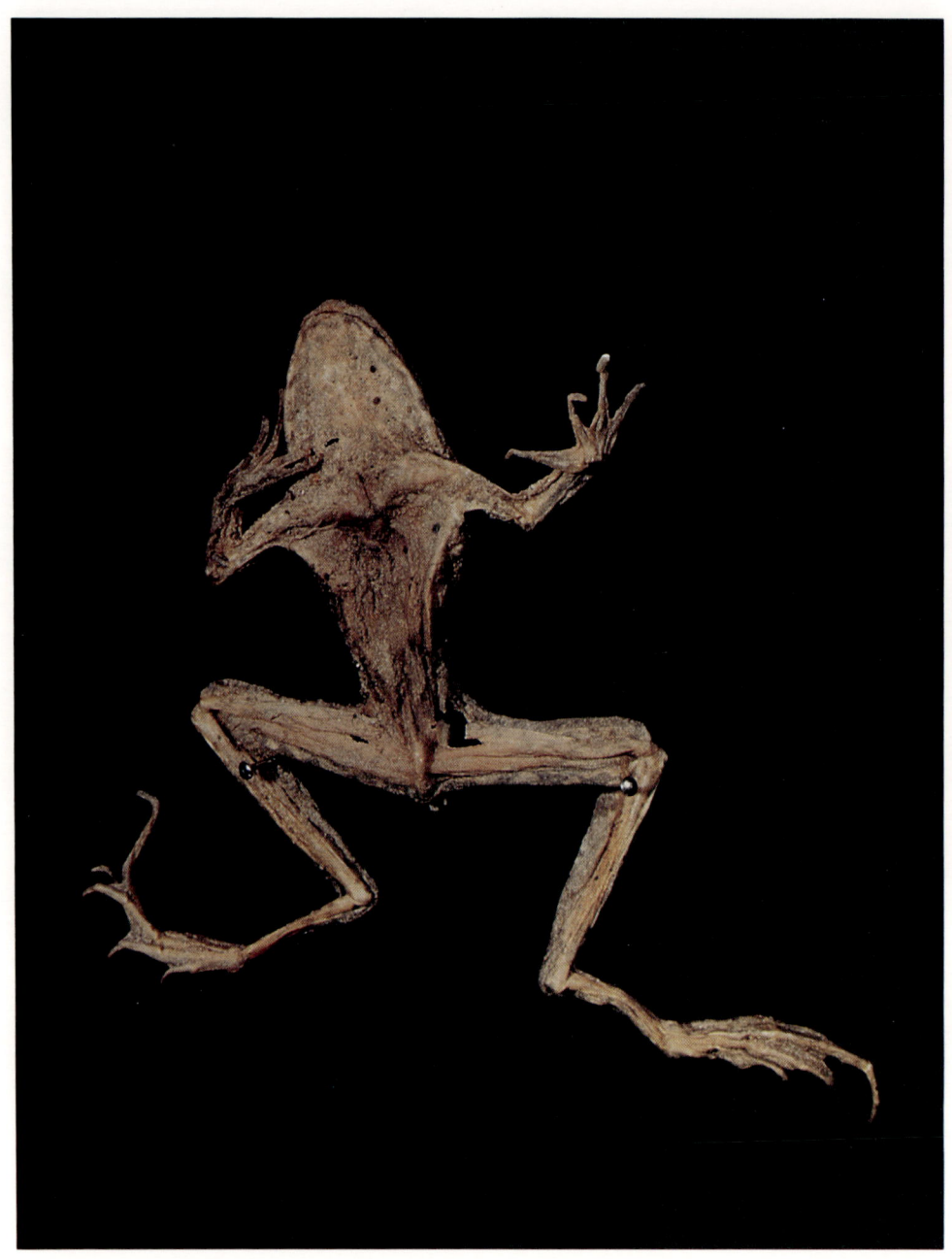

31k. *XI. GRASS FROG (Rana pipiens),* from
ADSVMVS ABSVMVS, 1982
Ektacolor photograph, 20 x 16, 7/14

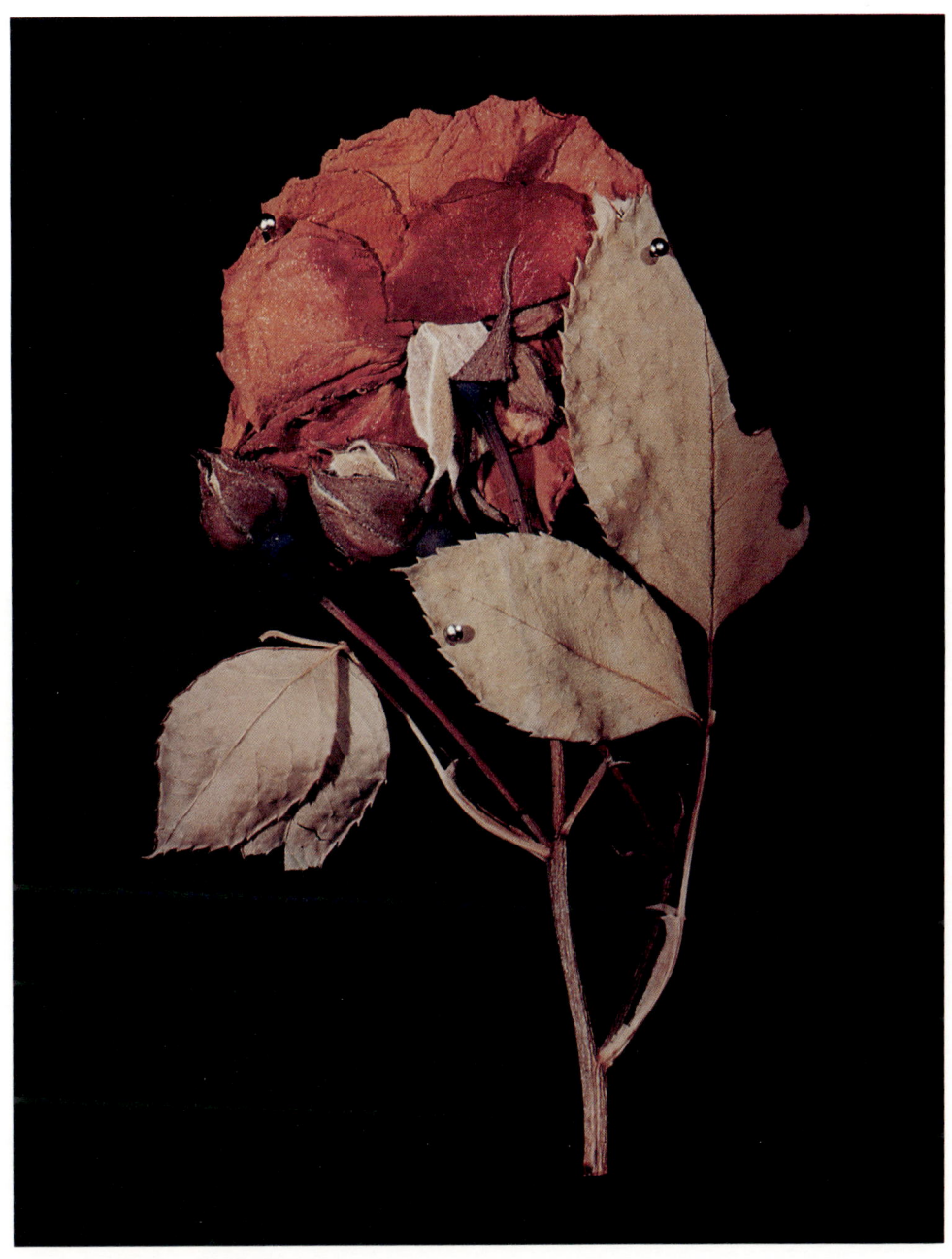

31n. *XIV. ROSE (Rosa damascena)*, from
ADSVMVS ABSVMVS, 1982
Ektacolor photograph, 20 x 16, 7/14

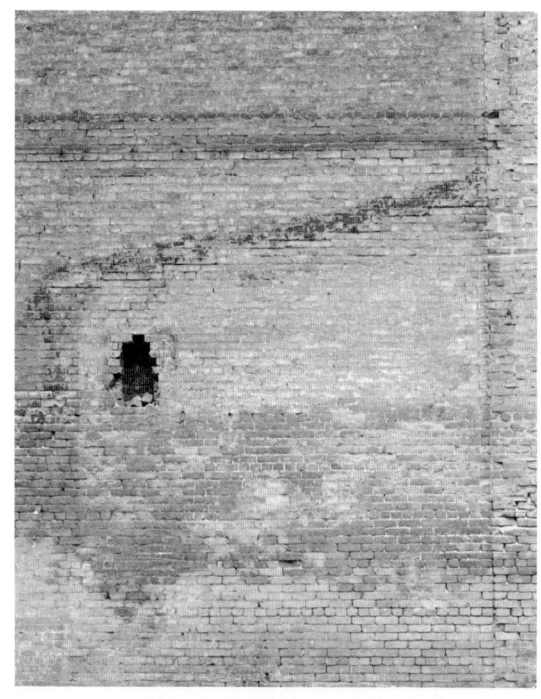

3c. *3. "40" Crosby Street,*
from *Ways to Purity,* 1959
black and white photograph, 9½ x 7½
(Minor White/brick wall)

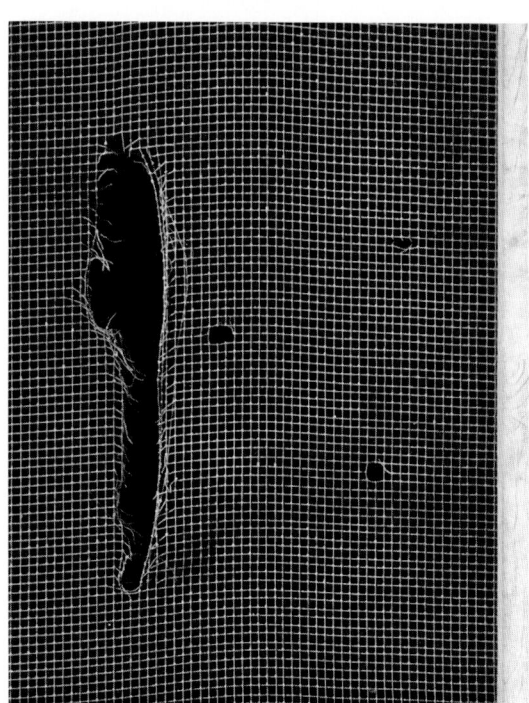

3d. *4. 154 Spring Street,*
from *Ways to Purity,* 1959
black and white photograph, 9½ x 7⁹⁄₁₆
(A. Burri/screen door)

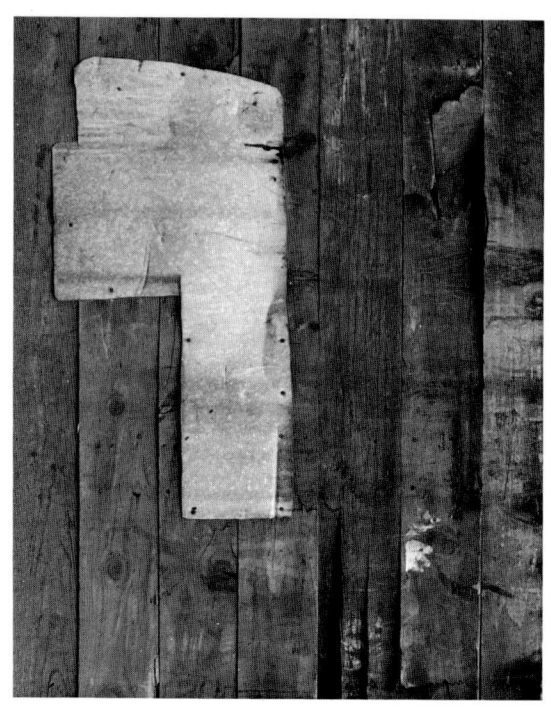

3e. *5. 400 West Broadway,*
from *Ways to Purity,* 1959
black and white photograph, 9½ x 7⁹⁄₁₆
("axe")

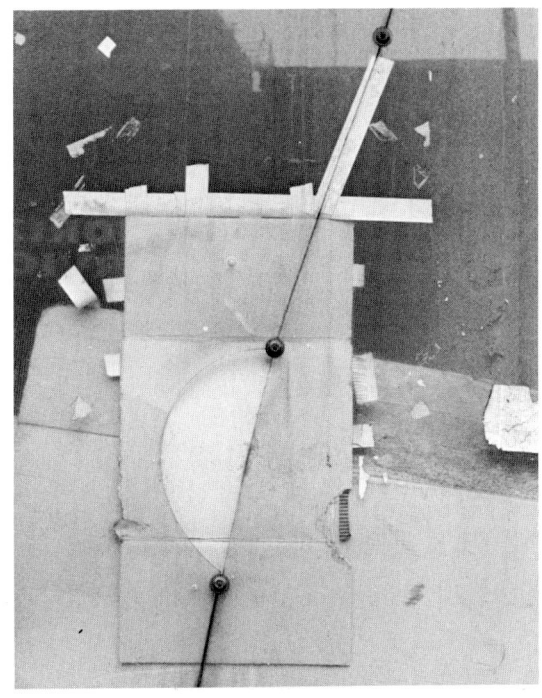

3f. *6. 49 Prince Street*,
   from *Ways to Purity*, 1959
   black and white photograph, 9½ x 7½
   (collage window)

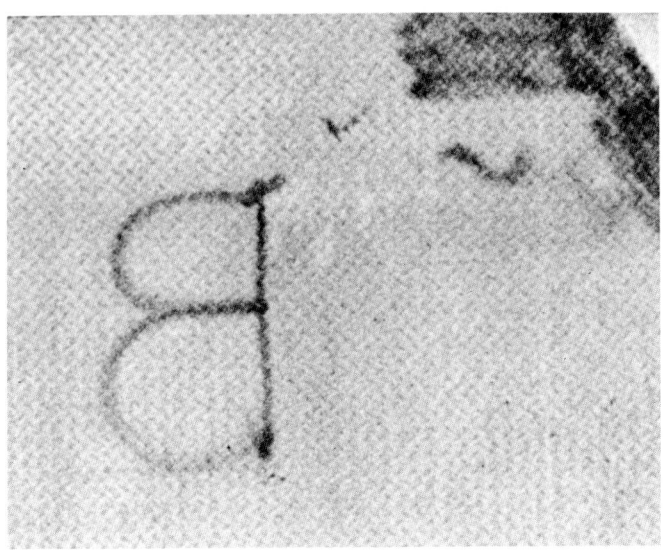

3g. *7. 409 West Broadway*,
   from *Ways to Purity*, 1959
   black and white photograph, 7½ x 9½
   (letter B)

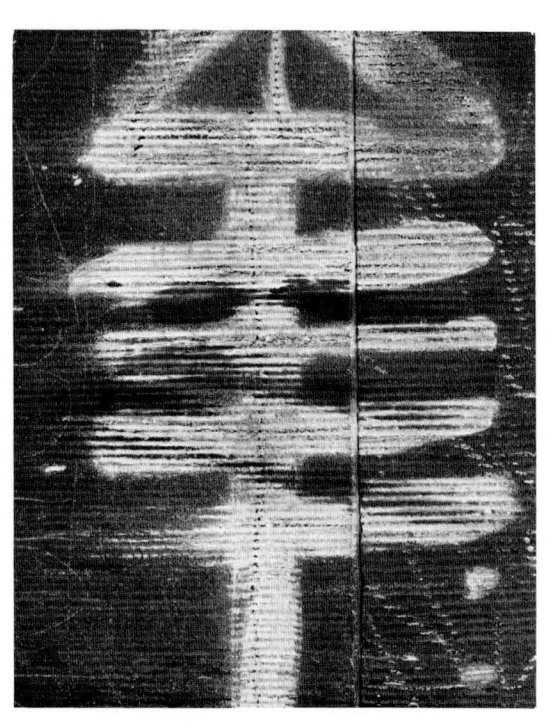 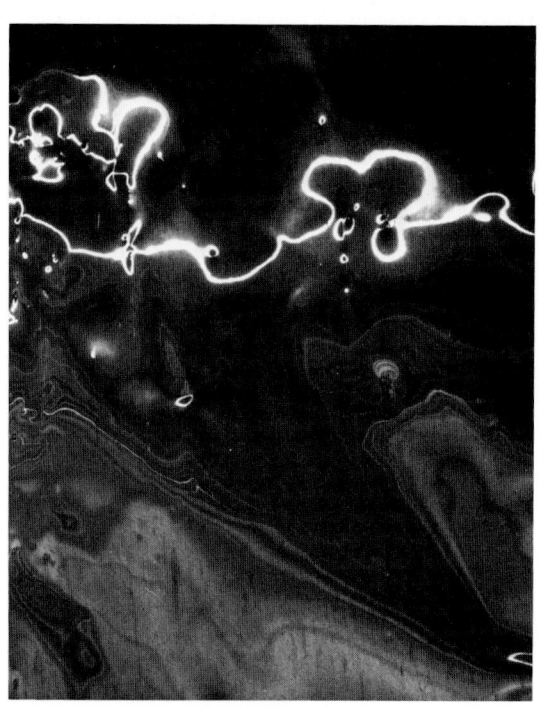

3h. *8. 137 Prince Street,*
from *Ways to Purity,* 1959
black and white photograph, 9⁷⁄₁₆ x 7⁹⁄₁₆
(Motherwell/fish skeleton)

3i. *9. 51 Crosby Street,*
from *Ways to Purity,* 1959
black and white photograph, 9⁷⁄₁₆ x 7⁹⁄₁₆
(Lauterwasser *[sic]*
/aluminum door)

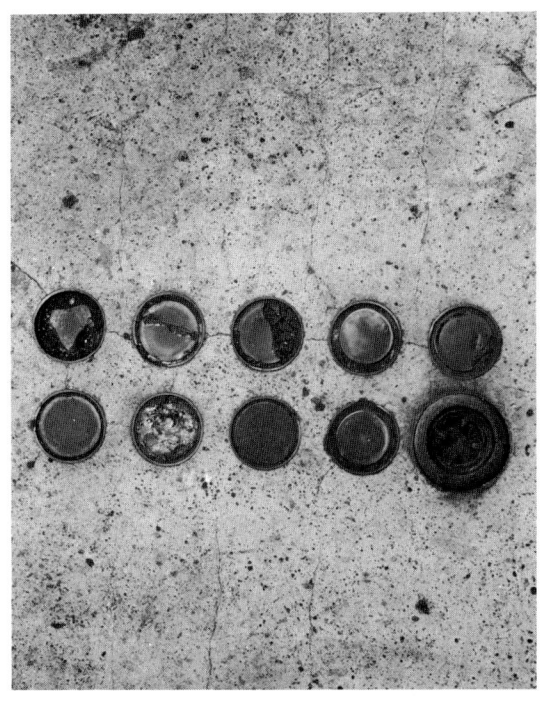

3j. *10. 464 Broome Street,*
from *Ways to Purity,* 1959
black and white photograph, 9 7/16 x 7 9/16
(circles)

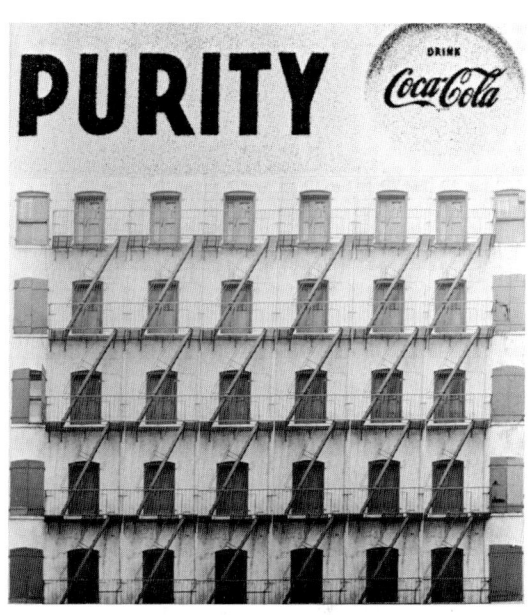

3l. *12. 366 West Broadway; 97 Crosby Street,*
from *Ways to Purity,* 1959
black and white photograph, 8 x 7 1/4
(terminal hoax)

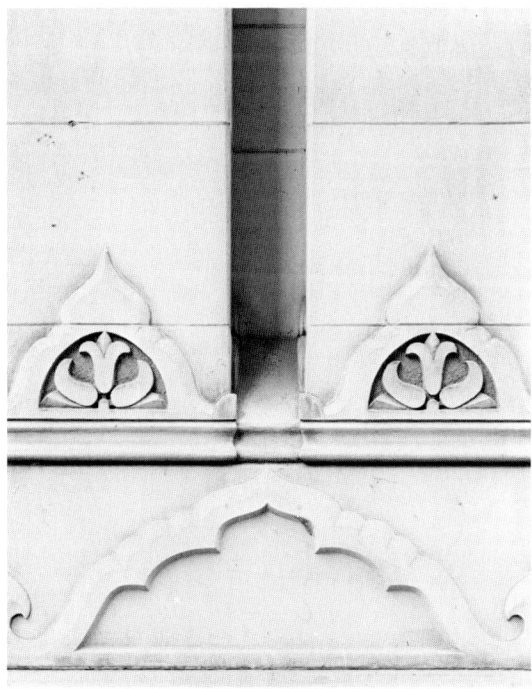

3k. *11. 450 Broome Street,* from *Ways to Purity,* 1959
black and white photograph, 9 7/16 x 7 9/16
(Louise Nevelson/stonework)

1. *THE SECRET WORLD OF FRANK STELLA,* 1958–1962

Frampton initially began this series of fifty-two black and white photographs as a parody of a recently published book, *The Private World of Pablo Picasso,* by David Douglas Duncan. He and Stella staged the shots casually on and off during the next few years. When seen in its entirety, the series of photographs, all bled mounted, is meant to be arranged in four "suits" of thirteen. The series is, as well, a spoof on photographic traditions and stock art historical images, a point Frampton elaborated in 1963:

. . . My intention was a massive *sottisier,* the prize-picture on the point of becoming cliche. A photographic cliche is not a set of *idées fixes* about how to organize a surface, it is a petrified notion about seeing. There *is* a photographic tradition of some sort, in precisely the sense that there is a literary or a painterly tradition. This series has reference to a critical attitude towards that tradition. I use the word "tradition" in the broad sense: what has been done. The photographs, to encompass my aim, had to be "bad."[1]

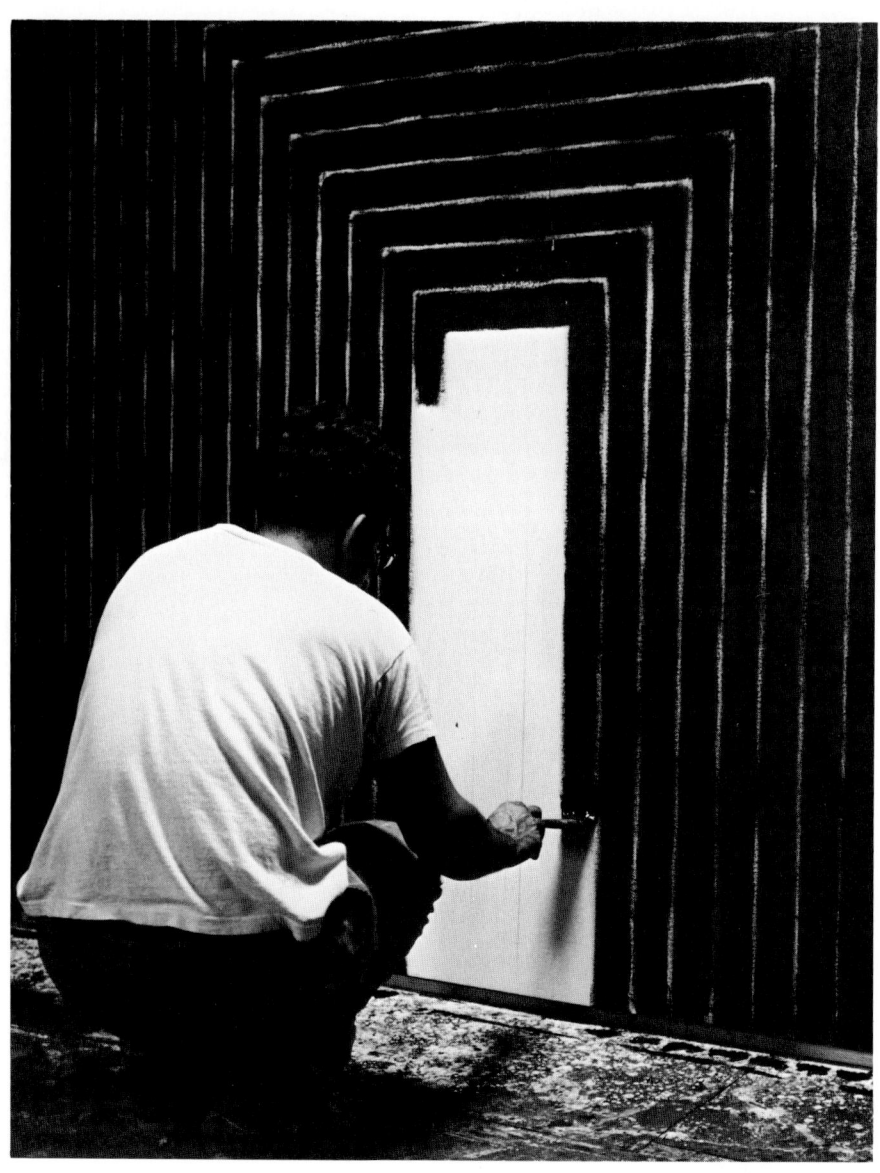

46

Notes to illustrations appear on p. 120.

left: 1a. *#3*, from *The Secret World of Frank Stella*, 1958–1962
black and white photograph, 9½ x 7½
(28 painting Getty Tomb)

below: 1c. *#14*, from *The Secret World of Frank Stella*, 1958–1962
black and white photograph, 7½ x 9⁷⁄₁₆
(360 "photos")

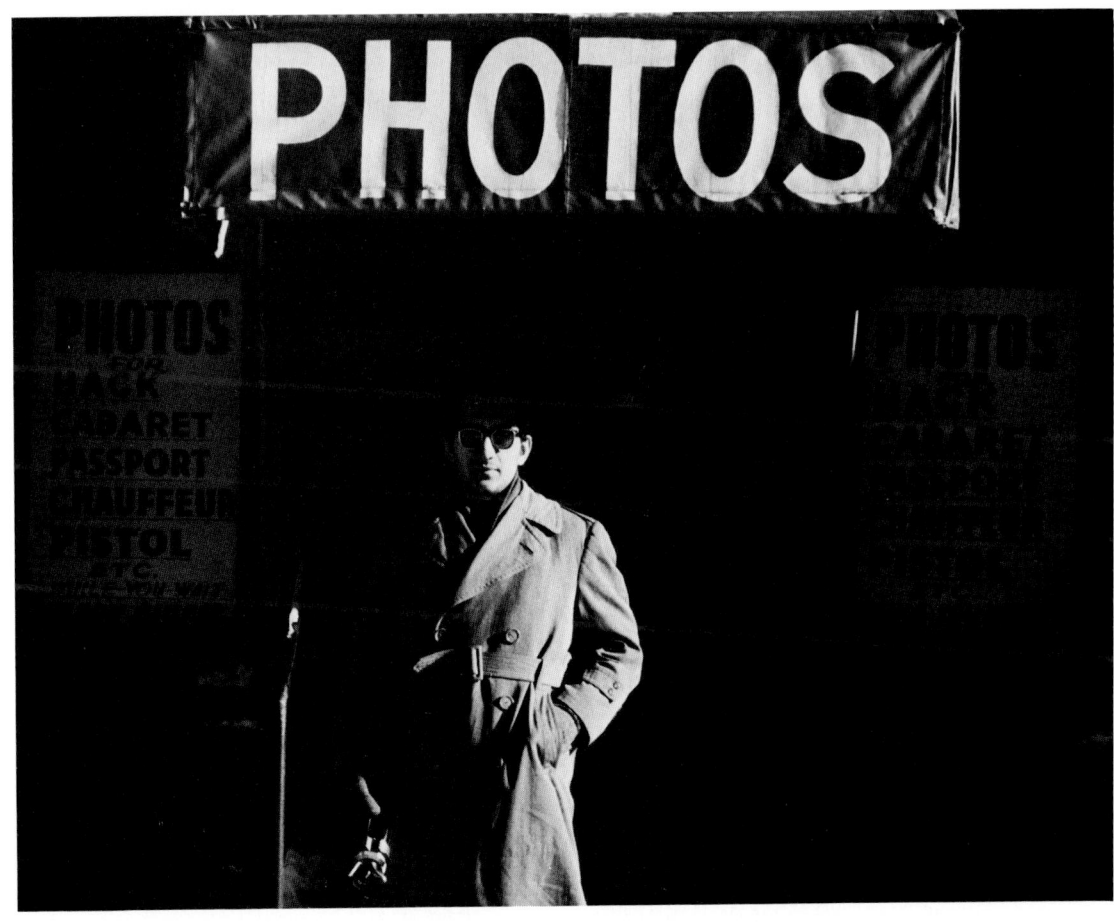

1e. *#33*, from *The Secret World of Frank Stella,*
   1958–1962
   black and white photograph, 7½ x 9⁷⁄₁₆
   (440 yogi & rubberplant, 3/17/61)

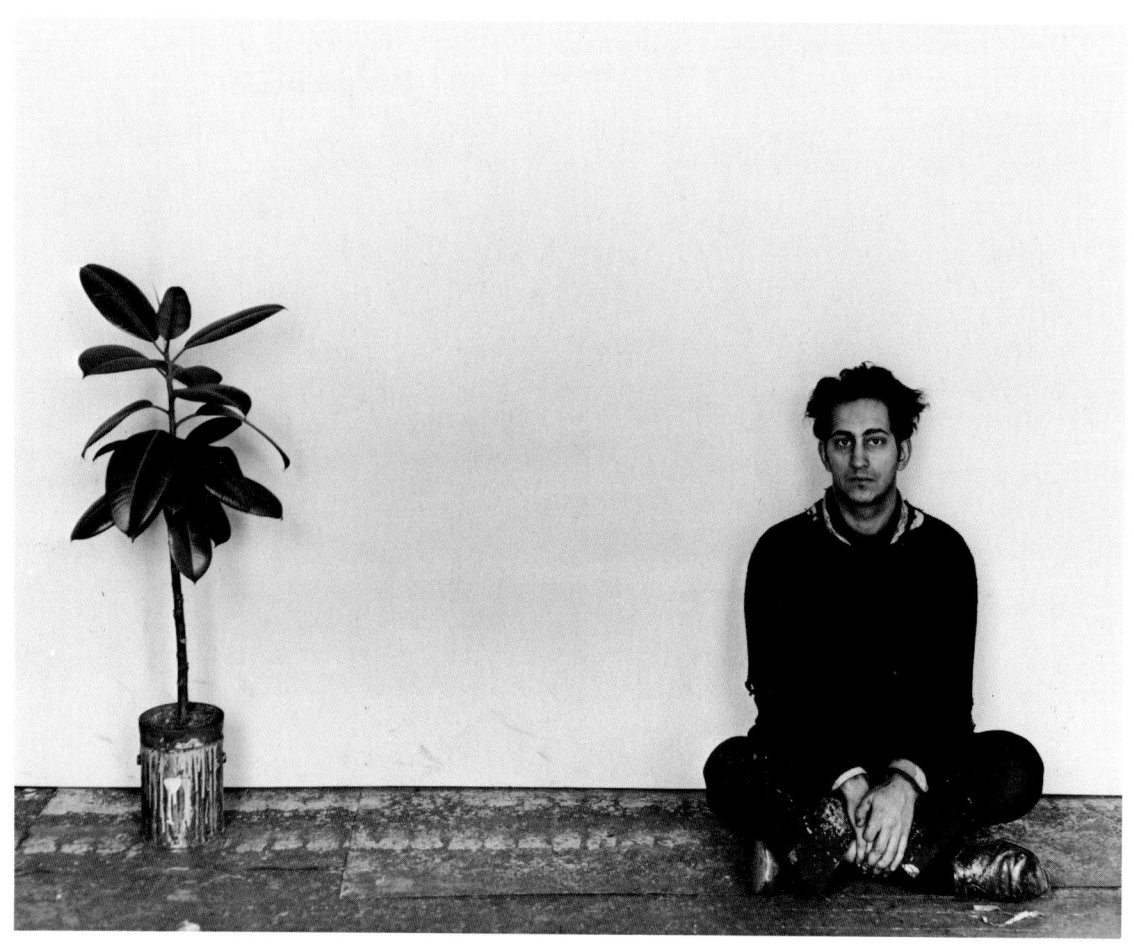

1h. *#52*, from *The Secret World of Frank Stella*, 1958–1962
black and white photograph, 7½ x 9⁷⁄₁₆
(444 Marat, 3/17/61)

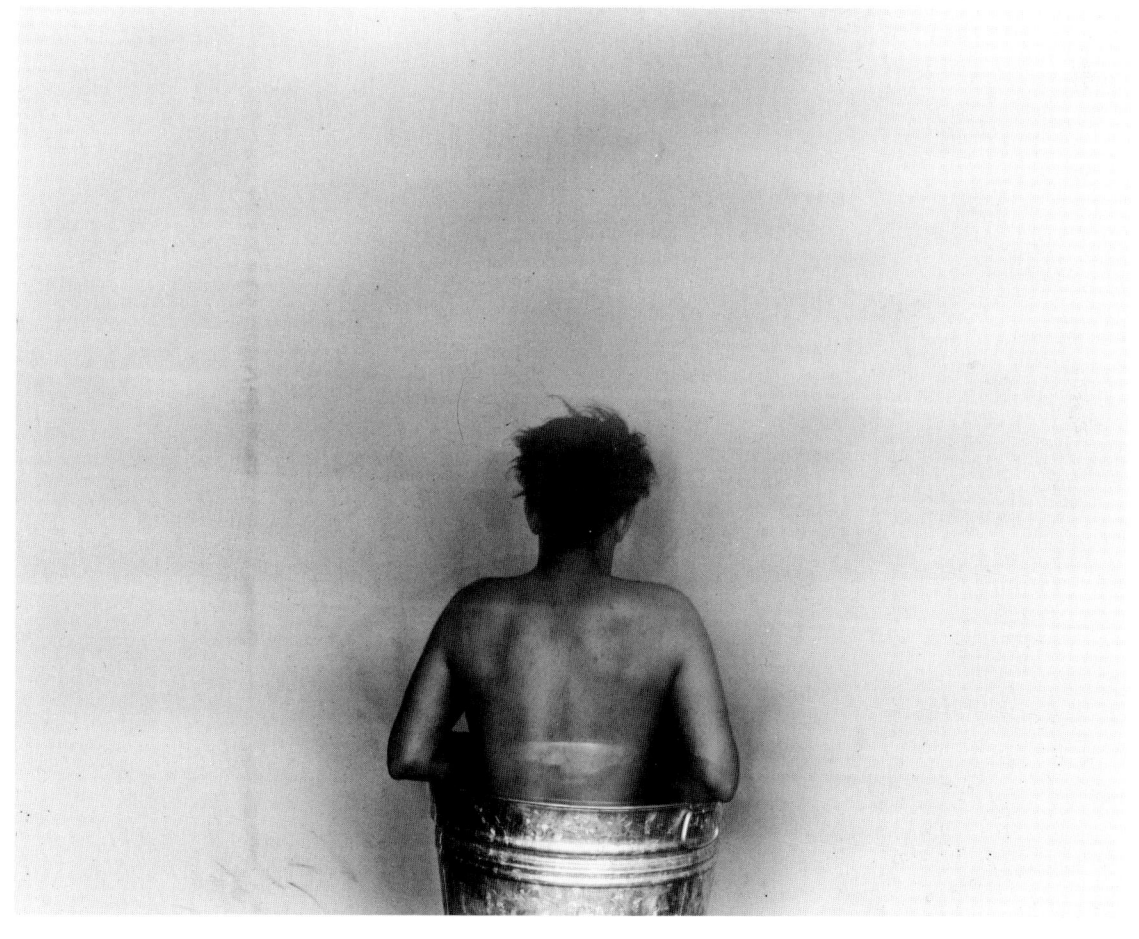

7. THE TEMPTATION OF ST. ANTHONY, 1962

Frampton heavily worked unexposed 8 x 10 inch negatives using photo chemicals and inks to produce these fluid surface patterns: The large scale reinforces their obvious connection with painterly abstraction. The work refers to photographic traditions, particularly the seductively "artful" photographic abstractions of Edward Weston and perhaps Minor White, here ironically emulated without a camera. Indicated, too, by these "tortured negatives" is Flaubert's *La Tentation de St. Antoine (The Temptation of St. Anthony)*, 1874, an enigmatic "tortured text" long admired by Frampton.

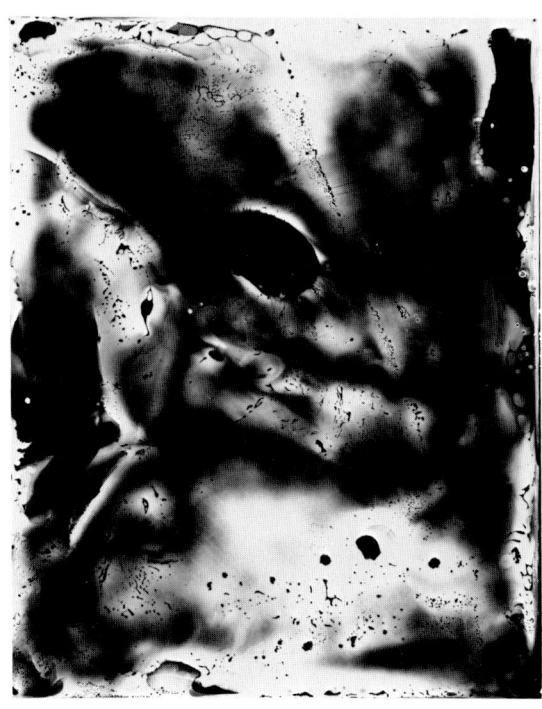

7a.–7c.: *The Temptation of St. Anthony*, 1962, third triad from a series of four triads of black and white cameraless photographs from manipulated negatives
each 24 x 20 [printed 1984]

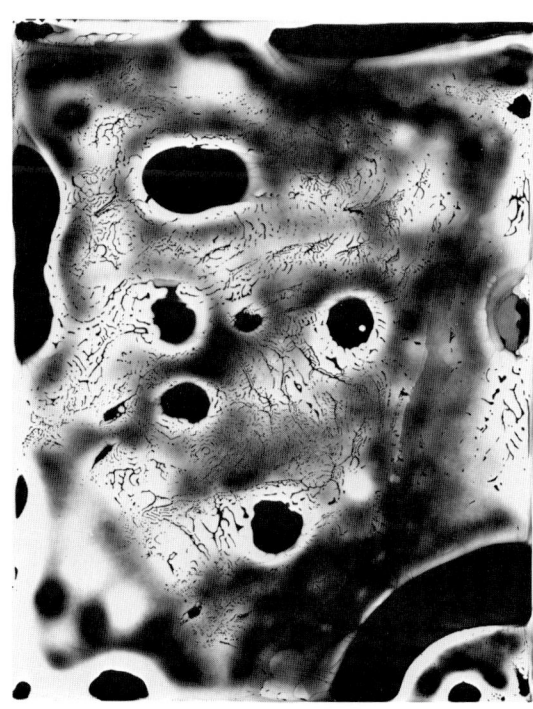
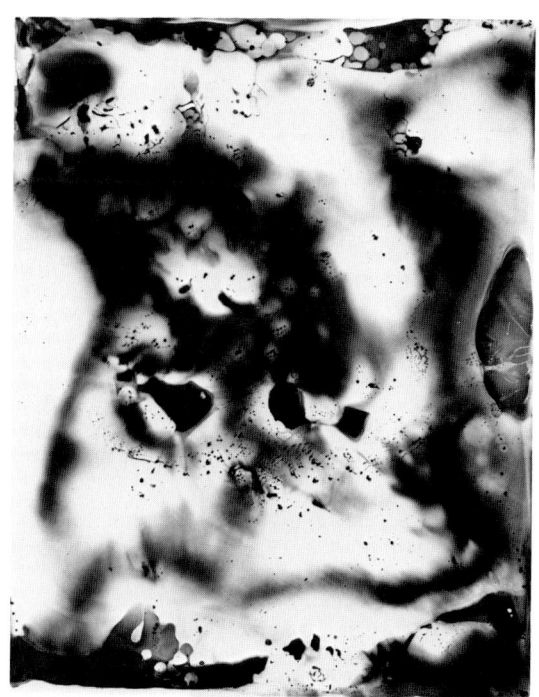

8. *WORD PICTURES*
   [Working title *WORDS*],
   1962–1963

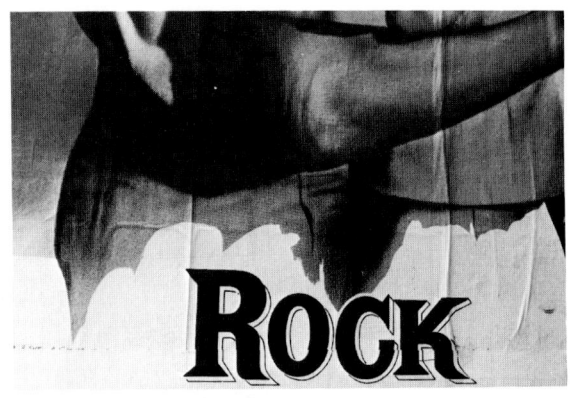

8e. *Rock*, from *Word Pictures*, 1962–1963
black and white photograph, 3¹⁵⁄₁₆ x 6

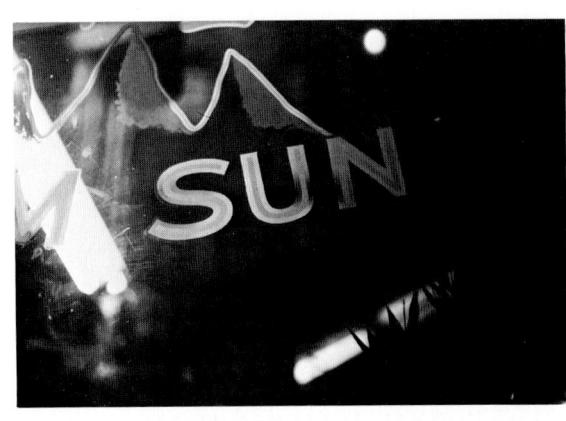

8f. *Sun*, from *Word Pictures*, 1962–1963
black and white photograph, 4⅝ x 6¹⁵⁄₁₆

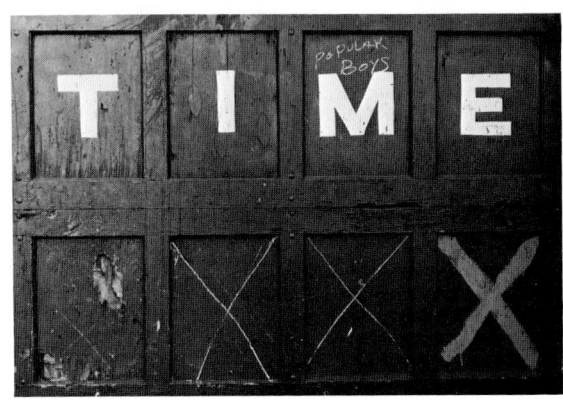

8g. *Time*, from *Word Pictures*, 1962–1963
black and white photograph, 4⅝ x 6½

2. *OFFICIAL PORTRAITS*, 1959

Frampton took an "official portrait" of Frank Stella for the catalogue of the *Sixteen Americans* exhibition at the Museum of Modern Art. He then made similar portraits of Carl Andre, Walter Darby Bannard and Richard Meier. All the portraits are deliberately—and mockingly—standardized. With the exception of one image, Frampton had none of these portraits in his possession. Some were printed in 1959, however, and presented to his subjects. These *Official Portraits* were recently selected from proof sheets by Bannard, Meier and Stella themselves.

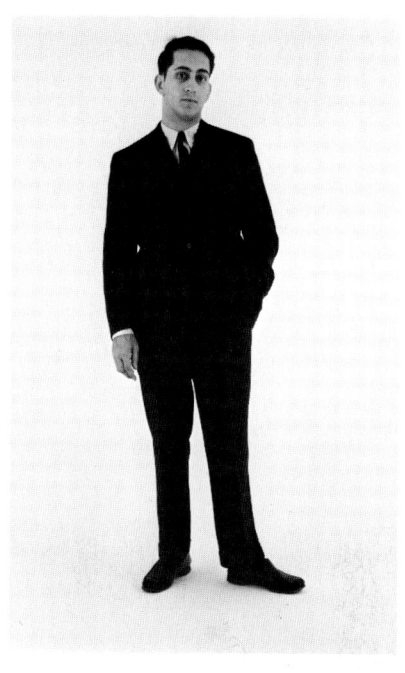

2a. *Frank Stella*, from *Official Portraits*, 1959
black and white photograph, 16⅝ x 10½
(10/9/59)

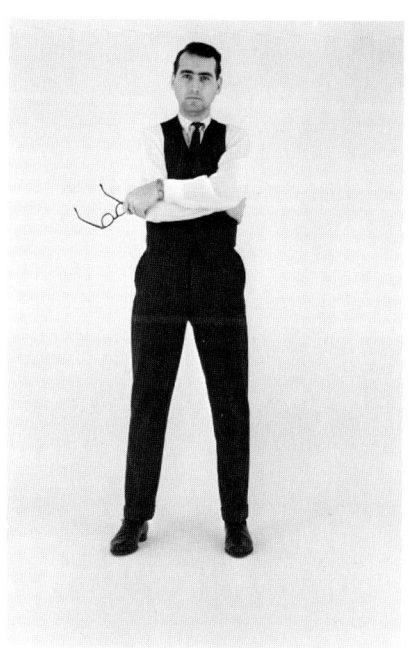

2b. *Richard Meier*, from *Official Portraits*, 1959
black and white photograph, 16⅝ x 10½
(10/27/59)

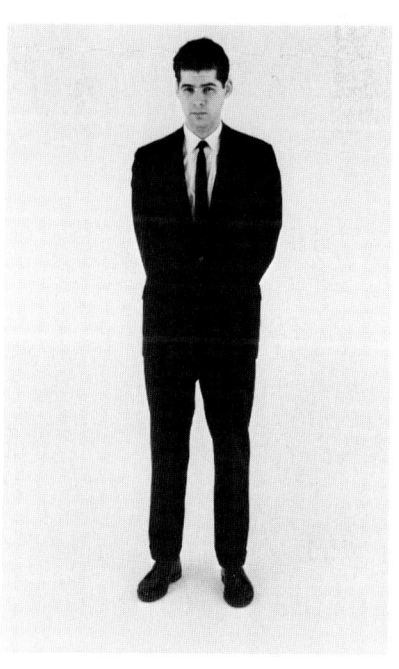

2c. *Walter Darby Bannard*, from
Official Portraits, 1959
black and white photograph, 16⅝ x 10½

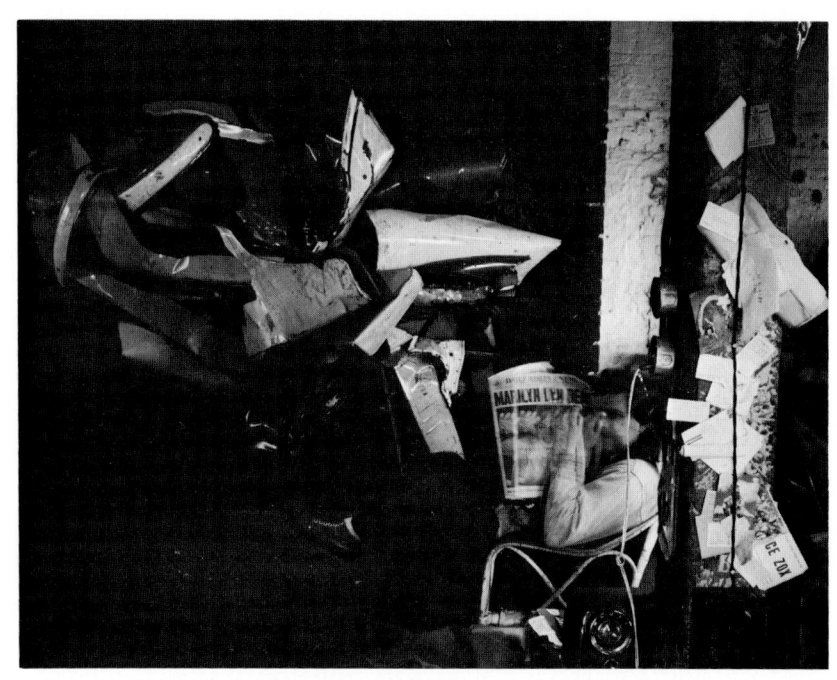

10. *John Chamberlain*, 1963
black and white photograph, 7½ x 9½

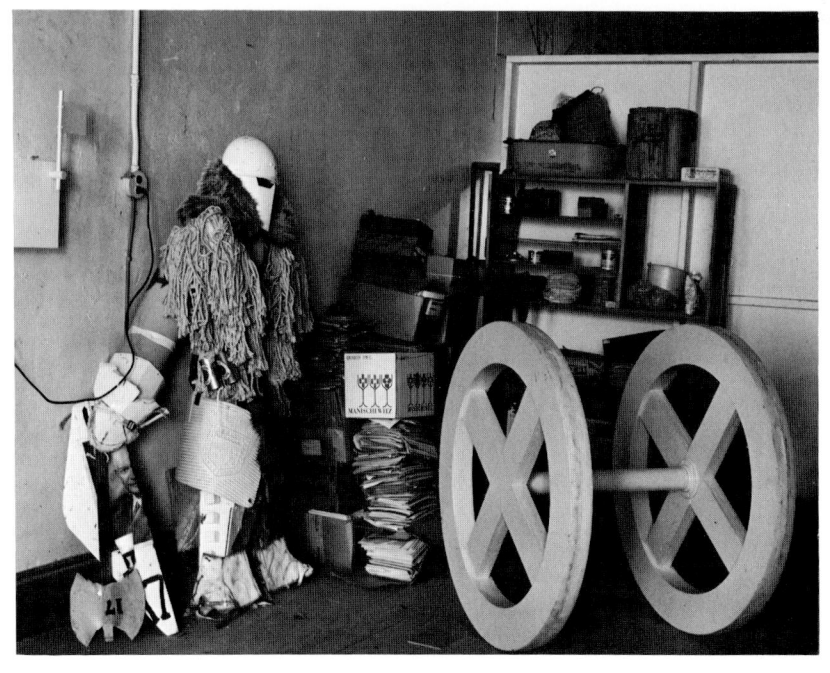

15. *Robert Morris* [studio], 1963
black and white photograph, 7½ x 9½

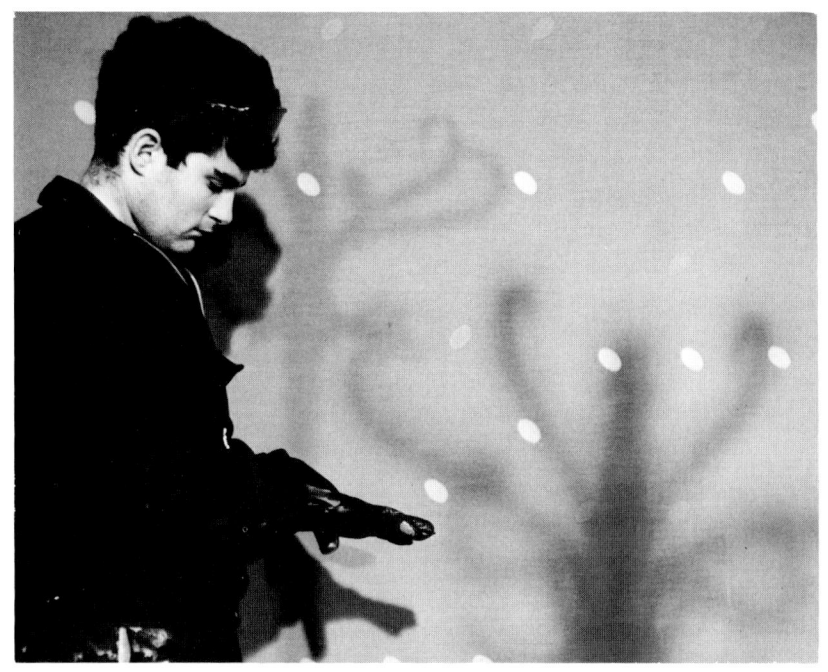

16. *Larry Poons*, 1963
black and white photograph, 7½ x 9½

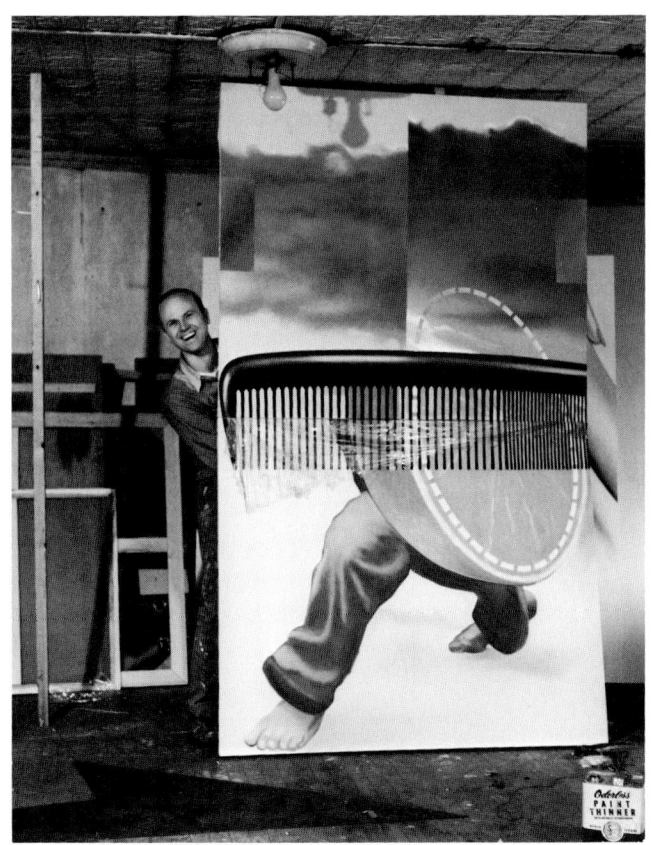

18. *James Rosenquist*, 1963
black and white photograph, 9½ x 7½

24. THE NOSTALGIA PORTFOLIO, 1971

In January 1971, Frampton assembled twelve of his earlier photographs to make the film *nostalgia,* during the course of which they are burned on camera. He recently decided to reprint the images and to reassemble them for exhibition using the script of the film verbatim for the texts accompanying these photographs. In doing so, he synchronized the voice-over narration of the film with the visuals, since their disjuncture is a major compositional element of the film. Some of the dates recounted in the commentary (of, for example, *5, 9,* and *11*) are purposefully fictitious in keeping with Frampton's idea that autobiography is a manipulation of one's past created for the public. As he explained:

> . . . In Greek the word means "the wounds of returning." "Nostalgia" is not an emotion that is entertained; it is sustained. When Ulysses comes home, nostalgia is the lumps he takes, not the tremulous pleasures he derives from being home again. In my film there is a remastering of a certain number of lumps I took during those years as a still photographer in New York. You noticed that there are no triumphs in the film; it was by no means a time that I look back to in the current pathetic sense of "nostalgia" at all . .[3]

In the portfolio, as in the film, the final image remains hidden: "that unseen thirteenth is Judas Iscariot."[4]

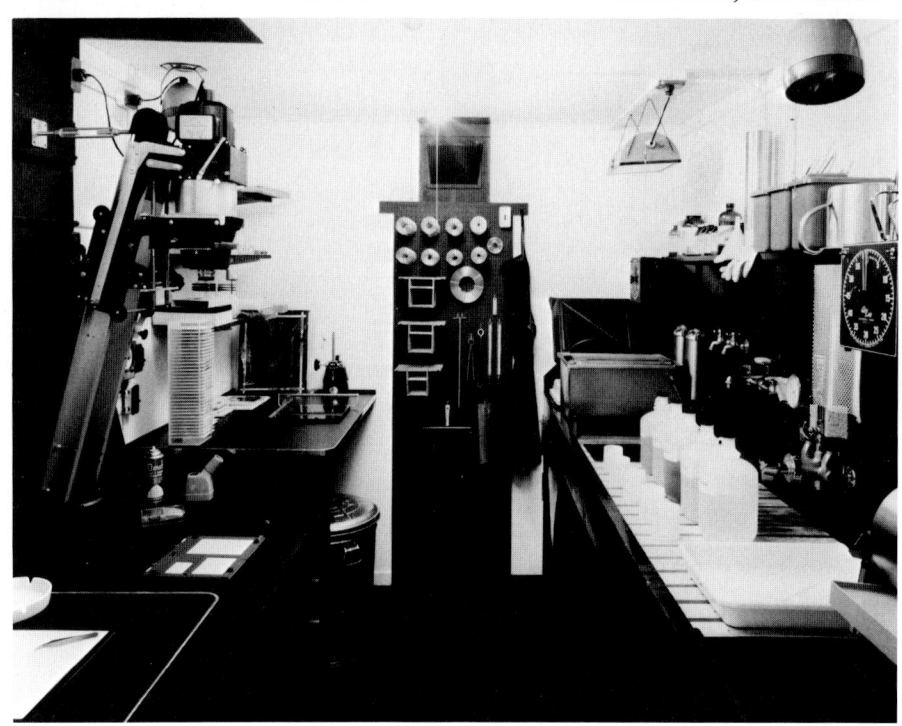

24a. *0,* n.d., from *The* nostalgia *Portfolio,* 1971
black and white photograph, 7⁵⁄₁₆ x 9⁷⁄₁₆

Blows into microphone: *It is all right?*
Voice off mike: *It's all right.*
Pause.
Reads: *These are recollections of a dozen still photographs I made several years ago.*
Pause. Blows into microphone. Pause. *Does it sound all right?*
Voice off mike: *Yes, yes, perfectly. It's fine.*
Pause.

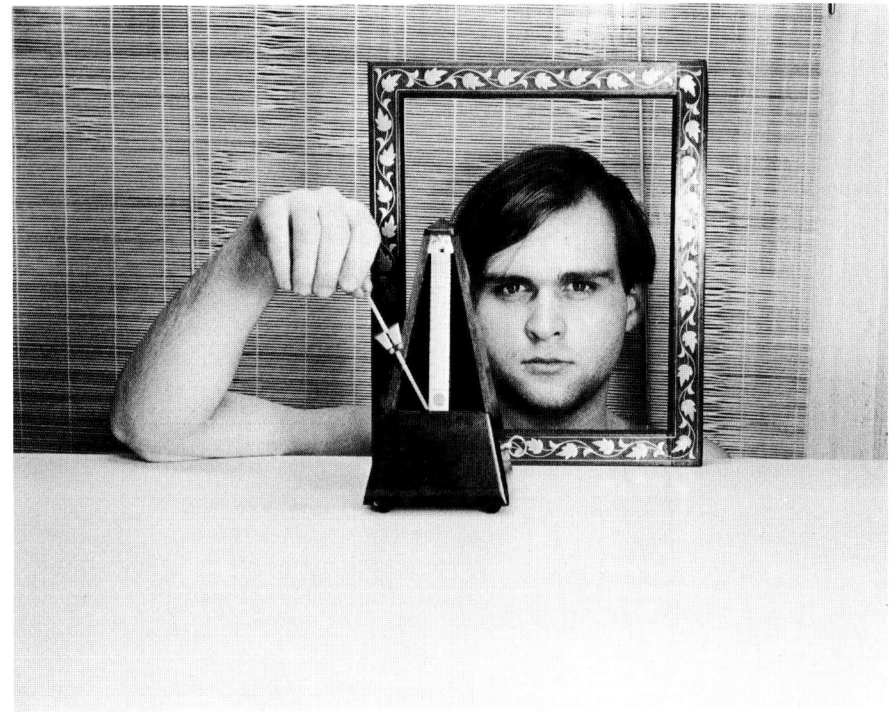

24b. *1*, 1958–1959, from *The nostalgia Portfolio*, 1971
black and white photograph, 7⅜ x 9½

Reads: *This is the first photograph I ever made with the direct intention of making art.*

I had bought myself a camera for Christmas in 1958. One day early in January of 1959, I photographed several drawings by Carl André, with whom I shared a cheap apartment on Mulberry Street. One frame of film was left over, and I suggested to Carl that he sit, or rather, squat, for a portrait.

He insisted that the photograph must incorporate a handsome small picture frame that had been given him a year or so before by a girl named North.

How the metronome entered the scheme I don't recall, but it must have been deliberately.

The picture frame re-appears in a photograph dated March, 1963, but there isn't time to show you that one now. I discarded the metronome eventually, after tolerating its syncopation for quite a while.

Carl André is twelve years older and more active than he was then. I see less of him nowadays than I should like; but then there are other people of whom I see more than I care to.

I despised this photograph for several years. But I could never bring myself to destroy a negative so incriminating.

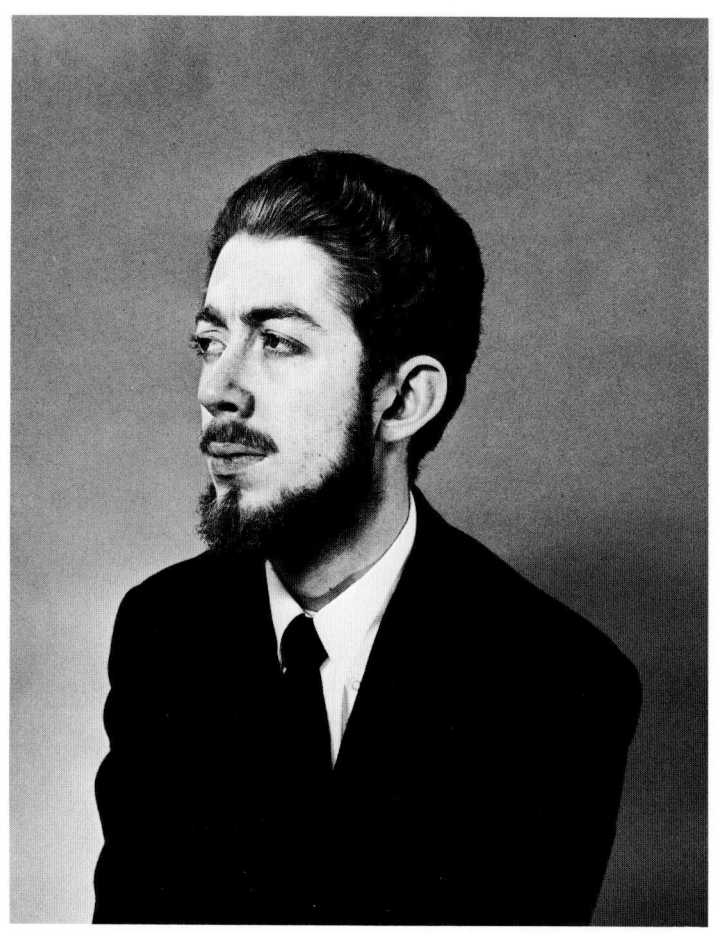

24c. *2*, 1959, from *The nostalgia Portfolio*, 1971
black and white photograph, 9½ x 7½

I made this photograph on March 11, 1959. The face is my own, or rather it was my own. As you see, I was thoroughly pleased with myself at the time, presumably for having survived to such ripeness and wisdom, since it was my twenty-third birthday.

I focussed the camera, sat on a stool in front of it, and made the exposures by squeezing a rubber bulb with my right foot.

There are eleven more photographs on the roll of film, all of comparable grandeur. Some of them exhibit my features in more sensitive or imposing moods.

One exposure records what now looks to me like a leer. I sent that one to a very pretty and sensible girl on the occasion of the vernal equinox, a holiday I held in some esteem. I think I wrote her some sort of cryptic note on the back of it. I never heard from her again.

Anyhow, photography had obviously caught my fancy. This photograph was made in the studio where I worked. It belonged to the wife of a friend. I daresay they are still married, but he has not been my friend for nearly ten years. We became estranged on account of an obscure mutual embarrassment that involved a third party, and three dozen eggs.

I take some comfort in realizing that my entire physical body has been replaced more than once since it made this portrait of its face. However, I understand that my central nervous system is an exception.

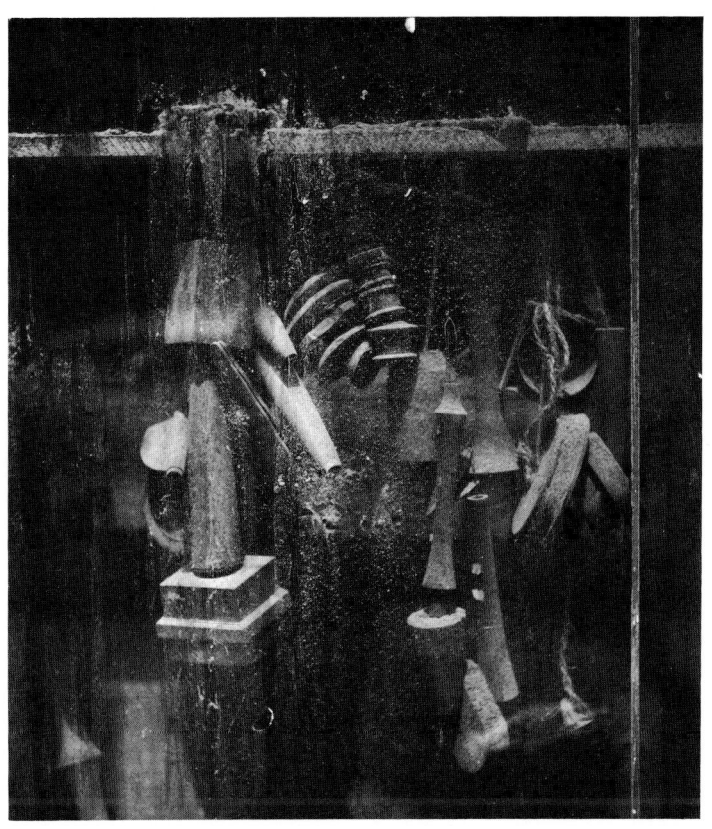

24d. *3, 1960*, from *The* nostalgia *Portfolio*, 1971
black and white photograph, 8 9/16 x 7 1/2

This photograph was made in September of 1960. The window is that of a dusty cabinetmaker's shop, on the west side of West Broadway, somewhere between Spring Street and West Houston.

I first photographed it more than a year earlier, as part of a series, but rejected it for reasons having to do with its tastefulness and illusion of deep space.

Then, in the course of two years, I made a half-dozen more negatives. Each time, I found some reason to feel dissatisfied. The negative was too flat, or too harsh; or the framing was too tight. Once a horse was reflected in the glass, although I don't recall seeing that horse. Once, I found myself reflected, with my camera and tripod.

Finally, the cabinetmaker closed up shop and moved away. I can't even remember exactly where he was, anymore.

But a year after that, I happened to compare the prints I made from the six negatives. I was astonished! In the midst of my concern for the flaws in my method, the window itself had changed, from season to season, far more than my photographs had! I had thought my subject changeless, and my own sensibility pliable. But I was wrong about that.

So I chose the one photograph that pleased me most after all, and destroyed the rest. That was years ago. Now I'm sorry. I only wish you could have seen them!

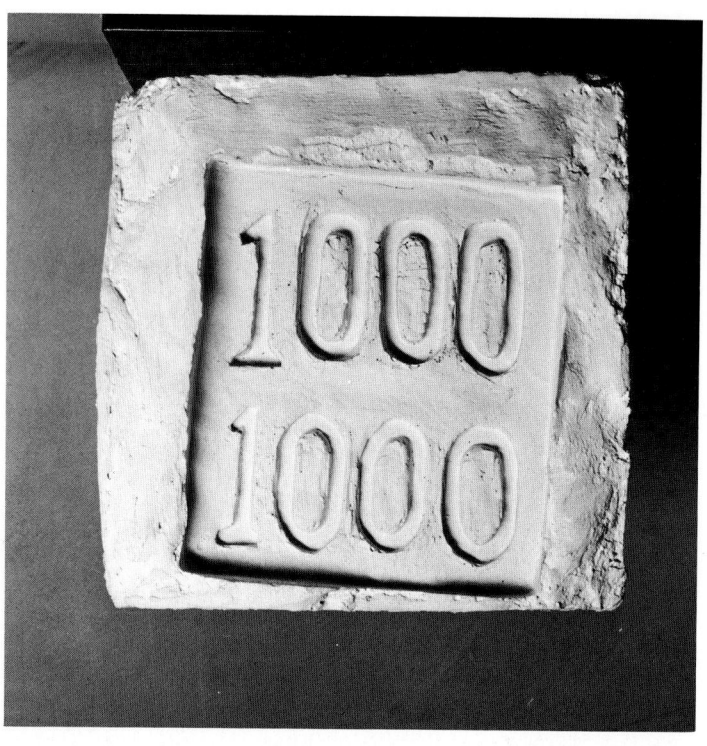

24e. *4, 1961,* from *The nostalgia Portfolio,* 1971
black and white photograph, 7½ x 7½

In 1961, for six or eight months, I lived in a borrowed loft on Bond Street, near the Bowery.

A young painter, who lived on the floor above me, wanted to be an Old Master. He talked a great deal about gums and varnishes; he was on his way to impastoes of record thickness.

The Spring of that year was sunny, and I spent a month photographing junk and rubble, in imitation of action painting. My neighbor saw my new work, and he was not especially pleased.

His opinion upset me . . . and for good reason. He lived with a woman (I believe her father was a Brazilian economist) who seemed to stay with him out of inertia. She was monumentally fair, and succulent, and indifferent. In the warm weather, she went about nearly naked, and I would invent excuses to visit upstairs, in order to stare at her.

My photographs failing as an excuse, decided to ingratiate myself in the household by making a realistic work of art. I carved the numerals you see out of modeling clay, and then cast them in plaster.

The piece is called "A Cast of Thousands." The numbers are reversed in the cast, of course, but I have reversed them again in printing, to enhance their intelligibility.

Anyway, I finally unveiled the piece one evening. I suppose the painter was properly horrified. But the girl, who had never said a dozen words to me, laughed, and then laughed outrageously, and then, outrageously, kissed me.

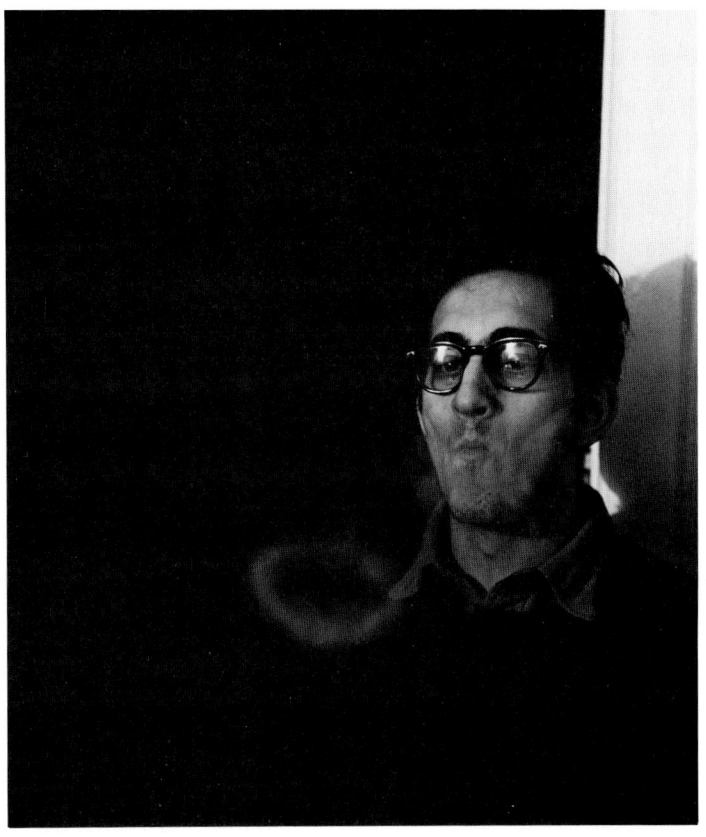

24f. *5*, 1962, from The nostalgia *Portfolio*, 1971
black and white photograph, 8⁹⁄₁₆ x 7½

Early in 1963, Frank Stella asked me to make a portrait. He needed it for some casual business use: a show announcement, or maybe a passport. Something like that. I only recall that it needed to be done quickly. A likeness would do.

I made a dozen likenesses and he chose one. His dealer paid me for the job.

Most of those dozen faces seem resigned, or melancholy. This one amuses me because Frank looks so entirely self-possessed. I suppose blowing smoke rings admits of little feeling beyond that.

Looking at the photograph recently, it reminded me, unaccountably, of a photograph of another artist squirting water out of his mouth, which is undoubtedly art. Blowing smoke rings seems more of a craft.

Ordinarily, only opera singers make art with their mouths.

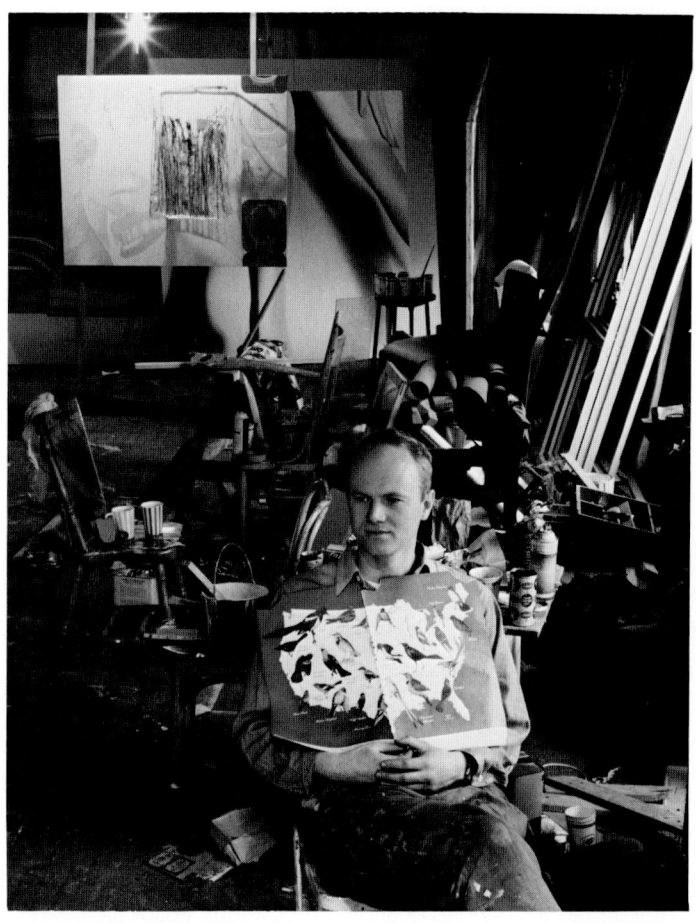

24g. 6, 1963, from The nostalgia Portfolio, 1971
black and white photograph, 9½ x 7½

I made this photograph of James Rosenquist the first day we met. That was on Palm Sunday in 1963, when he lived in a red brick building at number 5 Coenties Slip. I went there to photograph him, in his studio, for a fashion magazine. The job was a washout, but Rosenquist and I remained friends for years afterward.

He rented two floors in the building. The lower floor, where he lived with his wife Mary Lou, was cool, neat and pleasant. Mary Lou was relaxed, cool, neat, very tall, and extremely pleasant. Rosenquist was calm. It was a lovely, soft, quiet Sunday.

We talked for awhile and then went upstairs to his workroom. I made 96 negatives in about two hours. This was the last. It is unrelated to the others.

Rosenquist is holding open a copy of an old magazine. A map of the United States shows the distribution of our typical songbirds. I admire this photograph for its internal geometry, the expression of its subject, its virtually perfect mapping of tonal values on the grey scale. It pleases me as much as anything I did.

James Rosenquist and I live far apart now, and we seldom meet. But I cannot recall one moment spent in his company that I didn't completely enjoy.

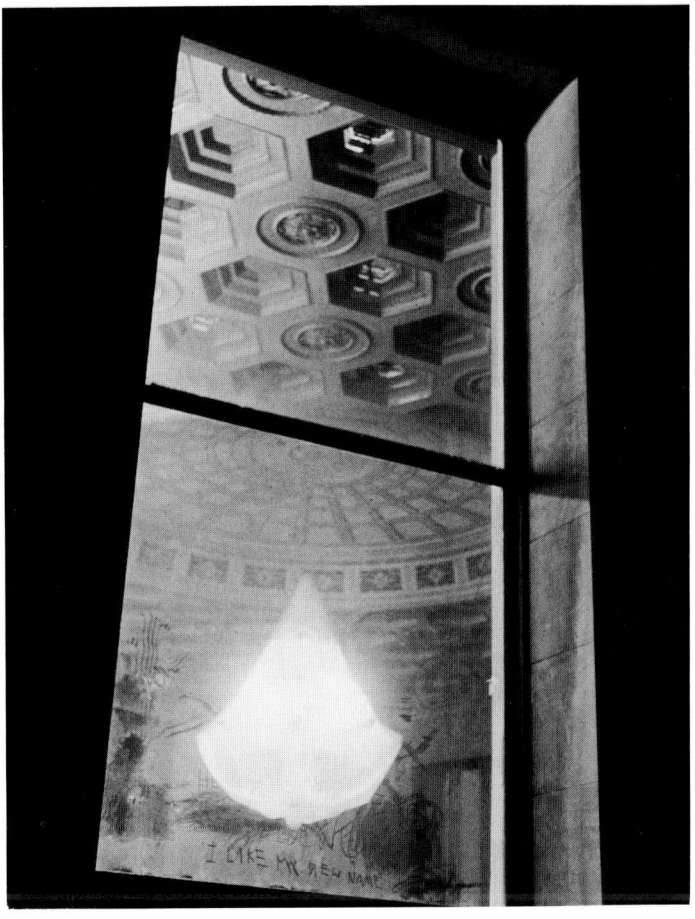

24h. *7, 1963*, from *The nostalgia Portfolio*, 1971
black and white photograph, 9½ x 7½

This photograph was made at about 3:00 o'clock on the morning of June 6, 1963, in lower Manhattan. It may even have been Wall Street.

It is seen from the sidewalk, through the window of a large bank that had been closed for renovation and partially demolished inside. A big crystal chandelier is draped in a dusty, translucent membrane that recalls the tents of caterpillars. Someone has written with a forefinger, on the dusty pane, the words "I like my new name."

This seemed mysterious to me. At that time, I was much taken with the photographs of Lartigue, and I wanted to make photographs as mysterious as his, without, however, attempting to comprehend his wit.

All I learned was that the two were somehow bound together. Anyway my eye for mystery is defective, and so this may be the only example I'll ever produce.

Nevertheless, because it is a very difficult negative to print, I find that I do so less and less often.

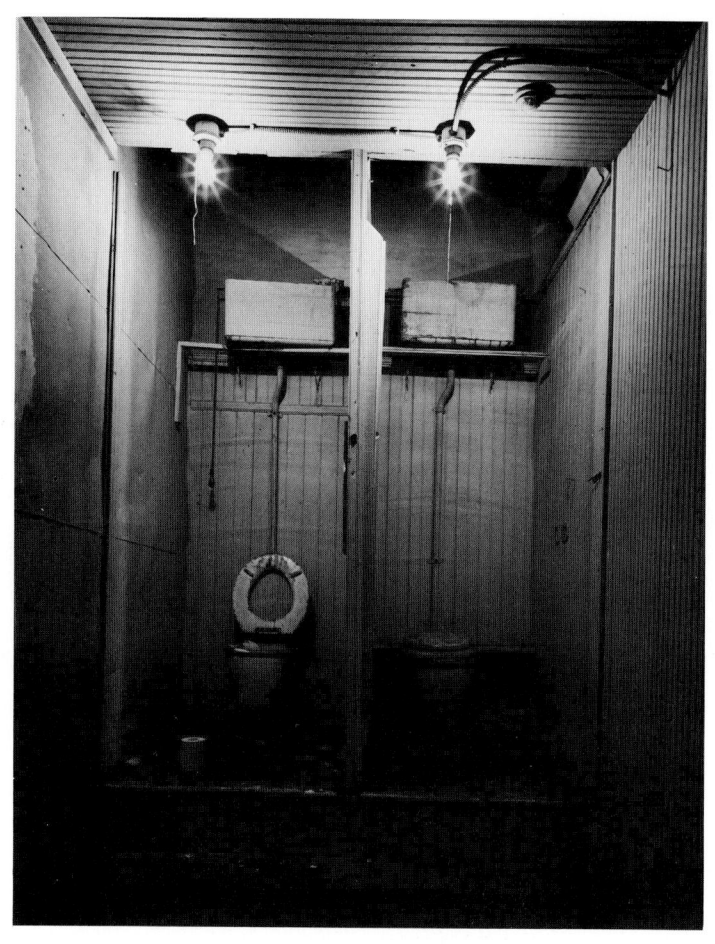

24i. *8*, 1964, from *The* nostalgia *Portfolio*, 1971
black and white photograph, 9½ x 7½

This photograph of two toilets was made in February of 1964, with a new view camera I had just got at that time.

As you can see, it is an imitation of a painted renaissance crucifixion.

The outline of the Cross is quite clear. At its foot, the closed bowl on the right represents the Blessed Virgin. On the left is St. Mary Magdalene: a bowl with its lid raised. The roll of toilet paper stands for the skull of Adam, whose sin is conventionally washed away by the blood the crucified Savior sheds. The stairs leading up to the two booths symbolize Calvary.

I'm not completely certain of the iconographic significance of the light bulbs, but the haloes that surround them are more than suggestive.

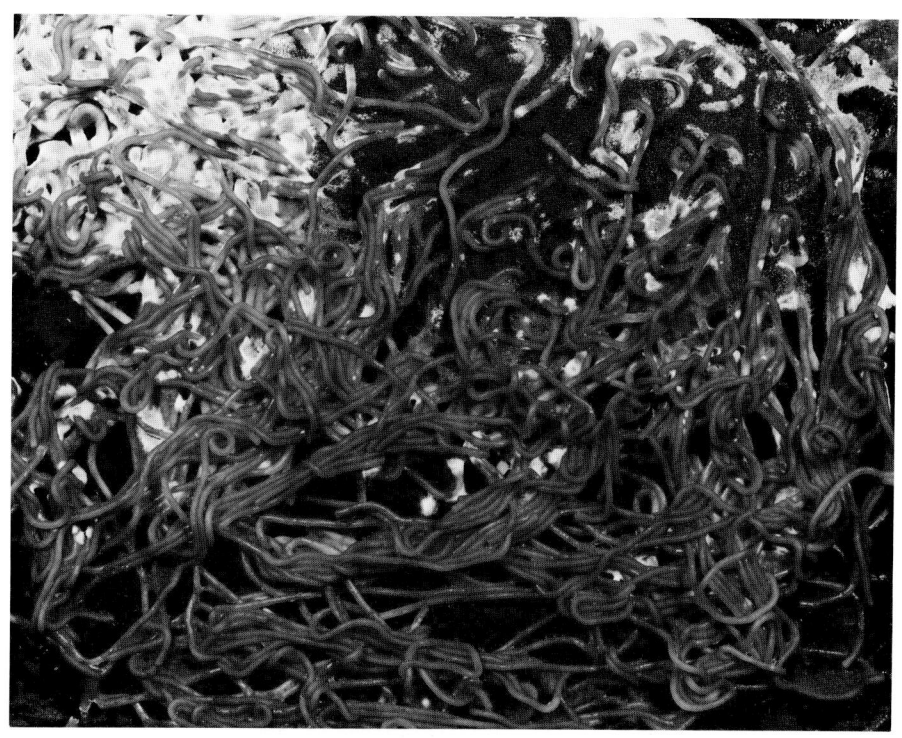

24j. *9,* 1964, from *The* nostalgia *Portfolio,* 1971
black and white photograph, 7½ x 9½

Late in the Fall of 1964, a painter friend asked me to make a photographic document of spaghetti, an image that he wanted to incorporate into a work of his own.

I set up my camera above an empty darkroom tray, opened a Number 2 can of Franco-American Spaghetti, and poured it out. Then I stirred it around until I saw a suitably random arrangement of pasta strands, and finished the photograph in short order.

Then, instead of disposing of the spaghetti, I left it there, and made one photograph every day. This was the eighteenth such photograph.

The spaghetti has dried without rotting. The sauce is a kind of pink varnish on the yellow strings. The entirety is covered in attractive mature colonies of mold in three colors: black, green and white.

I continued the series until no further change appeared to be taking place: about two months altogether. The spaghetti was never entirely consumed, but the mold eventually disappeared.

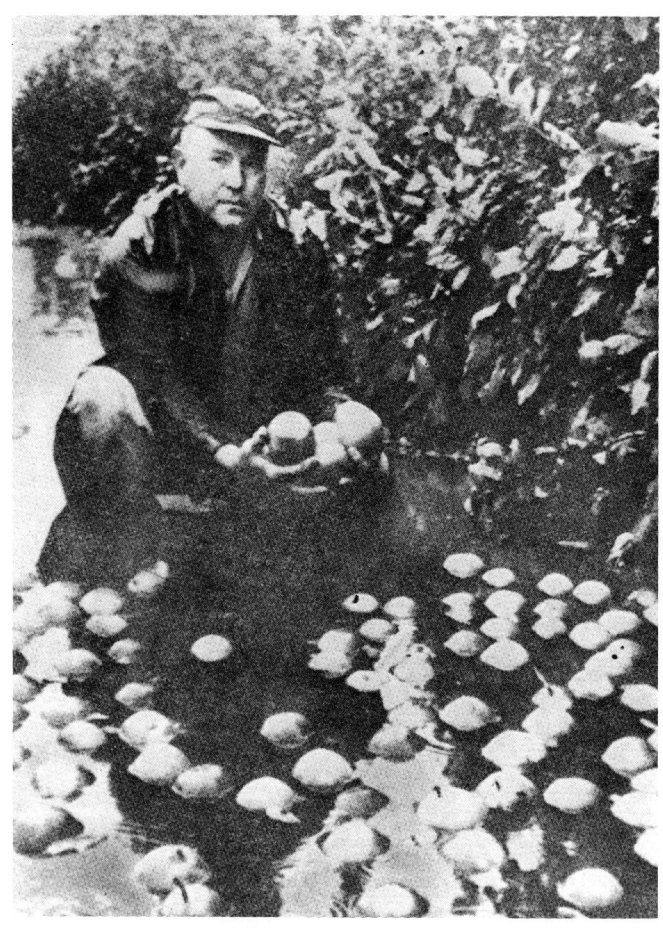

24m. *12*, n.d., from *The nostalgia Portfolio*, 1971
black and white photograph, 9¾ x 6¹⁵⁄₁₆

I did not make this photograph, nor do I know who did. Nor can I recall precisely when it was made. It was printed in a newspaper, so I suppose that any patient person with an interest in this sort of thing could satisfy himself entirely as to its origins.

The image is slightly indistinct. A stubby, middle-aged man wearing a baseball cap looks back in matter-of-fact dismay or disgruntlement at the camera. It has caught him in the midst of a display of spheres, each about the size of a grapefruit, and of some nondescript light color. He holds four of them in his cupped hands. The rest seem half-submerged in water, or else lying in something like mud. A vague, mottled mass behind the crouching man suggest foliage.

I am as puzzled and mildly distressed by the sight of this photograph as its protagonist seems to be with the spheres. They seem absolutely alien, and yet not very forbidding, after all.
What does it mean?

I am uncertain, but perfectly willing to offer a plausible explanation. The man is a Texas fruit-grower. His orchards lie near the Gulf of Mexico. The spheres are grapefruit. As they neared maturity, a hurricane flooded the orchard and knocked down the fruit. The man is stunned by his commercial loss, and a little resentful of the photographer who intrudes upon his attempt to assess it.

On the other hand, were photography of greater antiquity, then this image might date from the time of, let us say, Pascal; and I suppose he would have understood it quite differently.

24n. Closing text, from *The nostalgia Portfolio*, 1971

Since 1966 I have made a few photographs. This has been partly through design, and partly through laziness. I think I expose fewer than fifty negatives a year now. Of course I work more deliberately than I once did, and that counts for something. But I must confess that I have largely given up still photography.

So it is all the more surprising that I felt again, a few weeks ago, a vagrant urge that would have seemed familiar a few years ago: the urge to take my camera out of doors and make a photograph. It was a quite simple, obtrusive need. So I obeyed it.

I wandered around for hours, unsatisfied, and finally turned towards home in the afternoon. Half a block from my front door, the receding perspective of an alley caught my eye . . . a dark tunnel with the cross-street beyond brightly lit. As I focussed and composed the image, a truck turned into the alley. The driver stopped it, got out, and walked away. He left his cab door open.

My composition was spoiled, but I felt a perverse impulse to make the exposure anyway. I did so, and then went home to develop my single negative.

When I came to print the negative, an odd thing struck my eye. Something, standing in the cross-street and invisible to me, was reflected in a factory window, and then reflected once more in the rear-view mirror attached to the truck door. It was only a tiny detail.

Since then, I have enlarged this small section of my negative enormously. The grain of the film all but obliterates the features of the image. It is obscure; by any possible reckoning, it is hopelessly ambiguous.

Nevertheless, what I believe I see recorded, in that speck of film, fills me with such fear, such utter dread and loathing, that I think I shall never dare to make another photograph again.

Here it is!
Look at it!
Do you see what I see?

23. *A VISITATION OF INSOMNIA,* 1970–1973

Frampton had long been interested in time and motion, and discontent with the atemporal nature of most modern photographic images. These fundamental concerns spurred him to research and reinvestigate the history of photography, and to assimilate into his revisionist "metahistory" works previously discounted or misinterpreted. His fascination with the nineteenth-century photographs of Muybridge and Marey is reflected in writings, films, and photographs. His comments on Marey pertain directly to this series:

> The work of Etienne-Jules Marey, a scientist who switched from graphic to photographic notations of animal movement under Muybridge's direct tutelage, summarizes the point of disjunction between the still photograph and cinema; his studies consist of serial exposures made on a single plate. The photograph could no longer contain the contradictory pressures to affirm time and to deny it. It split sharply into an illusionistic cinema of incessant motion and a static photographic art that remained frozen solid for decades. So complete and immediate was the separation that by 1917 the photographer Alvin Langdon Coburn (an ex-painter, who is rumored to have collaborated on a Vorticist film, long since lost, with Ezra Pound) could speculate in print—and in ignorance—on the "interesting patterns" that might be produced if one were but to do what Marey had in fact done, mountainously, thirty-odd years before.[2]

A Visitation of Insomnia refers visually to Marey's chronophotographs, which similarly incorporated multiple exposures in one image. Frampton shot the series in 1970; the complicated process of its printing stretched into the next year. He later revised the series in preparation for an exhibition in 1973, the year he wrote his essay on Muybridge and was working on the film *Vernal Equinox,* 1975, in which the same woman is shown going through very similar movements.

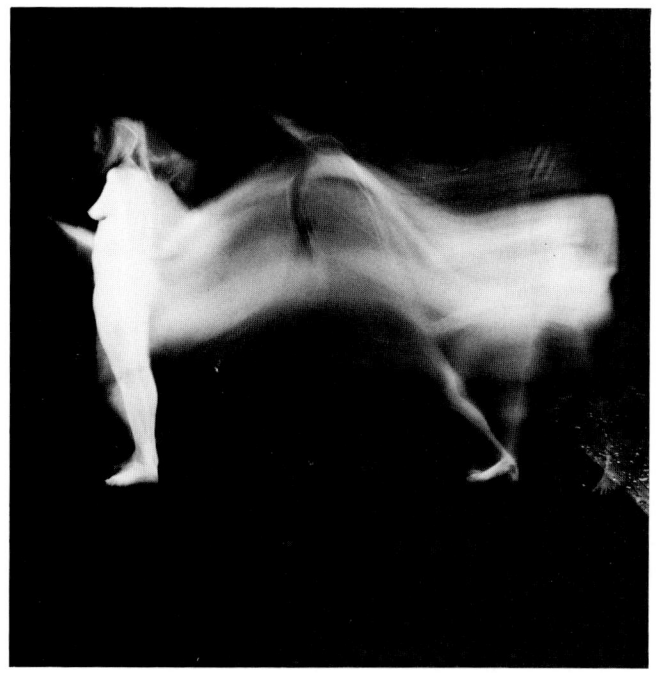
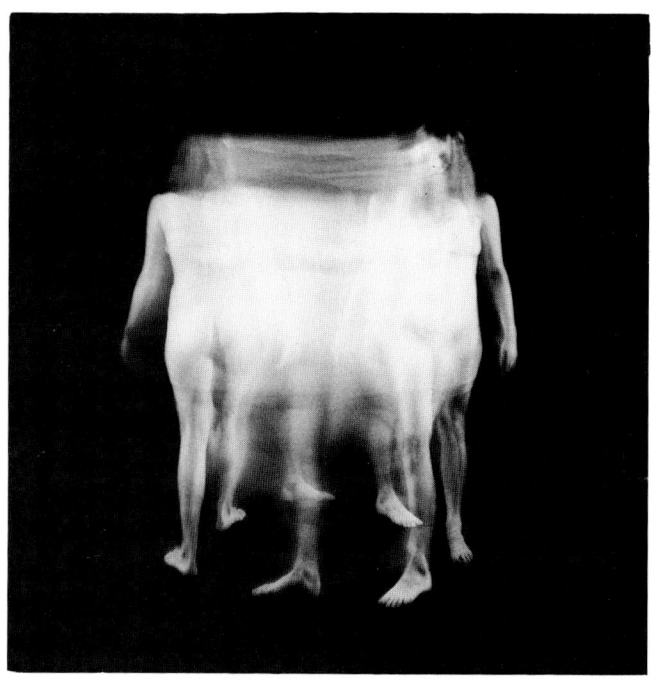
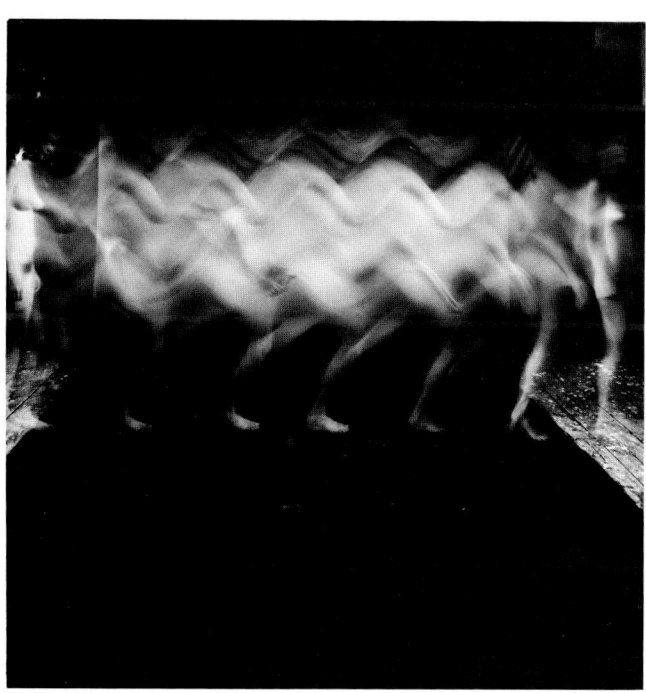
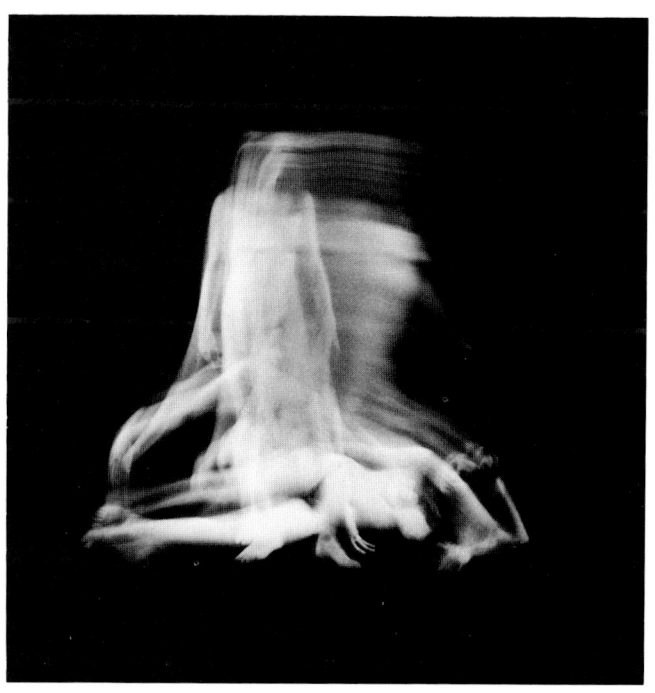

23. clockwise: *5, 12, 15* and *20* from *A Visitation of Insomnia*, 1970–1973
black and white photographs, each
10⅜ x 10⅜

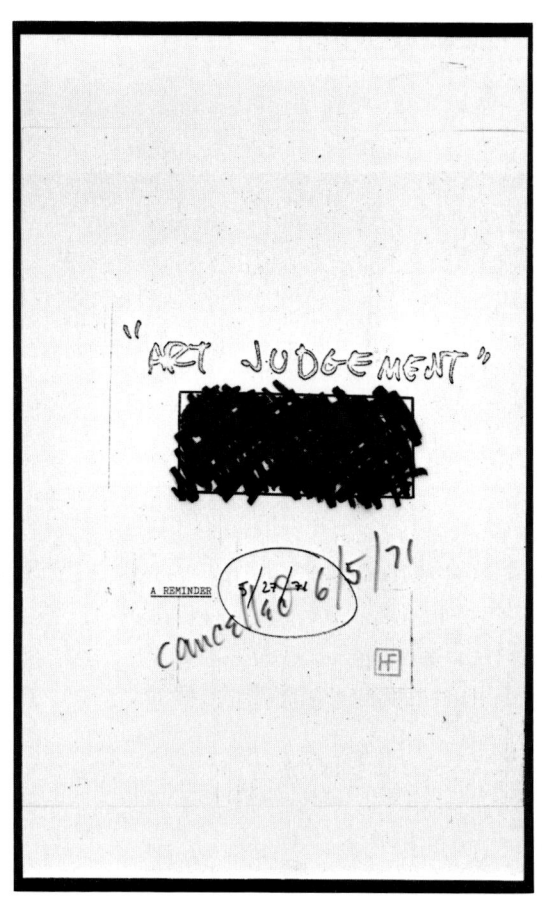

25f. *A Reminder*, from *Reasonable Facsimiles*, 1971
applied color on xerograph
13 11/16 x 8 7/8

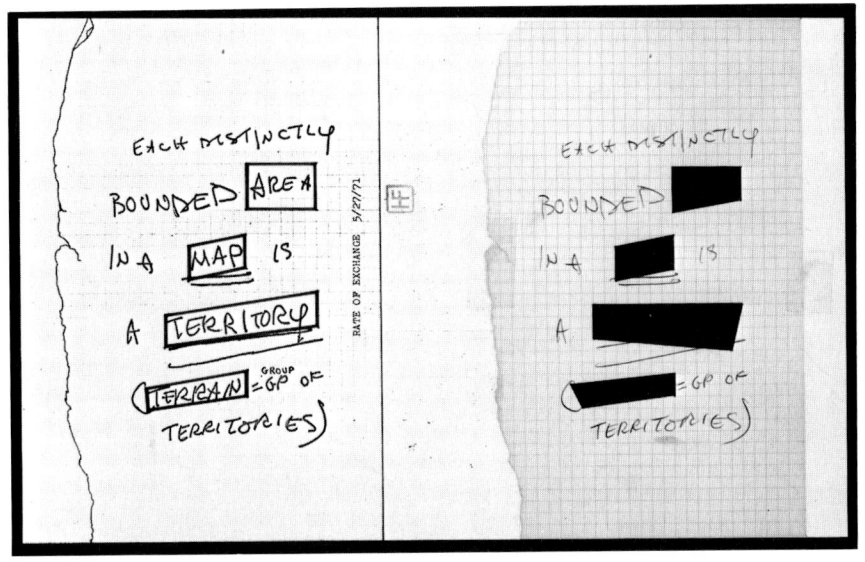

25e. *Rate of Exchange,* from *Reasonable Facsimiles,* 1971
applied color on xerograph, collage
8 7/16 x 13 11/16

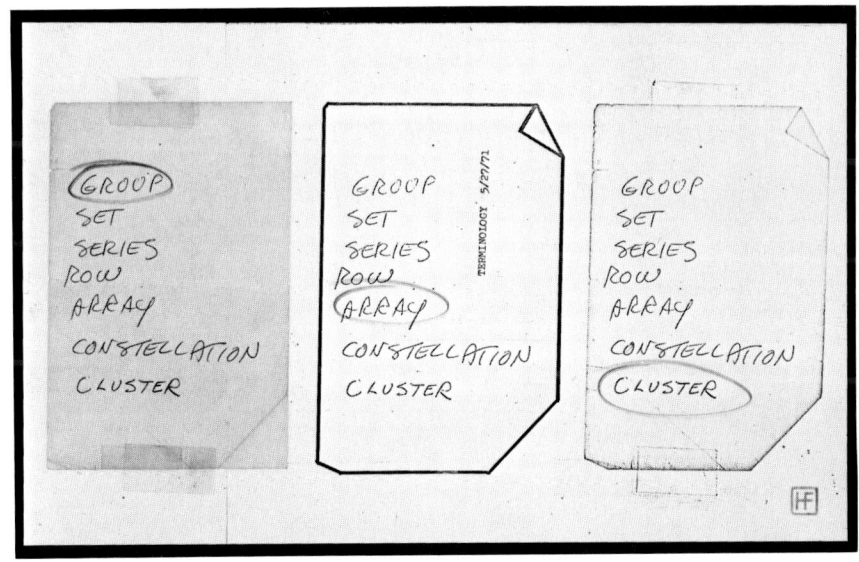

25g. *Terminology,* from *Reasonable Facsimiles,* 1971
applied color on xerograph, collage
8 3/8 x 13 11/16

28. *SIXTEEN STUDIES FROM VEGETABLE LOCOMOTION,* 1975
with Marion Faller

This series, Frampton's first major collaboration with Marion Faller, is a blatant, humorous pun on the animal locomotion photographs of Eadweard Muybridge. In 1973, Frampton wrote about Muybridge's famed motion studies:

> Having once consciously fastened upon time as his grand subject, Muybridge quickly emptied his images as nearly as he could of everything else. His animals, athletes, and subverted painters' models are nameless and mostly naked, performing their banalities, purged of drama if not of occasional horseplay, before a uniform grid of Cartesian coordinates, a kind of universal 'frame of reference,' ostensibly intended as an aid in reconciling the successive images with chronometry, that also destroys all sense of scale (the figures could be pagan constellations in the sky), and utterly obliterates the tactile particularity that is one of the photograph's paramount traits, thereby annihilating any possible feeling of place. About all that is left, in each case, is an archetypal fragment of living action, potentially subject to the incessant reiteration that is one of the most familiar and intolerable features of our dreams.[5]

The items Faller and Frampton photographed are, ironically, hopelessly immobile. Muybridge's study contains a total of 781 plates. When "re-doing" them, Frampton and Faller outdid Muybridge by one; thus the last in their series is purported to be 782. The images are not, however, based on the corresponding plates in Muybridge's series. The name listed in brackets is for the most part the actual variety of seed used for the vegetables, which were the indisposable remains of a bumper crop from their garden. "Dread" in *33. Zucchini squash encountering sawhorse [var. Dread]* is not a variety, but a dog that appears in Muybridge's plates.

The intellectual humor belies the importance of the autobiographical elements of *Sixteen Studies from VEGETABLE LOCOMOTION,* which was made the summer after Frampton and Faller moved from New York City to thirty acres of land in Eaton, New York. The series echoes of Frampton's description of old family photographs, and one in particular that amused him:

> The photo is of my father and my grandfather with an enormous number of crook neck squash and my grandfather's 1938 Buick. He has hung the crook neck squash all over the bumpers of the Buick, on the head lights and on the handles, and he's holding them. And my father is holding crook neck squash, and they have them hooked in their pockets and so forth. As a final touch, they unzip their flies and each of them has a crook neck squash hanging from their pants. They're both standing there with huge smirks of utter tom foolery and hell-bent mischief on their faces.[6]

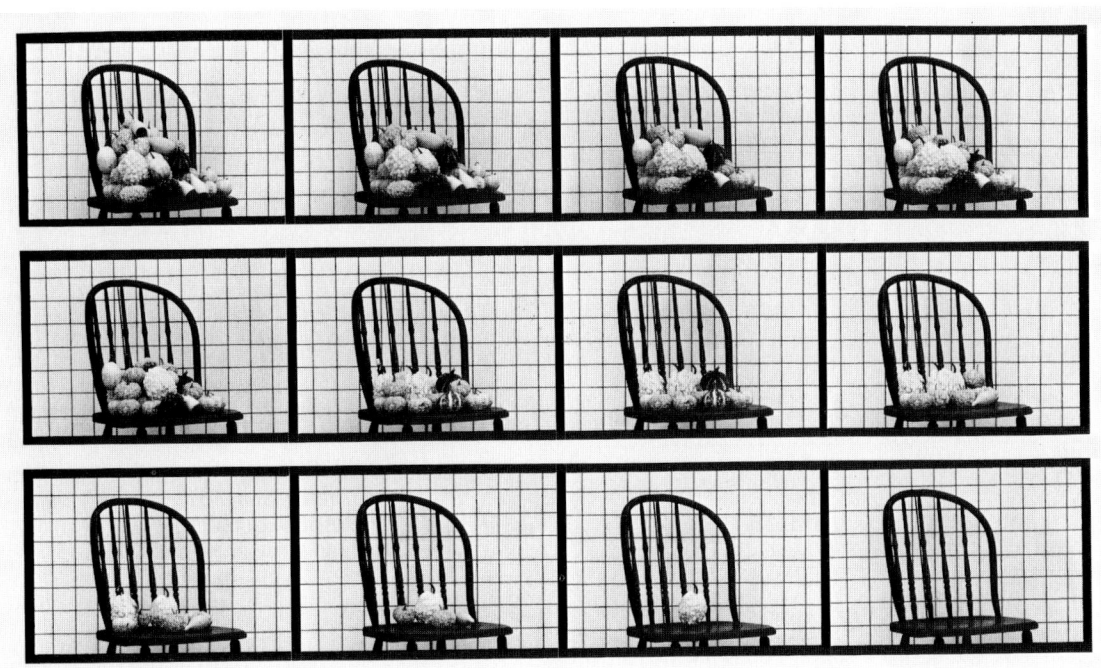

28a. *14. Gourds vanishing [var. "Mixed Ornamental]*, from *Sixteen Studies from VEGETABLE LOCOMOTION*, 1975
black and white photograph, 11 x 14

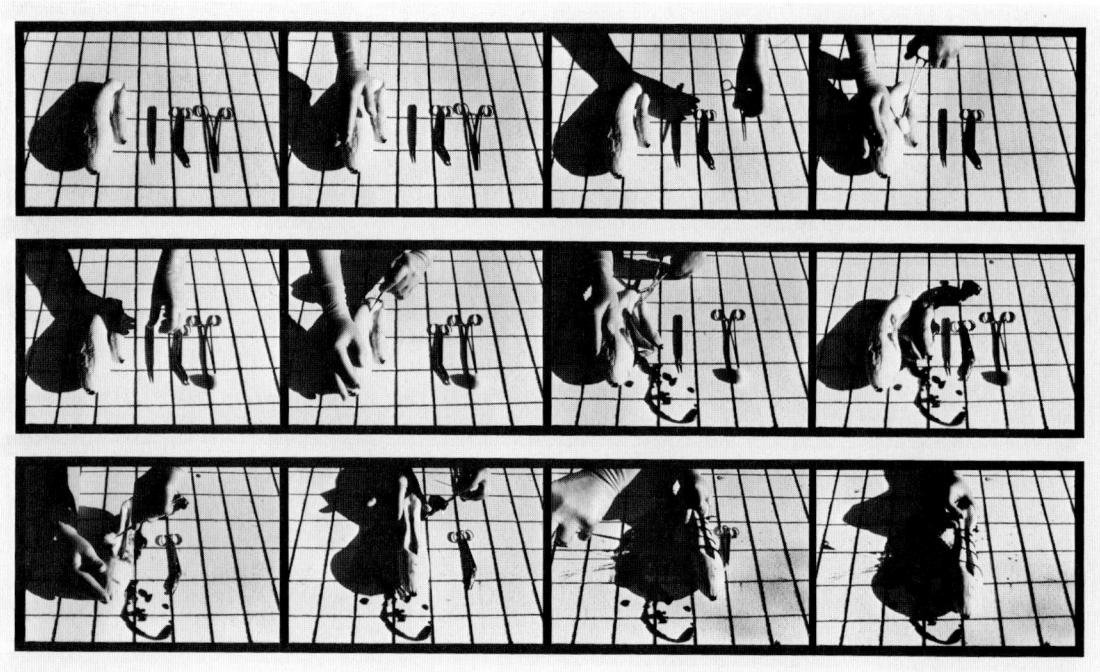

28f. *357. Summer squash undergoing surgery [var. "Yellow Straightneck"]*, from *Sixteen Studies from VEGETABLE LOCOMOTION*, 1975
black and white photograph, 11 x 14

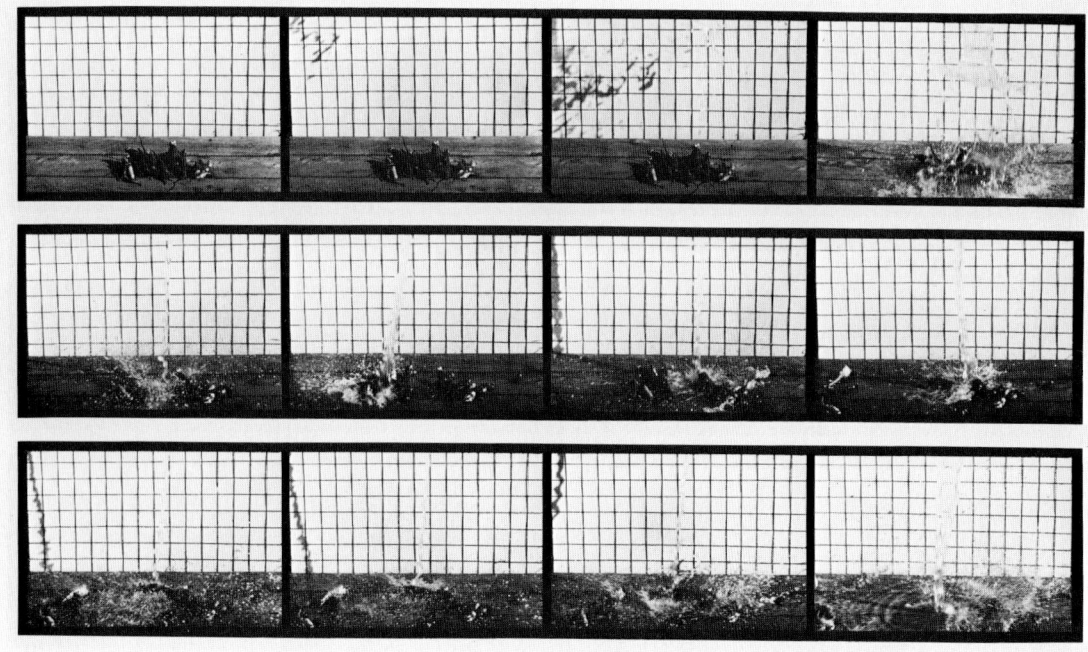

28g. *481. Mature radishes bathing [var. "Black Spanish"]*, from *Sixteen Studies from VEGETABLE LOCOMOTION*, 1975
black and white photograph, 11 x 14

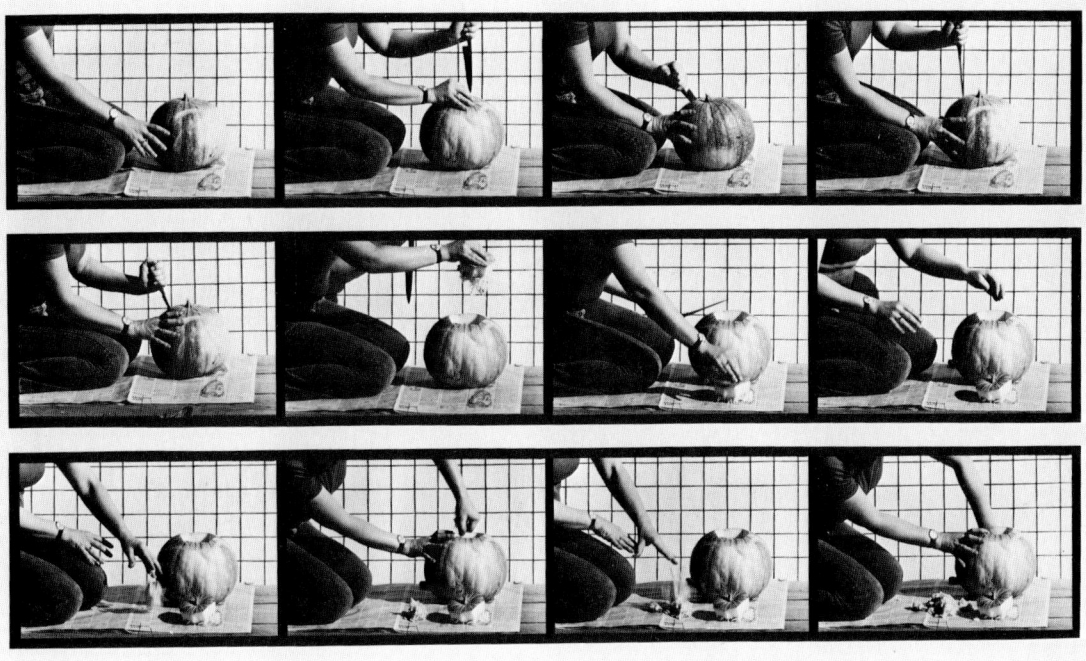

28h. *482. Pumpkin emptying [var. "Cinderella"]*, from *Sixteen Studies from VEGETABLE LOCOMOTION*, 1975
black and white photograph, 11 x 14

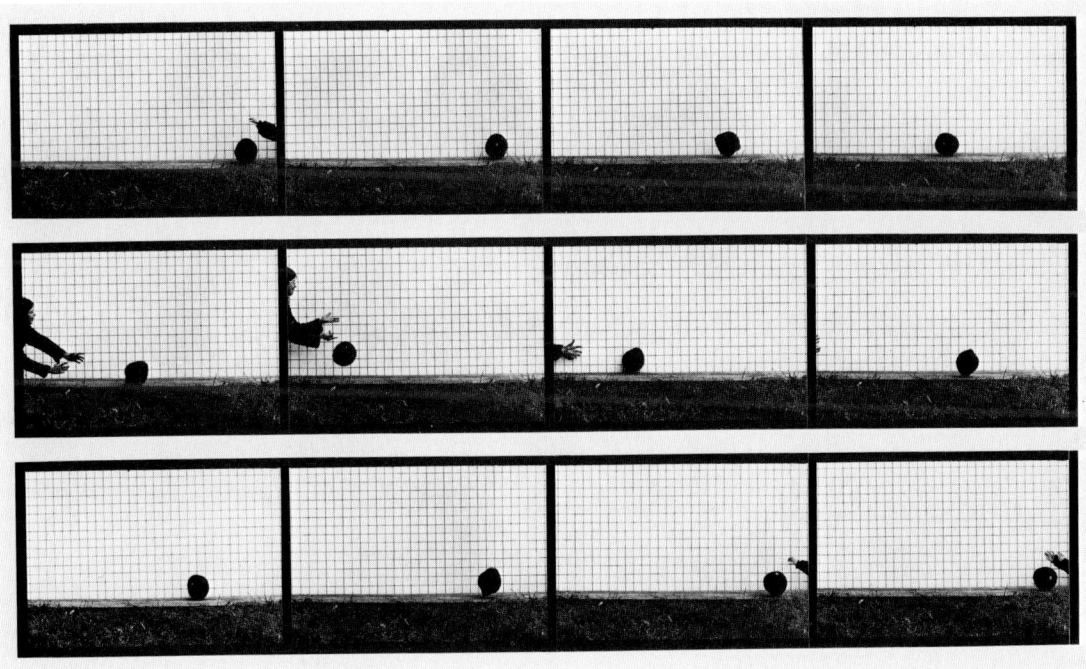

28i. *484. Winter squash vacillating [var. "True Hubbard"]*, from *Sixteen Studies from VEGETABLE LOCOMOTION*, 1975
black and white photograph, 11 x 14

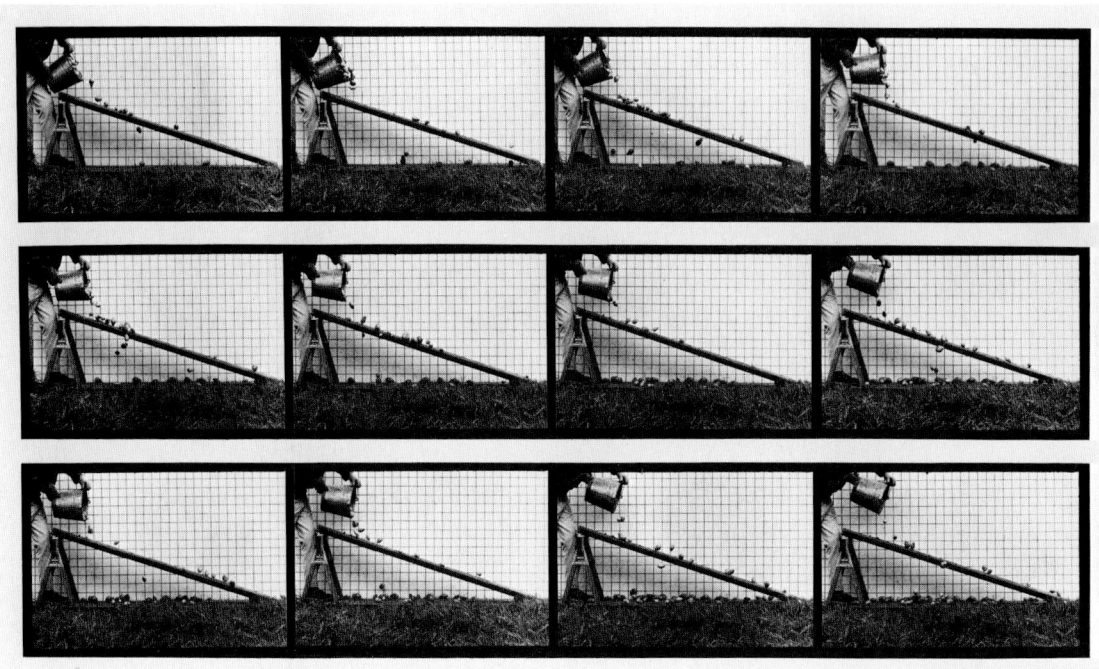

28j. *519. Tomatoes descending a ramp* [var. *"Roma"*], from *Sixteen Studies from VEGETABLE LOCOMOTION*, 1975
black and white photograph, 11 x 14

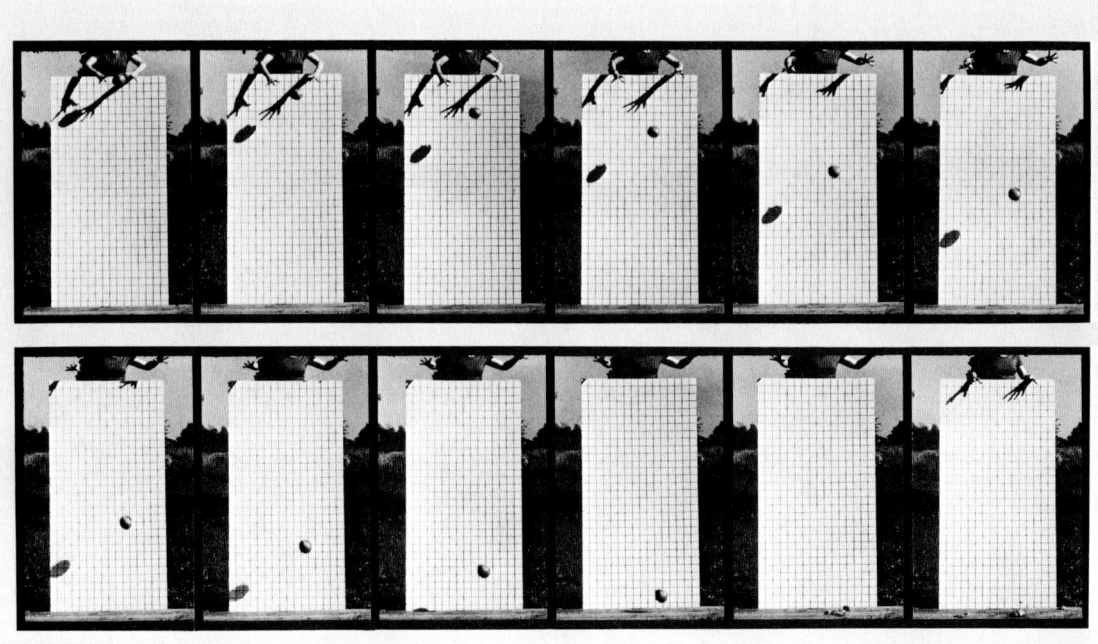

28k. *537. Watermelon falling* [var. *"New Hampshire Midget"*], from *Sixteen Studies from VEGETABLE LOCOMOTION*, 1975
black and white photograph, 11 x 14

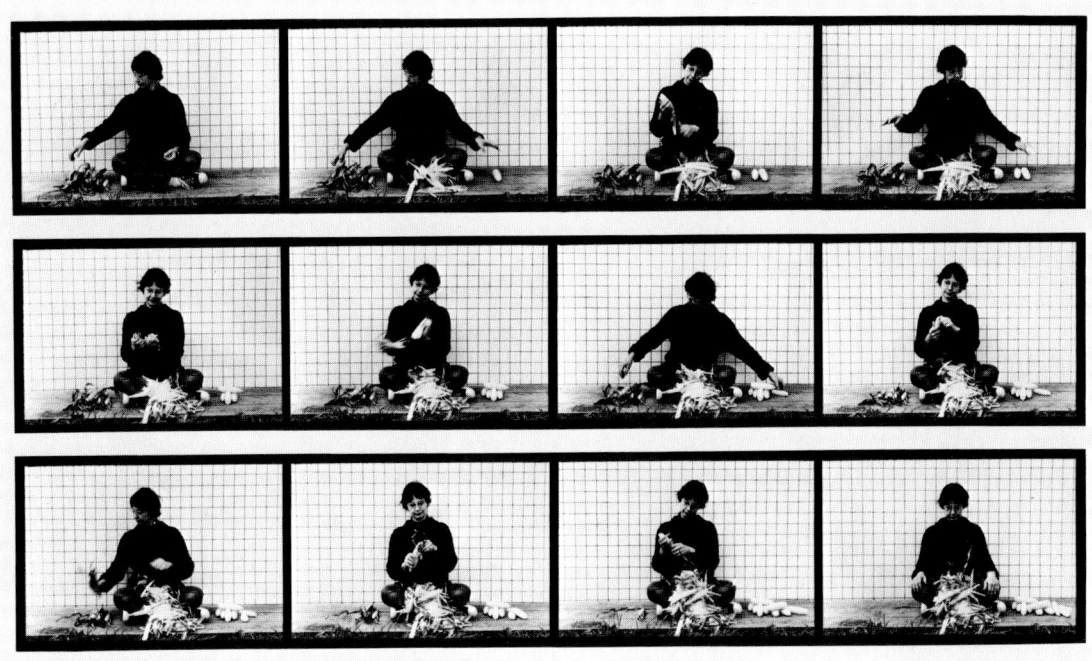

28l. *601. Sweet corn disrobing [var. "Early Sunglow"]*, from *Sixteen Studies from VEGETABLE LOCOMOTION*, 1975
black and white photograph, 11 x 14

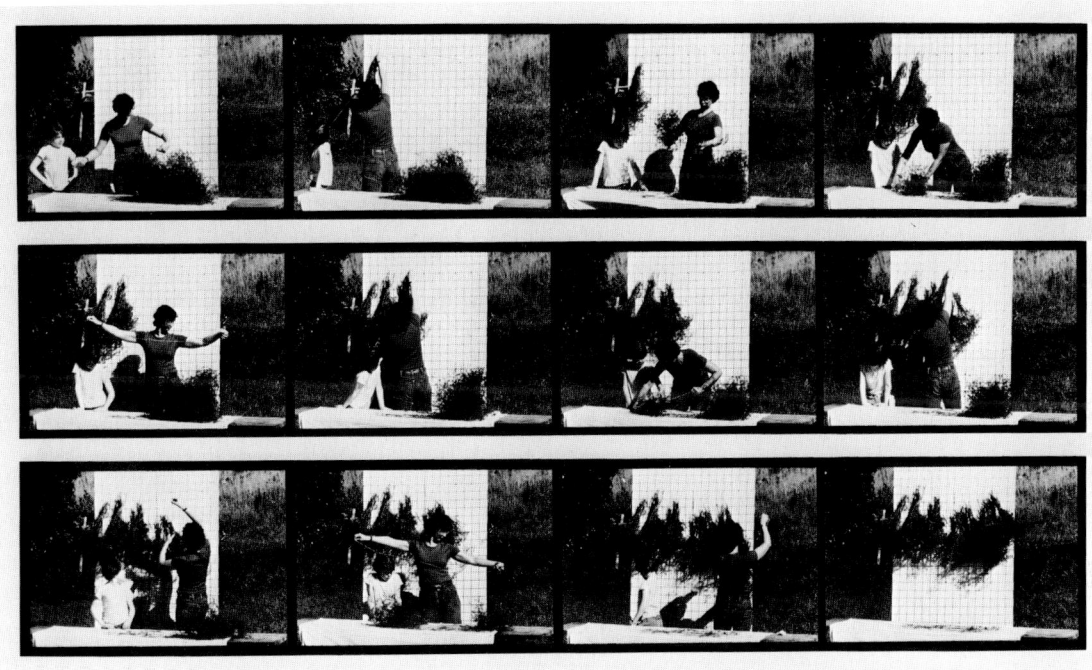

28m. *605. Dill bundling [var. "Rural Splendor"]*, from *Sixteen Studies from VEGETABLE LOCOMOTION*, 1975
black and white photograph, 11 x 14

30. *FALSE IMPRESSIONS,* 1979
with Marion Faller

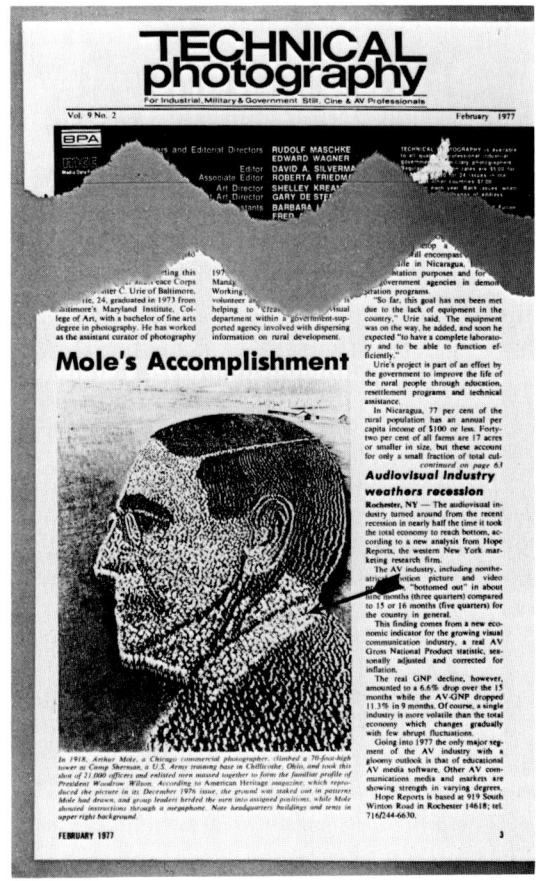

30b. *Uncle Rudy at the fourth cervical vertebra,* from *False Impressions,* 1979
color xerograph, 13¼ x 8⁵⁄₁₆, 6/14

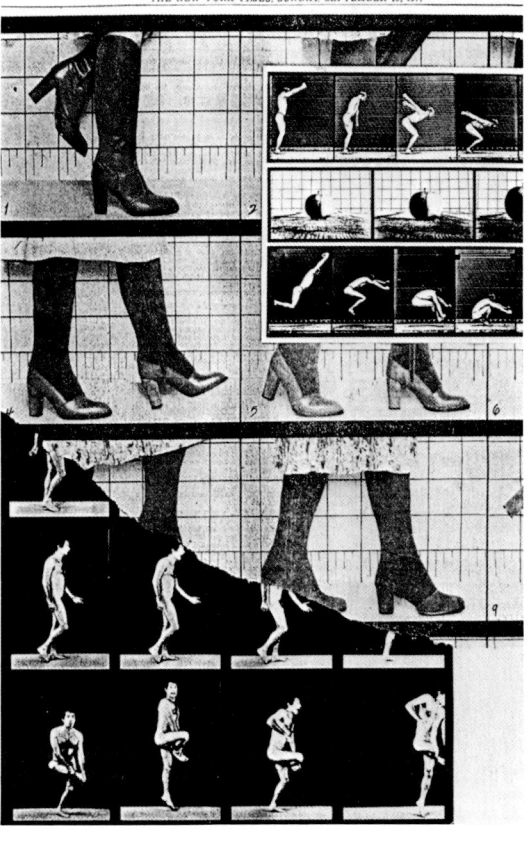

30d. *If Muybridge were alive today, he'd turn over in his grave,* from *False Impressions,* 1979
color xerograph, 12⅝ x 8¼, 6/14

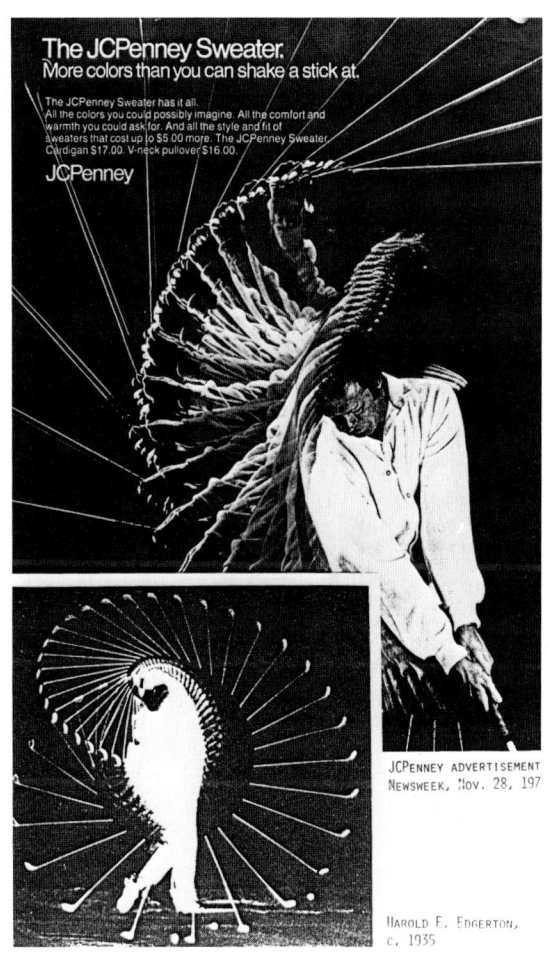

30e. *Which one is the professional golfer? Hint: check the follow-through,* from *False Impressions,* 1979
color xerograph, 13¾ x 8⅛, 6/14

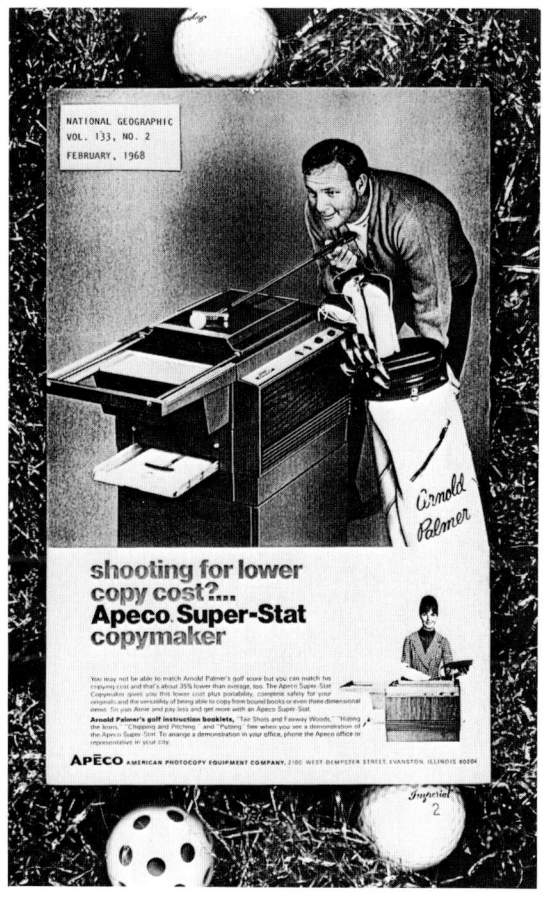

30f. *An Early Practitioner,* from *False Impressions,* 1979
color xerograph, 13⅛ x 8⅛, 6/14

29 and 33. *BY ANY OTHER NAME,*
1979-1983

Frampton made a total of six series of *By Any Other Name;* the first in 1979, the remaining five in 1983. The initial conceit of the project was to reproduce in series of color xerographs product labels in which one thing was used to sell another. There is no specific order to the series, yet each purposefully includes specimens from different "realms" of imagery, that is, oriental goods, animals, etc. The labels used were from his ongoing collection of cultural memorabilia, contributed to by friends and fellow devotees. The issues of scale, syntax, and perspective raised by these found objects fascinated him. Many used for the later series are "antique" labels purchased at flea markets. Xerox art, like photography, was for Frampton an inherently democratic medium, one he felt should be made widely available. Thus the images were produced in editions.

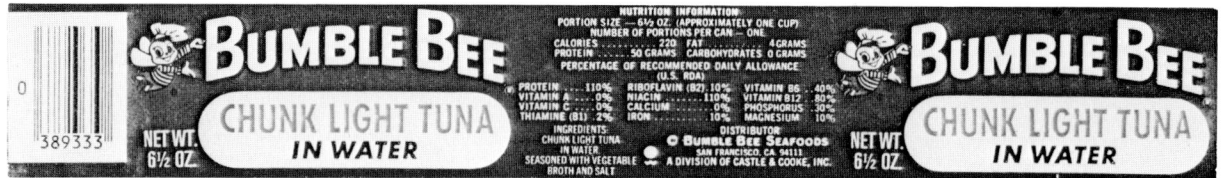

29b. *Tuna Brand Chunk Light Bumblebees*, from
By Any Other Name—Series 1, 1979
color xerograph, 1½ x 10⅝, 1/14

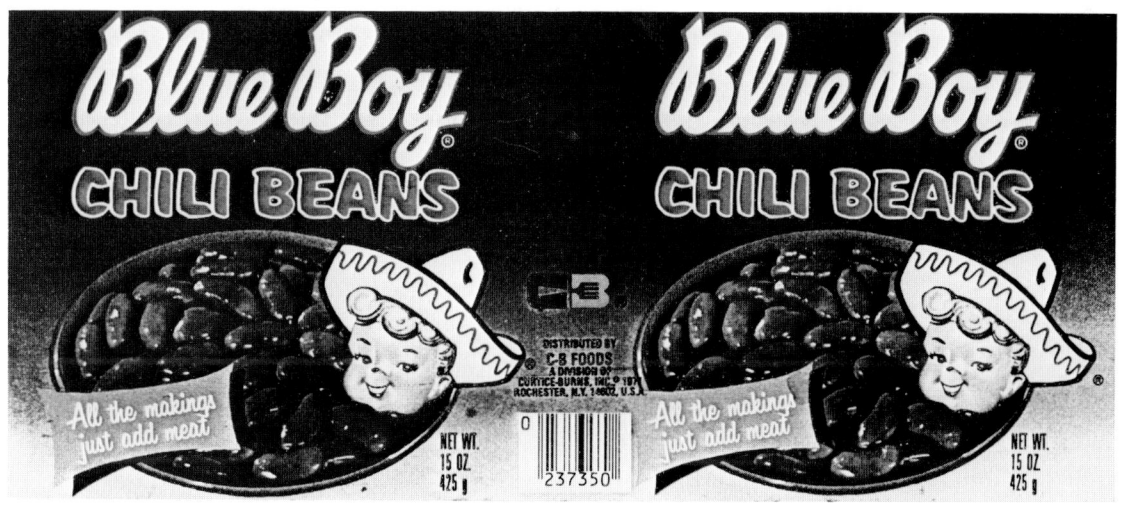

29c. *Chili Bean Brand Blue Boys*, from *By Any Other Name—Series 1*, 1979
color xerograph, 4⅛ x 9⅞, 1/14

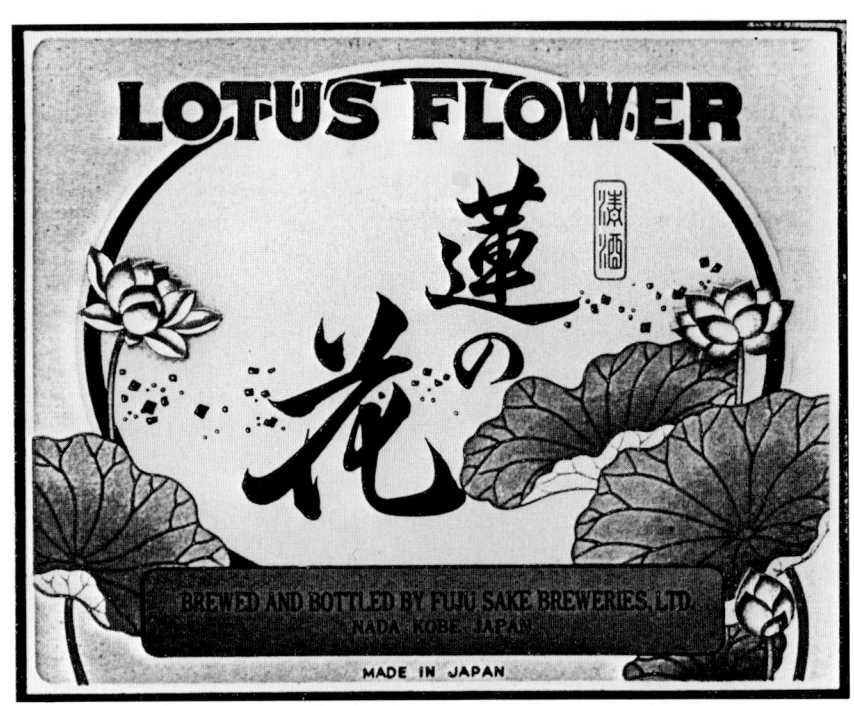

29k. *Sake Brand Lotus Flowers*, from *By Any Other Name—Series 1*, 1979
color xerograph, 3 9/16 x 4 7/16, 1/14

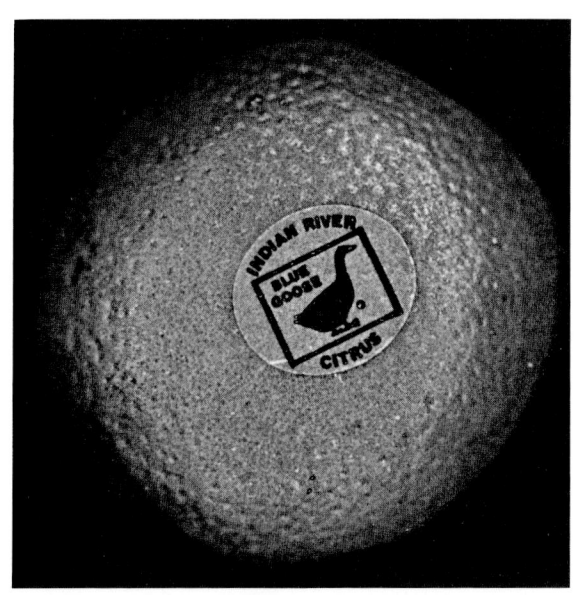

33b. *Blue Citrus Brand Goose*, from *By Any Other Name—Series 2*, 1983
color xerograph, 2¾ x 2¾, 2/4

31. *ADSVMVS ABSVMVS*, 1982

These photographs with accompanying texts were made in memory of the artist's father, Hollis Frampton, Sr. (1913–1980).

The author has come to suppose that he conserved the things represented herewith against the day when they were to be photographed, understanding them to harmonize with photographs then unmade according to a principle within the economy of the intellect. A photographic text and its proper pretext bear the following resemblance to one another: each is a sign of the perfective absence of the other.

In the unimaginable or ordinary case of their copresence, an object and its picture, contending for the center of the spectatorial arena, induce, out of mutual rejection, an oscillation of attention whose momentary frequency is the implicit cantus firmus *of our thought. If we understand but poorly our own notion of likeness between paired entities, we understand even less the manner in which entities are like, or unlike, or may come to be like, or unlike, themselves. This indisposition depends from a temporary defect: that we have not yet evolved to comfort in the domain of time, our supreme fiction, that parses sets of spaces in favor of successiveness.*

But before there were photographs, there are autographs, or happenstances whereunder bounded vacations of matter generate asexual artifacts, reproductions of themselves, necessarily incomplete: desiccations, fossils, memories, mummies, traces indistinguishable from residues. Appearances like these, found free in nature, command our attention, for they present to us, hovering at the margins of legibility, a collocation of failed instants when matter seems about to invent, in comparison and its precedent recollection, the germ of consciousness. Nature, or the customary behavior of matter, implies the photographic image at least as certainly as it implies ourselves. Accordingly, since they predate us, photographs may be treated scientifically.

Fourteen argued plates are appended. The author acknowledges that their identifications are as probabilistic as the captions of all photographs, thereby suggesting that taxonomy is an incomplete discipline.

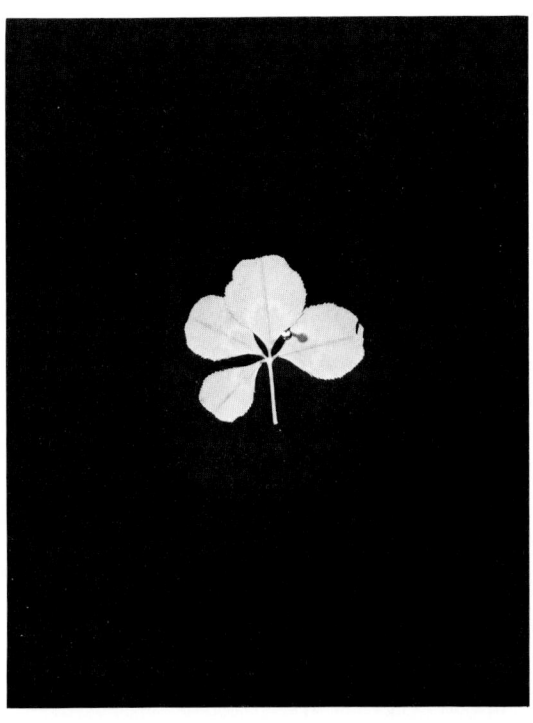

31a. *I. WHITE CLOVER (Melilotus alba),* from *ADSVMVS ABSVMVS,* 1982
Ektacolor photograph, 20 x 16, 7/14

This specimen was found by Marion Faller in an established escape well within the dripline perimeter of a Crack Willow in the Town of Eaton, New York in July, 1977. Good fortune emanates from ownership of the consequence of a chromosomal ambiguity in this leguminous herb. As the number of leaves is incremented, luck increases exponentially. For related but inferior species, that increase is merely arithmetic. Even numbers greater than three govern cards, odd numbers, love. The nectar is edible, but disappointingly weak considering the exercise required to extract it.

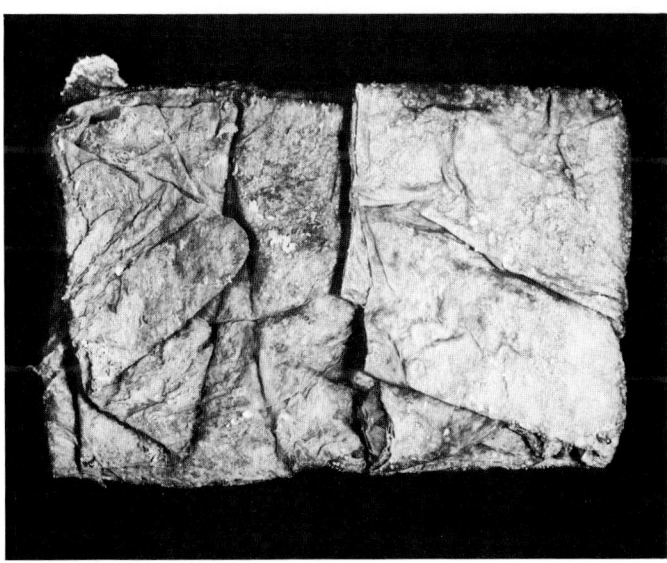

31b. *II. JELLY (Physalia physalis),* from *ADSVMVS ABSVMVS,* 1982
Ektacolor photograph, 16 x 20, 7/14

This remnant of a specimen was purchased by the author in February, 1982 from J & S Oriental Grocery on Erie Boulevard in Syracuse, New York. The stinging coelenterate, not a true jellyfish, is perfectly congruent with the virulent Portuguese Man O' War of the Atlantic, and is fished for food in the Sea of Japan. Only the flotation bladder is available at market, since the jellyfishermen reserve for their own households the finest portion, the mouth parts, which they call the head. Once desalinated and rehydrated, the bladder is sliced into strips and eaten raw, alone, or perhaps with cold chicken, juliennes of cucumber, and a light purée *of sesame. In appearance and first texture, this food resembles classic india rubberbands, but it retrieves for the palate something of the childish adventure of jumping on beached bell jellies after a hard sea storm: ever so momentarily, they resist, and then, suddenly, pressed, liquify and vanish, leaving behind an everlasting sensation.*

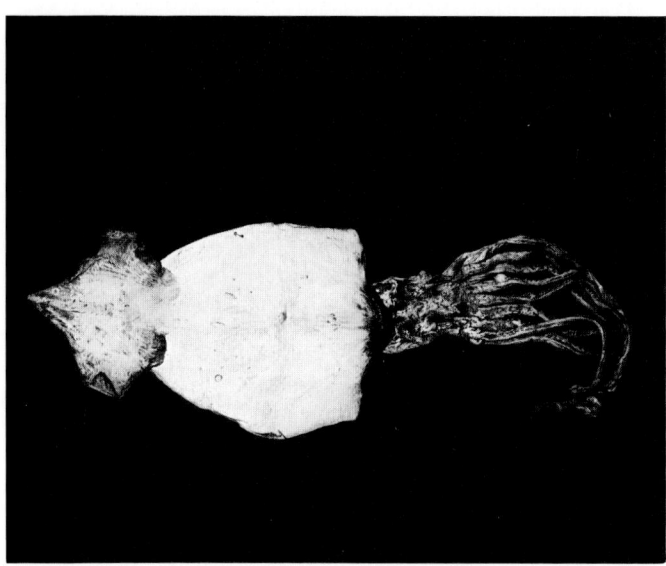

31c. *III. CUTTLEFISH (Rossia mastigophora)*,
from *ADSVMVS ABSVMVS*, 1982
Ektacolor photograph, 16 x 20, 7/14

This specimen, one of a pair costing $1.39, was purchased by the author at King Chong Company, Bayard Street, Manhattan, in November, 1981. Its chalky or calcaerous braincap, called ossa sepia, *has been excised for sale to the canary trade, as well as the little sac in which it carried with it a calamitous portable tint of night. The flesh of the genus is more savory, more pensive, less yielding to the teeth, than that of other caphalopods, who invite being eaten carelessly, with quick, flashing bites.*

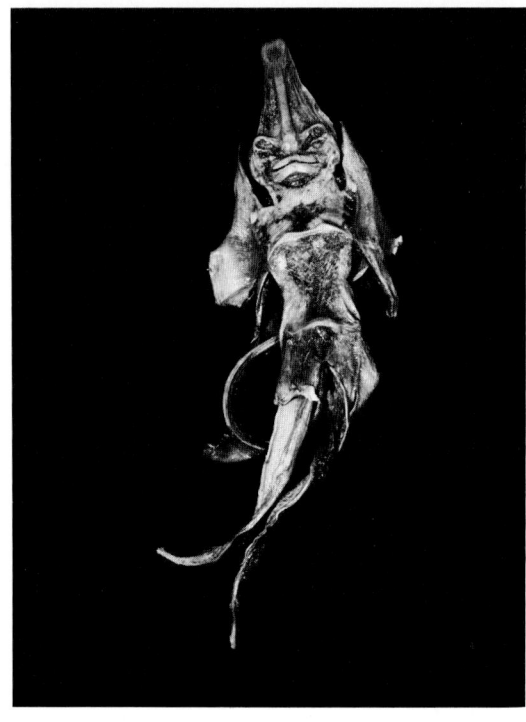

31d. *IV. CHIMÆRA (Challorhynchus capensis)*,
from *ADSVMVS ABSVMVS*, 1982
Ektacolor photograph, 20 x 16, 7/14

This specimen was purchased by the author at a marine curio shop on Fisherman's Wharf, San Francisco, in April, 1980, for five dollars. Its stated provenance was Hong Kong, and we may conjecture that the genus appears as an adulterant among edible catches dragnetted in easterly effluents from the Indian Ocean. The present apparition is an artificial fetish, made by incising the fish along its dorsal edge. It is then opened like a pamphlet, drawn, dried, varnished, and the result prepared for hanging as a wall decoration by twisting a noose of thin cooper wire about what passes for a neck. That wire has been removed: its presence implied a false narrative, since fish are never garotted or executed by hanging.

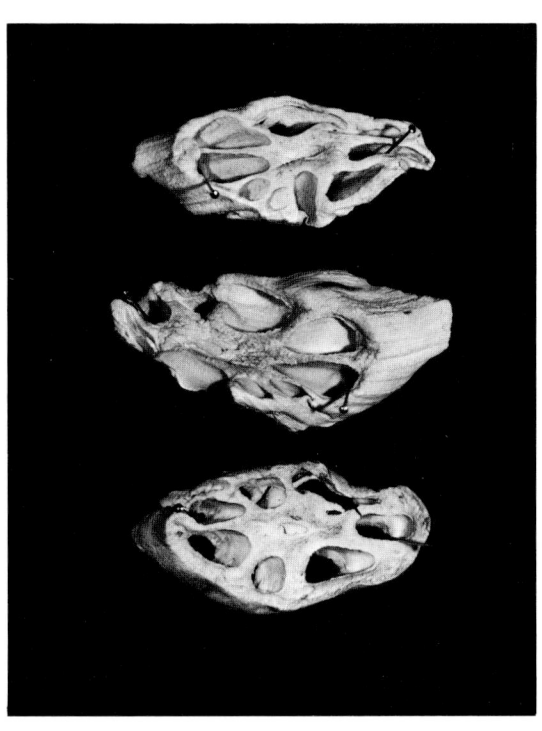

31e. *V. LOTUS (Nelumbo nucifera)*, from *ADSVMVS ABSVMVS*, 1982
Ektacolor photograph, 20 x 16, 7/14

These specimens were purchased by the author in June, 1980 from J & S Oriental Grocery on Erie Boulevard in Syracuse, New York as part of a packet of fourteen costing seventy-nine cents. The species is prized only for the edibility of the immature tuber represented here; unlike the sort from Gondwanaland, it never harbors jewels. The ancient euphoriac psychotropin of the Nile valley derived from the fruit of a tree, Zizyphus lotus, of the buckthorn family.

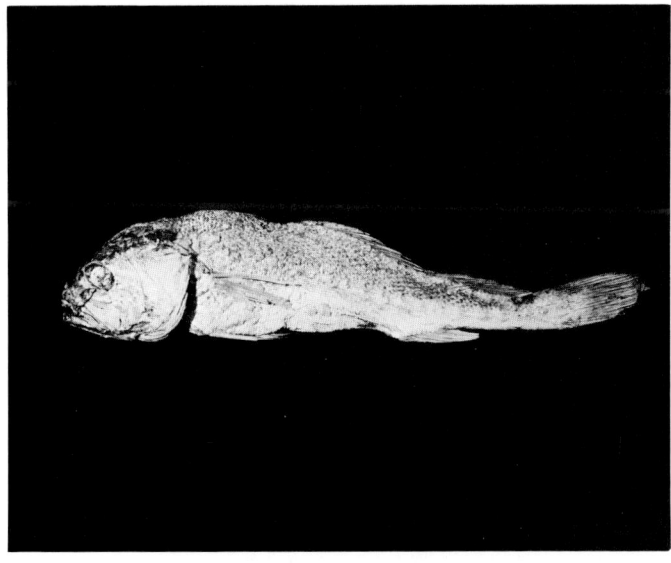

31f. *VI. MIDSHIPMAN (Porichthys notatus)*, from *ADSVMVS ABSVMVS*, 1982
Ektacolor photograph, 16 x 20, 7/14

This specimen, one of a pair costing $1.49, was purchased by the author at William's Market in Mattydale, New York, in October, 1979. Its tail is bowdlerized, having been surreptitiously gnawed some months later by Maxwell, a cat. The species, a notorious whistler and a schooler of subtropical shallows, is customarily seined, by hand or from rowboats, in Thai waters, where it is often chopped or shredded and pickled in a sour, peppery escabeche. From anatomical evidence, it is clear that this fish subsists on a diet of smaller fish, and possesses only moderate vertical mobility. It was mislabeled, though, as pollack (Pollachius virens), a commercially important codlike fish of the North Atlantic, shaped less like a cudgel, which appears at table even more seldom than hake.

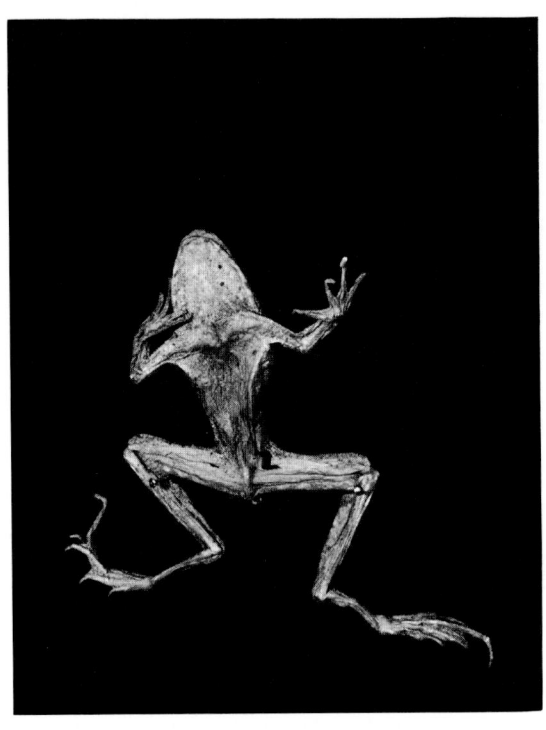

31k. *XI. GRASS FROG (Rana pipiens)*, from *ADSVMVS ABSVMVS*, 1982
Ektacolor photograph, 20 x 16, 7/14

This specimen was discovered by Will Faller, Jr. in May, 1981 on the shoulder of a macadam road in Randallsville, Town of Lebanon, New York. The timid soprano amphibian becomes highly vocal under collective sexual arousal, improvising stochastic nocturnal choruses of considerable elegance. It is nominally edible but meager.

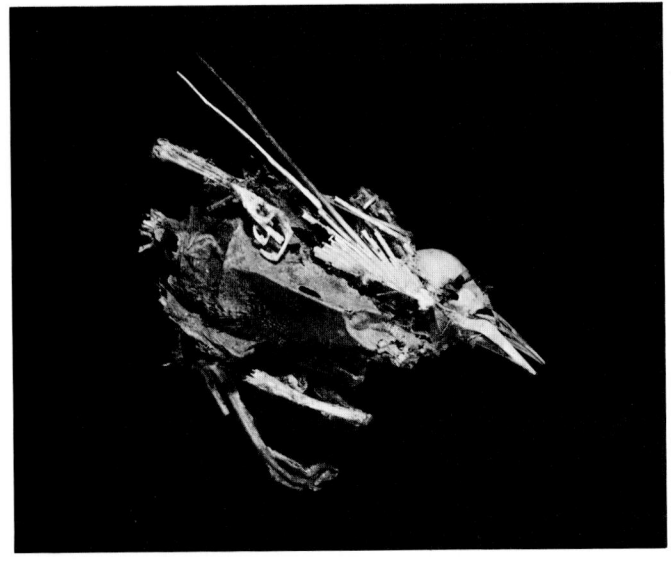

31l. *XII. MOURNING DOVE (Zenaidura macroura)*, from *ADSVMVS ABSVMVS*, 1982
Ektacolor photograph, 16 x 20, 7/14

This immature specimen was found by Bill Brand during the demolition of a wall in the Town of Eaton, New York, in July, 1975. The genus is never iridescent, but it is soothing in appearance as in voice, and graceful in its habits. The squabs are reputedly delicious, but are rarely to be gathered in quantity.

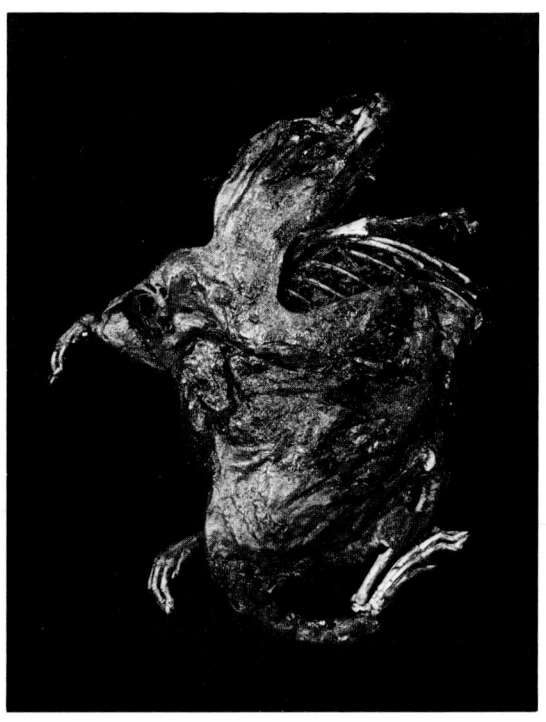

31m. *XIII. BROWN RAT (Rattus rattus)*, from *ADSVMVS ABSVMVS*, 1982
Ektacolor photograph, 20 x 16, 7/14

This young adult specimen, enhanced by two spray applications of a cellulose acetate fixatif, was discovered by Adam Mierzwa in May, 1973 in the course of partially dismantling a house in the Town of Eaton, New York. The cause of its virtually total depilation is unknown. A rural pest, graminivorous by preference, the species constitutes the permanent North American reservoir of bubonic plague, and must not be confused with Rattus norvegicus, its urban counterpart. Inedible by custom, the genus Rattus is prized as a delicacy in Easter Island, whither it was brought by European explorers. The author wishes that its site of delectation might have been displaced to Yap, in proximity to superior megaliths.

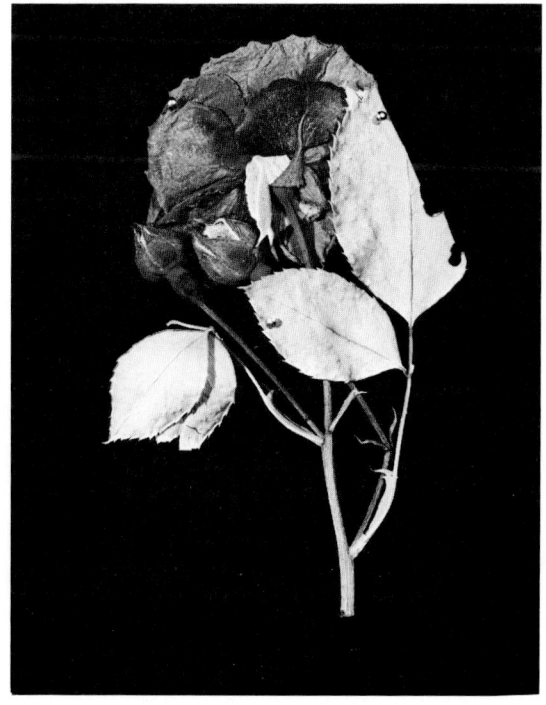

31n. *XIV. ROSE (Rosa damascena)*, from *ADSVMVS ABSVMVS*, 1982
Ektacolor photograph, 20 x 16, 7/14

This specimen was taken by the author as a keepsake from a funeral wreath at Millersburg, Ohio on March 5, 1980. The mature fruit, a hip, anatomically cognate with apples and pears, but unusual among most cultivars of this species, is edible, and contains appreciable quantities of ascorbic acid. Formerly, petals were smoked by the Queen of Siam, and offered for that use to guests during royal audiences; when strewn in the paths of the brilliant, or of heads of State, they are a sign of acclaim.

35. *RITES OF PASSAGE,* 1983–1984
with Marion Faller

Faller and Frampton shot this series of twenty black and white photographs (35a.–35t.), each 14 x 11 inches, over Thanksgiving weekend 1983. The images are meant to be viewed in strict sequence, as indicated by the letters at the upper left.

a.
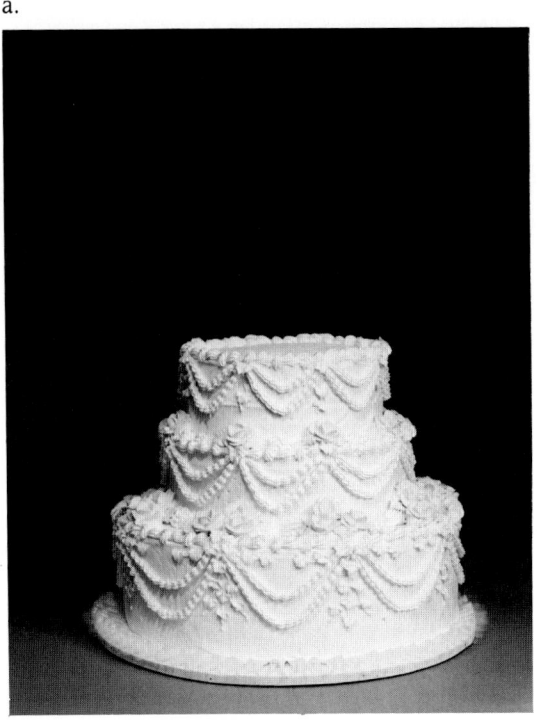

b.
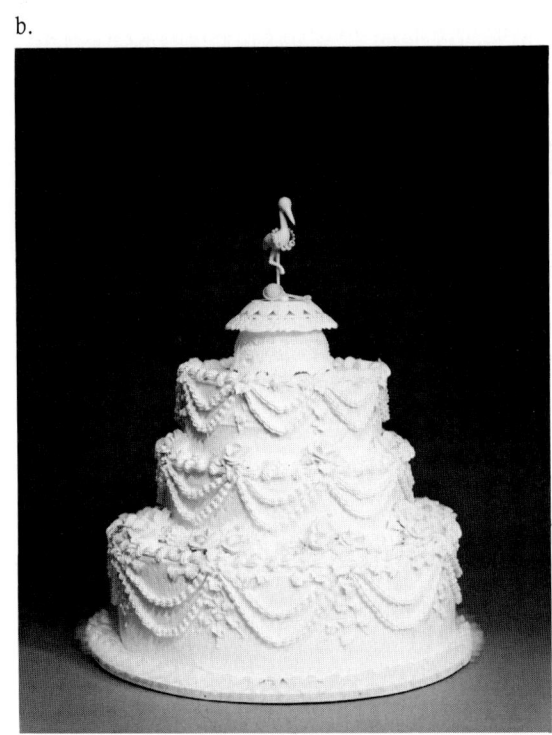

c. d.

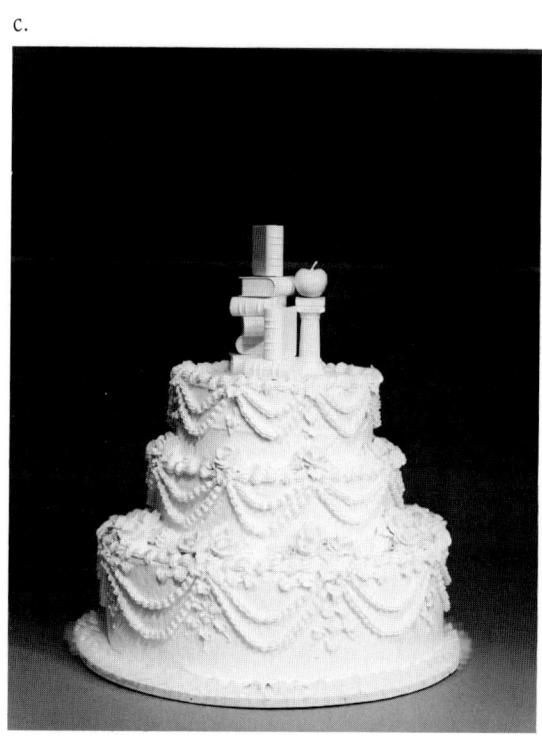
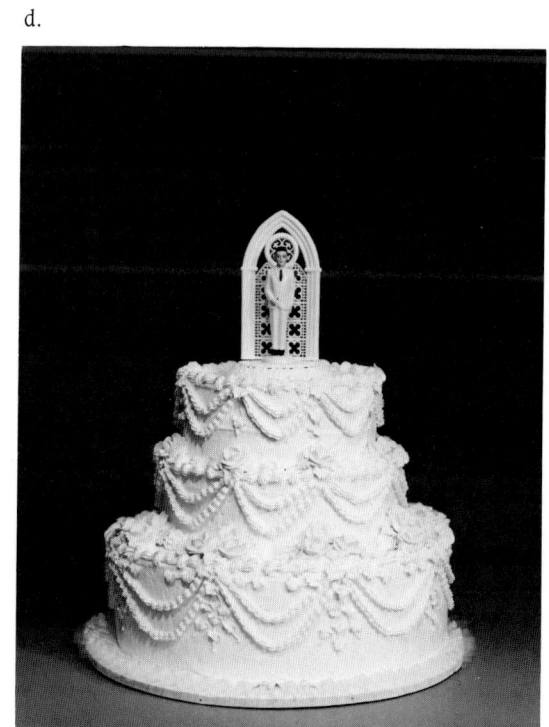

101

e.

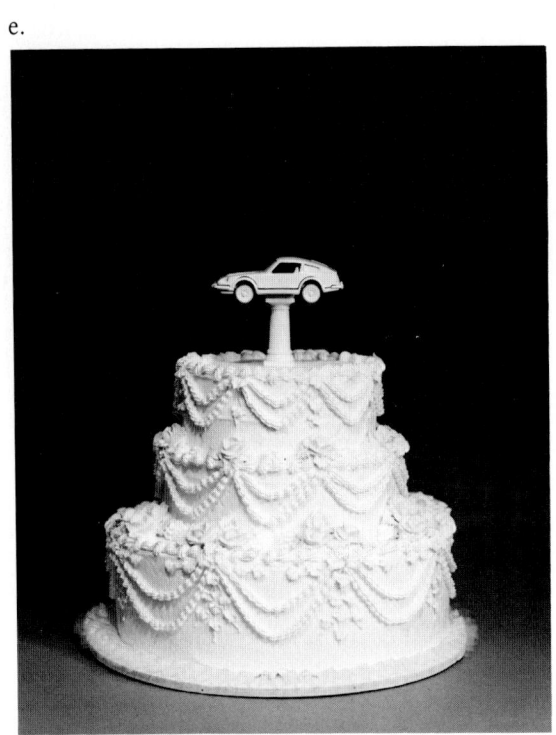

f.

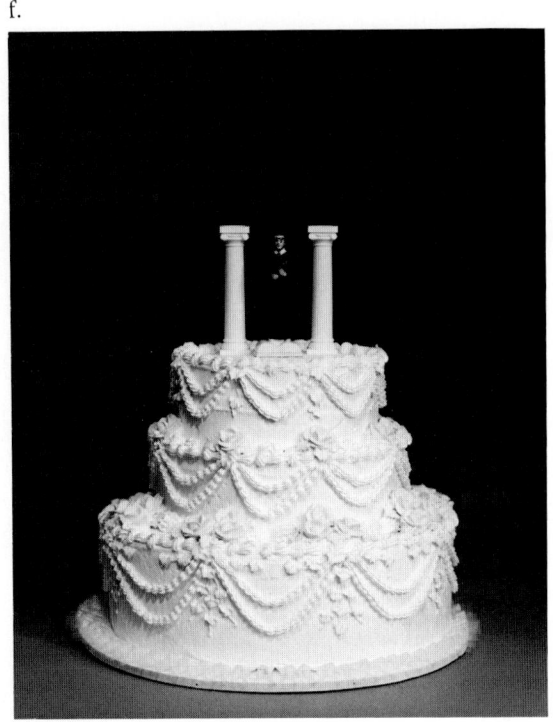

i.

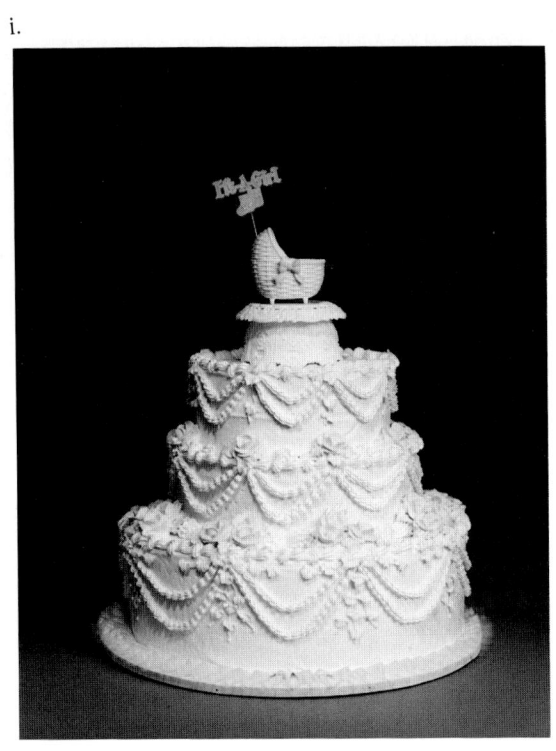

j.

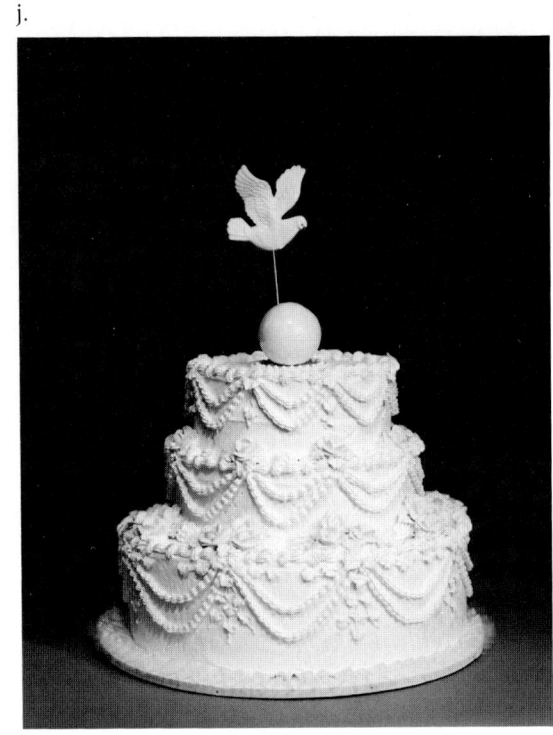

g.

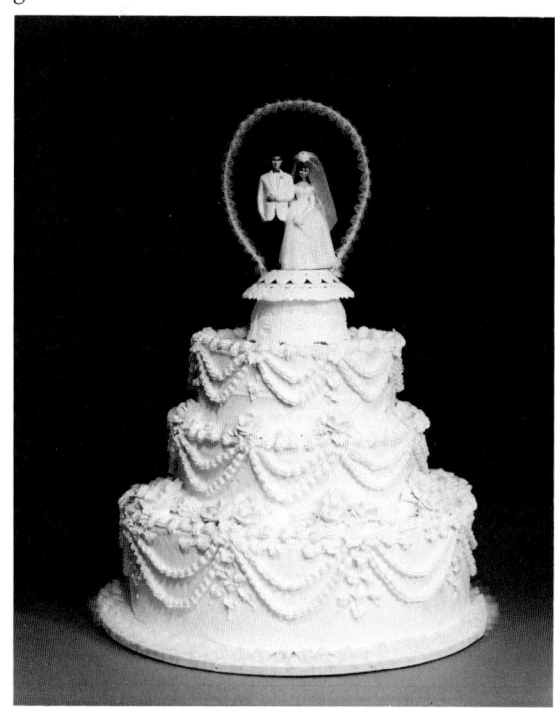

h.

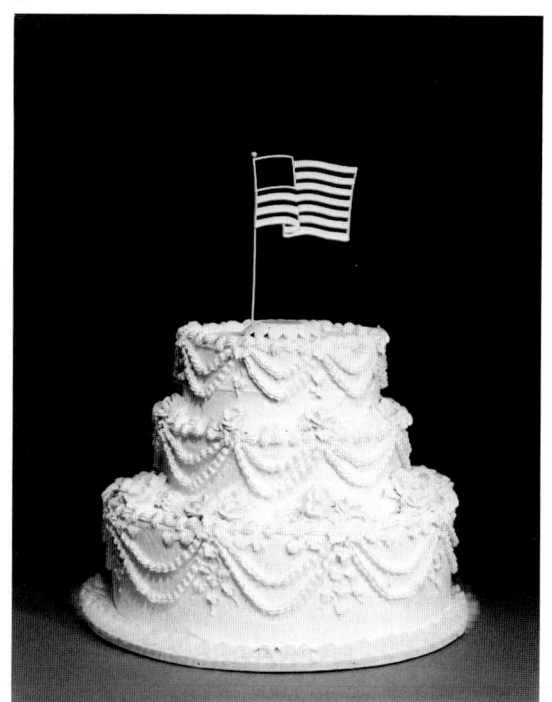

k.

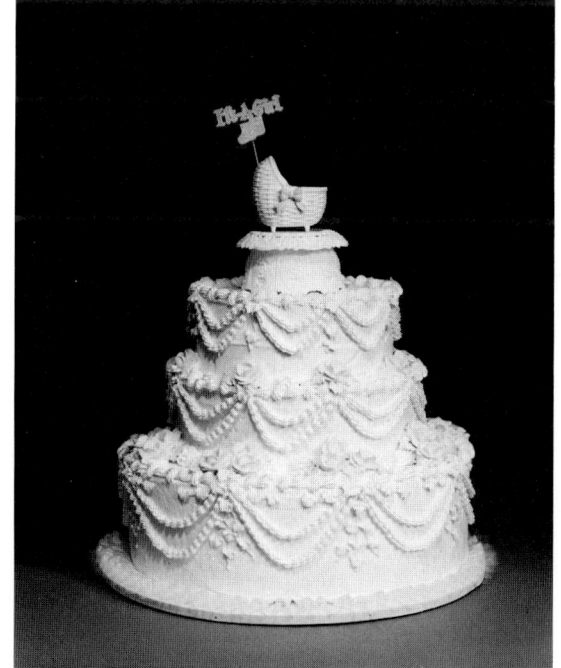

l.

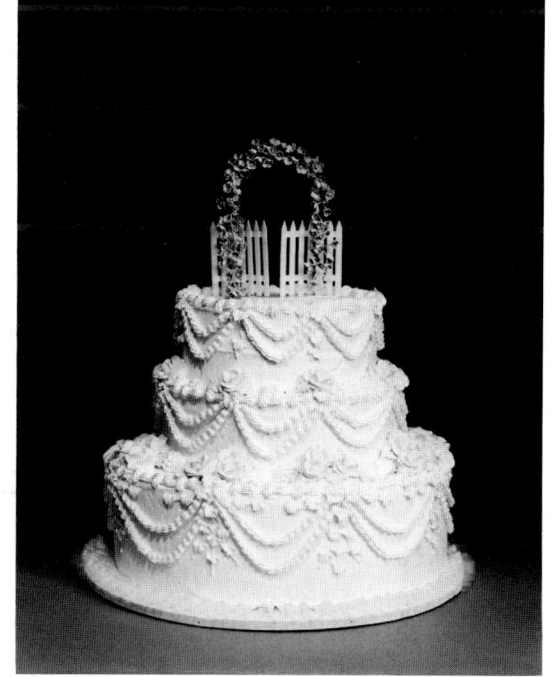

m.

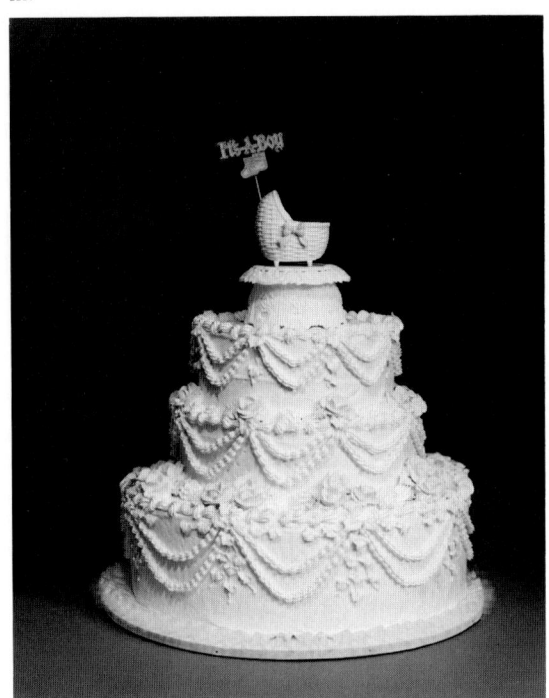

n.

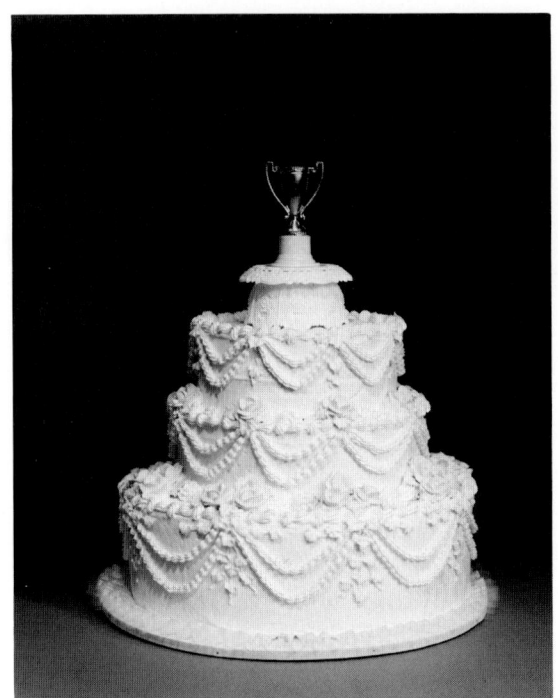

q.

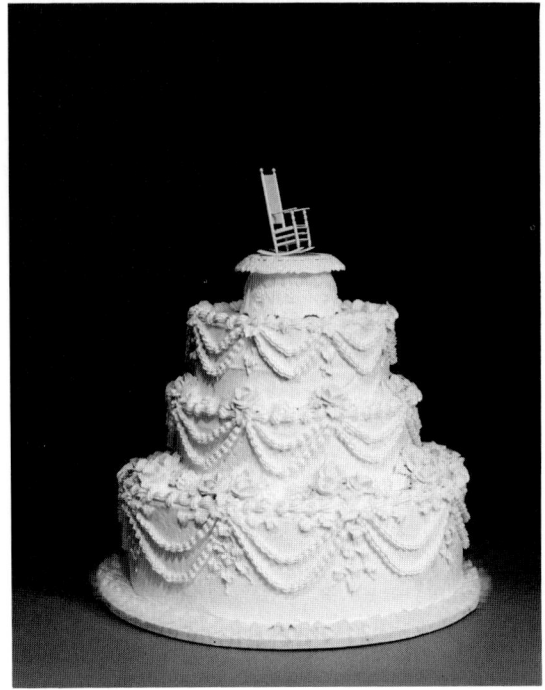

r.

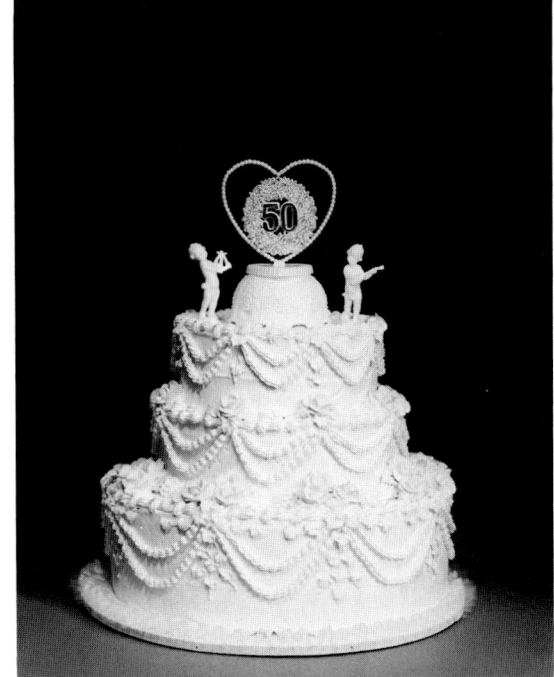

o.

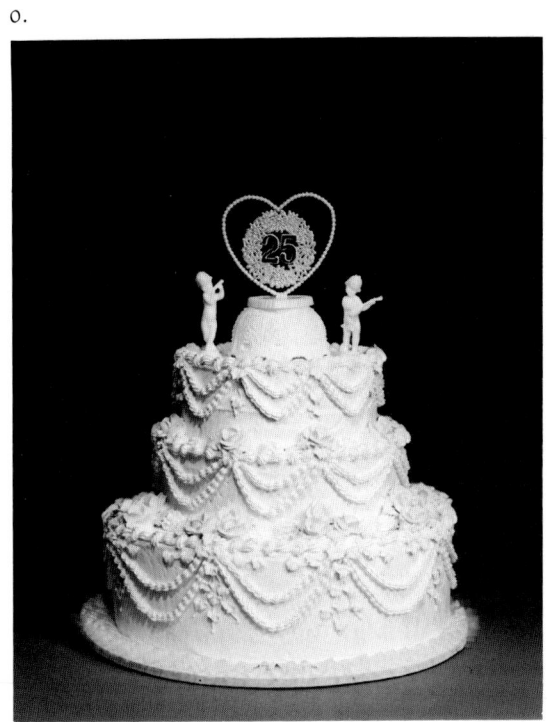

p.

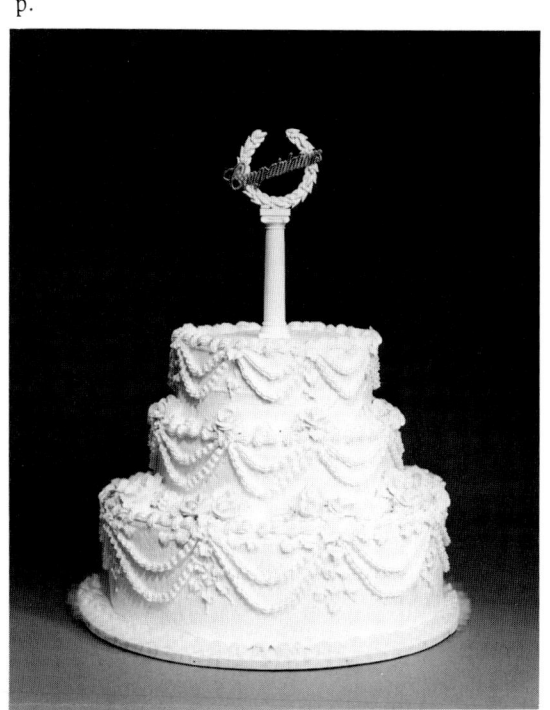

s.

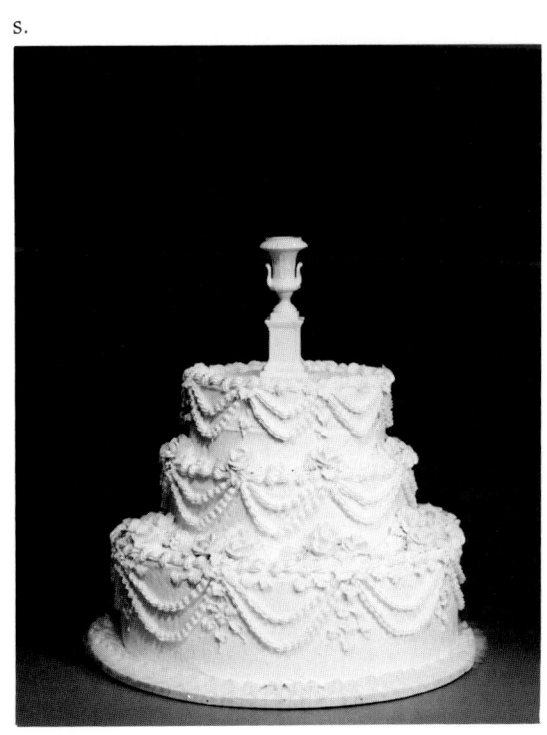

t.

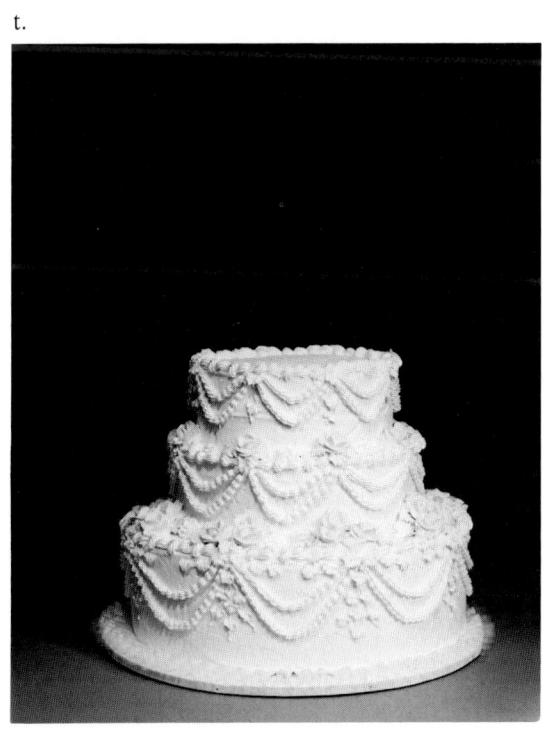

CHRONOLOGY

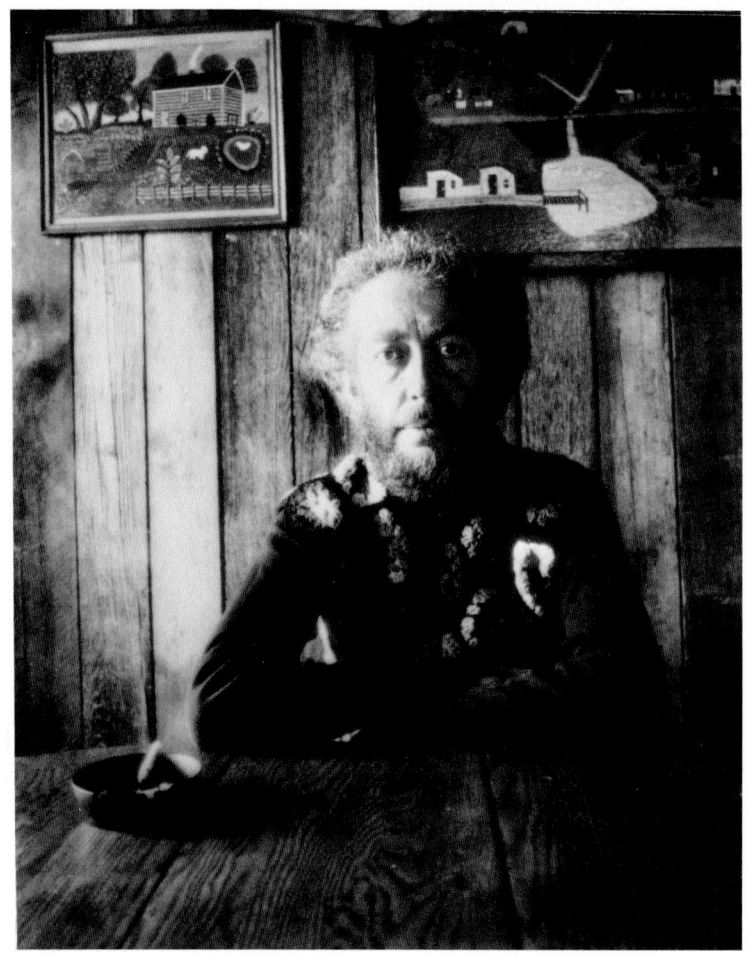

Marion Faller, Portrait of the artist at home in Eaton, New York, 1977, black and white photograph from color transparency, 4 x 5

[Hollis Frampton was a compelling raconteur: speech was another of his art forms. His insights and even his casual meanderings were immensely informative, as well as entertaining. Some of the tales (related repeatedly, as they were, from memory) perhaps lean toward the apocryphal; they are telling nonetheless. A filmography is incorporated, as are the dates of major photographic projects. Citations of Frampton's published theoretical pieces may be found in the bibliography. The artist's frequent domestic travels in conjunction with film showings and residencies have been excluded. S.K.]

1936 Born Hollis William Frampton, Jr. on March 11 (to Nellie Cross Frampton and Hollis William Frampton) in Wooster, Ohio:

> I was the first and only child of the marriage. At that time my father was working in a strip coal mine for a dollar and fifteen cents a day. It was one of the two bottom years of the depression. It was also one of the two times in the history of the U.S. when the birth rate was at the absolute lowest. Thirty years later it would make it far easier for me to get a decent job because there are far fewer of me than there are of you so that we're more in demand and, needless to say, the supply being less, the price is higher.[1]

Raised in large part in the country by his maternal grandparents, primarily his grandmother Fanny Elizabeth Catlett Cross, "my Irish grandma with the style of a drunken sailor"[2] [to whom the film *Gloria!*, 1979, is a tribute] who taught him to read at the age of three with the aid of an old typewriter. As a child, rarely spoke and was by his own account, "borderline autistic." Read voraciously:

> I had established that I could read and that I was careful and responsible and had got an adult library card when I was six from the local small town library where each Saturday I took my American Flyer wagon and loaded it with books and took it home. The librarian must have thought I was fairly amusing and anyway she was cordial. While it [the library] was small, it *was* open stack . . . I got hooked off onto hard science at a fairly early age. So that by the time I was nine and they said that they had dropped an atom bomb I had a smattering of what that meant, at least in terms of its physics and technology.[3]

1943 With maternal grandfather, John Cross (an amateur painter), makes primitive movie out of six-foot belt collaged with images from Sears, Roebuck Company and farm equipment catalogues, and driven by handcranked phonograph motor.[4]

1945 Given Brownie box camera:

> I was the victim of the doting uncle syndrome. The doting uncle gives you, [as] you come downstairs on the Christmas morning of your ninth year, this big, yellow box. It has the little camera in it and a couple rolls of film, MQ developer and hypo and a little tank, etc . . . Really. So that was it. And I really liked it a lot.[5]

Moves to west side of Cleveland with parents. Still speaks only infrequently: tested at age nine years eleven months and found to have mental age of eighteen years six months. Removed from special education classes and enrolled in classes for gifted children, Wilbur Wright Junior High School. Studies French. Volunteers at the Cleveland Museum of Natural History. Receives scholarship to classes at Cleveland Museum of Art; studies predominantly life drawing for six semesters.

1951–54   Applies entirely on his own accord to Phillips Academy, Andover, Massachusetts; accepted on full scholarship. Classmates included painter Frank Stella ('54), composers David Behrman ('54) and Frederic Rzewski ('54), and sculptor Carl Andre ('53), who was his roommate the first year:

> We [H. F. and C. A.] had both read a physicist named Arthur Eddington during the summer and had a long discussion as do fifteen-year-olds about Eddington's representation of time. That is, thirty-two years ago. My class had Frederic Rzewski in it. It had David Behrman in it, both of them composers. It had me, it had Frank Stella. I found later that Frank had spent his Saturday mornings since he was a child copying Degas in the Museum of Fine Arts in Boston—the pastels. It was interesting because I had spent mine—my Saturday mornings—at the Cleveland Museum of Art drawing pictures of Chinese sculpture or the big Rodin *Thinker* outside, before it was dynamited or what have you. But he began to paint, of course, when he was there . . . I edited the school literary magazine [*The Mirror*] during my senior year and was associate editor during my junior year and I believe I was responsible for the first publication of Frank's paintings, as a matter of fact.[6]

Active in photography club. Writes poetry. Interest in art is fostered by painting teacher Patrick Morgan and his wife Maud, both of whom studied with Hans Hofmann in Munich. Paints. Studies German, Latin, then Greek.

Introduced by teacher and friend Dudley Fitts to works of Rimbaud, Flaubert, Mallarmé, Joyce, and Pound. Sees exhibitions of works by action painters and Hans Hofmann at the Addison Gallery of American Art, Phillips Academy. Often goes to New York by train to visit galleries:

> Maud Morgan had massive contacts in New York and really did know what was going on, and came and went to that city every two weeks or something like that. She was of course by the mid-early fifties ('52, '53 and '51 even) bringing back tales of extremely shaggy goings-on on 10th Street. I made my own first stop overs in New York at that time . . . Seeing Jackson Pollock operating in the flesh was a considerable experience even as far as attitude, not only for an extremely hostile and wickedly smart-ass fifteen-year-old of any persuasion, but for a fifteen-year-old who the year before on his fourteenth birthday had been six feet tall and weighed 106 lbs. (That was no fun, believe me.) Of course the action painters, whatever their other attributes might have been, were uniformly not your image of an artist at all—not seemingly very intellectual (at least to use that term crudely) and rather ill-tempered and truculent and extremely stubborn, all of which reinforced some of my own worst tendencies.[7]

Does not receive diploma because he fails (purposefully) required American history class, yet has highest average in class. Scholarship received to Harvard is then rescinded.

Arthur Kres, Photograph of the artist, c. 1954, in Cleveland, Ohio, black and white photograph, 4¼ x 3⅝

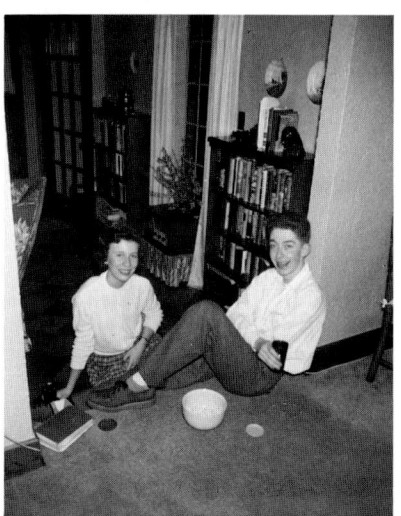

1954–57	Attends Western Reserve University in Cleveland:	1957	Travels by car to Seattle, down the coast and to Mexico over the course of about six months. In fall, moves to Washington, D.C., where he visits Ezra Pound, then confined to St. Elizabeth's Hospital in Congressional Heights:

1954–57 Attends Western Reserve University in Cleveland:

> I allowed myself to be admitted on the condition, which indeed I have in writing, that I not be required to take any required courses if I felt them irrelevant. They agreed to that—I don't know why.[8]

Studies primarily Latin and Greek, also German, French, Russian, Sanskrit, Chinese, mathematics. Briefly has radio program at Oberlin College. Works for Republic Steel, then Jones and Laughlin Steel Company (in the open hearth). Considers himself a poet ". . . tentatively." Studies at the Institute of Design, Chicago, in summers of 1955 and 1956, and "sneaks" into lectures in classical Chinese at the University of Chicago. Becomes interested in literary generation of the 1880s. Begins correspondence with Ezra Pound in 1956.

> . . . After three and a half years I was summoned by the Dean who once more asked me if I intended to take a degree. By that time I already had 135 hours of credits and I said that I more or less figured that I would, or something like that. He said in that case I have to tell you that you still have unfulfilled requirements in speech, western civilization, and music appreciation. To which I replied: I already know how to talk, I already know who Napoleon was and I already like music. For that reason I hold no bachelor's degree. I was very sick of school.[9]

1957 Travels by car to Seattle, down the coast and to Mexico over the course of about six months. In fall, moves to Washington, D.C., where he visits Ezra Pound, then confined to St. Elizabeth's Hospital in Congressional Heights:

> So away I went to Washington, sat in the Library of Congress, sat around St. Elizabeth's, earned a living by being an electrician in Washington's only live burlesque theatre—a theatre in the round by the way, abandoned by a Shakespeare Company that couldn't make it—right across from the Carnegie Library and two blocks from the Greyhound Station.[10]
>
> . . . I visited Pound nearly every day during this time, while he was finishing that part of his *Cantos* called *Section: Rock-Drill* [85–95], commencing work on *Thrones*—and had undertaken, for the benefit of his visitors, to read aloud . . . and to annotate, orally, the entirety of the epic poem. Thus I became privy to a most meaningful exposition of the poetic process by an authentic member of the "generation of the '80s." At the same time, I came to understand that I was not a poet.[11]

Completes the translation into English of the seven volume *Erlebte Erdteile* (Frankfurt-am-Main, West Germany: Societatsdruckerei, Abt. Buchverlag, 1925–1929) by German anthropologist Leo Frobenius, a project suggested by Pound [unpublished].

1958   Renews correspondence with Andre, Stella and Rzewski [all now in New York]. With Pound's departure imminent, leaves for New York in March.

> Loading my possessions level with the three seats and into the trunk of my genuine 1950 Studebaker complete with torpedo nose I hurtled northward, negotiated the Pulaski Skyway, passed through the Lincoln tunnel, and arrived in Manhattan at 5:20 a.m. on the sixth of March, 1958, five days before my twenty-second birthday, turned north into the odor of chicken soup and went up 11th Avenue until I petered out and found my way to Broadway and 113th Street where Carl [Andre] was staying in a rooming house around the corner from the West End Bar in the Columbia Hotel run by two old Swedish ladies who feared God, strangers and Puerto Ricans and had had cause to have painted on the south side of their hotel an enormous sign that said "The Wages of Sin is Death." The Big Apple . . . .[12]

Works briefly as a framer at the Renaissance Print Shop. Moves to fourth floor walkup apartment at 219 Mulberry Street, initially shared with Andre and Stella, then with Andre only.

> Painting in particular, and the plastic arts at large, were swinging very very high. My peers were mostly interested in that. The people I met were young painters and young sculptors who naturally wanted to drink in the same bars where Kline and de Kooning had been and so forth and so on had, and did and so spent endless evenings nursing one forty cent bottle of Ballantine beer in the Cedar Street Bar . . . . [sic]. I finally decided that while painting was something I respected, and it was very nice that other people did it, there were things that I didn't like about doing it. It seemed to be a kind of performance first of all, indeed it certainly was at that time. It seemed to have a lot to do with first refining and then expressing (or perhaps vice versa) your personality. The last thing in the world that I wanted to do was express my personality. It is still the last thing. It's almost inevitable that one will in any case, but above all I couldn't entertain the idea of seriously doing that for a long time. For awhile I liked the results; I did not like the activity. I finally didn't enjoy smearing goo on flat surfaces: it was not enchanting.[13]

Begins shooting *The Secret World of Frank Stella,* 1958–1962.
Buys Nikon for Christmas.

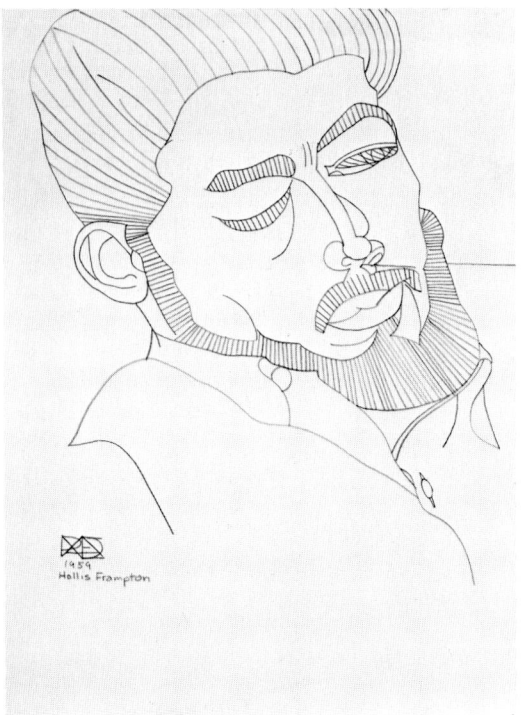

Carl Andre, *Portrait of Hollis Frampton,* 1959, pencil on paper, 13^{15}/$_{16}$ x 10¾ . © the artist.

Hollis Frampton, Poster (with type at bottom) for exhibition of Frank Stella's work at Ferus Gallery, New York, Feb. 1963. Black and white offset, 13⅛ x 12¼ . The image is cat.1b., #11 from *The Secret World of Frank Stella,* 1958–1962, (432 Leonardo after Vitruvius)

1959	In January, begins to photograph Andre's work. Works variously as assistant in commercial photo studios, as electrician, and as freelance photographer of painting and sculpture for New York galleries.	1960–61	Resides at 237 East Broadway then, with widespread evictions in lower Manhattan, lives in thirteen locales over a period of nineteen months. Begins full-time work as technician specializing in dye imbibition color processes in photographic laboratories [primarily Technicolor, Inc.], which he continues through 1969:

1959 — In January, begins to photograph Andre's work. Works variously as assistant in commercial photo studios, as electrician, and as freelance photographer of painting and sculpture for New York galleries.

> I didn't want to announce or to give out as something that I had done, something that showed the direct signature, the imprint of my having without mediation manipulated it. I liked to do things with machines so I took up still photography, which seemed to offer that advantage, that of mediation, that of signaturelessness, of a certain kind at least. The signature was in such things as framing and tonal scalings, abstractions as imperceptible as the infinitely thin clean line. So that one was not, as it were, the person hovering behind the artifact but rather behind the thing that made the artifact. And on the other hand, one did not have to laboriously build up this image. It was not made serially but came forward as a kind of matrix of thought instantaneously, in a manner that criticized the maker . . . .[14]

His photograph of Frank Stella is published in catalogue for the exhibition *Sixteen Americans,* the Museum of Modern Art.[15]

Makes *Ways to Purity.*

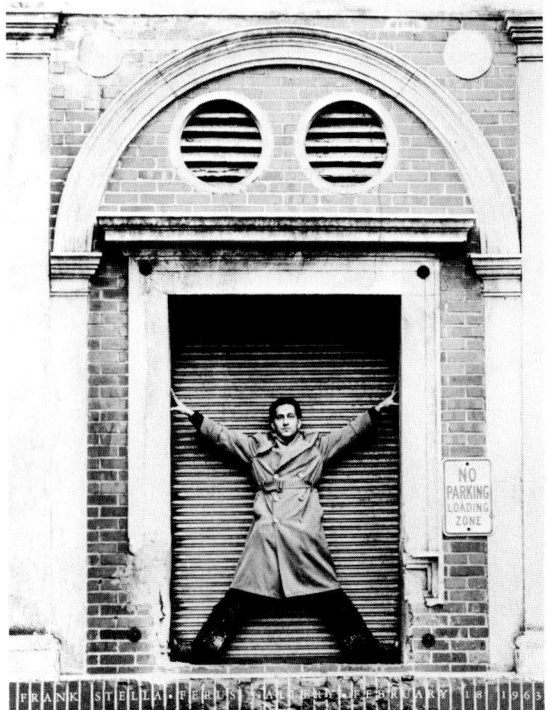

1960–61 — Resides at 237 East Broadway then, with widespread evictions in lower Manhattan, lives in thirteen locales over a period of nineteen months. Begins full-time work as technician specializing in dye imbibition color processes in photographic laboratories [primarily Technicolor, Inc.], which he continues through 1969:

> ". . . incidentally designing and building two entire professional facilities in the course of rising to the managerial level . . . something I had never intended."[16]

Photographs avidly, heavily influenced by formalism of Edward Weston.

1962 — Hospitalized for over six months. When released borrows a friend's Bolex camera and begins filming. In fall, continues "tentative experiments in film."

Clouds Like White Sheep (16mm, 25 min., black and white, silent, destroyed).

> In the late fifties, still photography was still locked in the grip of the 8 x 10″ view-camera F-64 school that included people like Weston and Strand, and which had become massively academicized. It had produced such entities as Ansel Adams and Minor White. There was an enormous stasis; photography was obviously something only old masters did. It produced a stasis in me, too, because to a degree I identified with it and got myself up a tree that I was never quite able to climb down until I completely got out of it. . .[17]

Makes *Word Pictures,* which becomes basis for the film *Zorns Lemma* (1970).

1962–63 — Undertakes a series of "dialogues" on art, responses composed alternately at the typewriter, with Carl Andre during Frampton's frequent visits to Andre and painter Rosemarie Castoro's one-room apartment in Brooklyn:[18]

> Briefly, though, we were both of us: in the arena of language, which is that of power. So, first, I would urge that these dialogues be read, if they are to be read, as anthropological evidence pertaining to a rite of passage and to the nature of friendship.[19]

Lives at 404 East Tenth Street.

1963	His photograph of James Rosenquist is published in the exhibition catalogue *Americans 1963,* the Museum of Modern Art.[20]	1966	Increasingly interested in film, buys himself Bolex equipment for his thirtieth birthday.

1963 — His photograph of James Rosenquist is published in the exhibition catalogue *Americans 1963,* the Museum of Modern Art.[20]

> I didn't find it a picnic to be a photographer, through the sixties, not because photography was disregarded, although of course that was true, but because my predicament was that of a committed illusionist in an environment that was officially dedicated to the eradication of illusion and, of course, utterly dominated by painting and sculpture. At that time I didn't understand how luxurious it was to find myself alienated in that way. Nothing is more wonderful than to have no one pay the slightest attention to what you are doing; if you're going to grow, you can grow at your own speed.[21]

1964 — ***A Running Man*** (16mm, 22 min., color, silent, destroyed).
Ten Mile Poem (16mm, 33 min., color, silent, destroyed).
Moves to 84 Walker Street.

1965 — ***Obelisk Ampersand Encounter*** (16mm, 1:30 min., color, sound, lost).

Photograph of Larry Poons appears in August issue of *Vogue.* Lives with artist Lee Lozano.

1966 — Increasingly interested in film, buys himself Bolex equipment for his thirtieth birthday.

> I believe that one reason I stayed with still photography as long as I did was an attempt, fairly successful I think, to rid myself of the succubus of painting. Painting has for a long time been sitting on the back of everyone's neck like a Muse "in heat," whispering in our ears and . . . it has crept into territories outside its own proper domain. I have seen, in the last year or so, films which I have come to realize are built largely around what I take to be painterly concerns and I feel that those films are very foreign to my feeling and my purpose. As for sculpture, I think a lot of my early convictions about sculpture, in a concrete sense, have affected my handling of film as a physical material. My experience of sculpture has had a lot to do with my relative willingness to take up film in hand as a physical material and work with it. Without it, I might have been tempted to more literary ways of using film—or more abstract ways of using film.[22]

In September, marries Marcia Steinbrecher (separated summer 1971, divorced 1974).

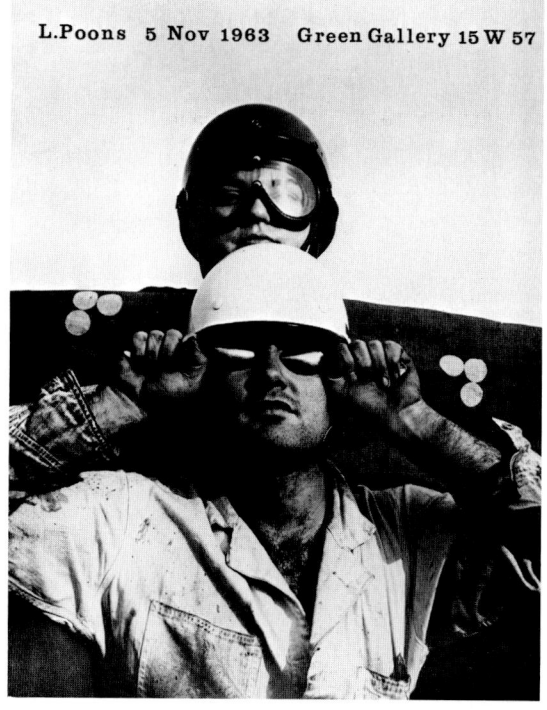

Hollis Frampton, Poster (with type) for exhibition of Larry Poons' work at Green Gallery, New York, Nov. 1963, black and white offset, 14 x 10⅞. The image is cat. 17. *Larry Poons,* 1963 (L. Poons, T. Poons and Spoons, 10/63)

Manual of Arms (16mm, 17 min., black and white, silent). Composed of film portraits of friends: sculptor Carl Andre, photographer Barbara Brown, painter Rosemarie Castoro, dancer Lucinda Childs, Bob Goldensohn [sic], filmmaker and painter Robert Huot, Eric Lloyd, sculptor Lee Lozano, Linda Meyer, painter Larry Poons, filmmaker and sculptor Michael Snow, historian Marcia Steinbrecher, dancer Twyla Tharp, filmmaker Joyce Wieland.

Process Red (16mm, 3:30 min., color, silent)

Information (16mm, 4 min., black and white, silent). A collaboration requested by Twyla Tharp, for whom he previously made short, incidental films as birthday gifts:

> . . . I had thought to project the film into the performance space and use it as a lighting system. Since the light beams are narrow, the projected light itself became an artifact, particularly if there were a little smoke in the room. In fact, Twyla did use the film as part of a piece. She had it projected *across* the stage, from the wings, so that one saw the columns of light fluctuating. She asked a lot of people to come and smoke, so they could see it. It was done only one time.[23]

1967

Teaches filmmaking at Free University of New York.

States (16mm, 17:30 min., black and white, silent).

Heterodyne (16mm, 7 min., color, silent). Makes use of "blank" footage:

> There are problems which can be dealt with by annihilation. I don't see why, just because you *can* be seeing something all the time, you *must* be seeing something all the time. I've called these passages silences; in doing so, I indicate a debt to Cage. Cage proposed that just because you could be hearing something all the time, didn't mean that you had to be. That struck me as a strategic option in film. In any case, because film stock is not truly opaque, you are always seeing something, the outline of the frame at least, and that itself is an enormous cultural icon: it tells you where the image would be if there were one. I am, as I think many filmmakers are, as preoccupied by the film frame as painting has been at various times by the limits of its support.[24]

1968

Snowblind (16mm, 5:30 min., black and white, silent). Features Michael Snow.

Maxwell's Demon (16mm, 4 min., color, sound). First surviving sound film.

Surface Tension (16mm, 10 min., color, sound). Features Kasper Koenig.

1969	Receives grant from Friends of New Cinema. Assistant professor of photography, film, design, at Hunter College, CUNY. Faculty included, among others, Mark Rothko, Raymond Parker, Tony Smith, Leo Steinberg, Robert Morris [through 1973]. **Palindrome** (16mm, 22 min., color, silent). **Carrots and Peas** (16 mm, 5:30 min., color, sound). **Lemon** (16mm, 7:30 min., color, silent). For Robert Huot. **Prince Ruperts Drops** (16mm, 7 min., color, silent). Features Robert Huot and Marcia Steinbrecher. **Works & Days** (16mm, 12 min., black and white, silent). **Artificial Light** (16mm, 25 min., color, silent). Robert Huot, Twyla Tharp, Lee Lozano, Carl Andre, Rosemarie Castoro.	1970	**Zorns Lemma** (16mm, 60 min., color, sound). Audio features Rosemarie Castoro, Ginger Michaels, Twyla Tharp, Susan Weiner, and Joyce Wieland. Visual features Hollis Frampton, David Hamilton, Robert Huot and Marcia Steinbrecher. First feature-length experimental work to be included in New York Film Festival at Lincoln Center: wins wide critical acclaim. Uses the alphabet and mathematical systems to structure the film, which becomes a "cryptic autobiography:"

> Film, even in its physical attributes, has become a kind of metaphor for consciousness for me. And I think of the incremental frame . . . as a dim but still appealing metaphor for the quantum nature, the chunk nature, of light itself. If you're watching a film, you believe you're watching a complete illusion of something real, but you're actually watching an illusion of only half of what took place. The camera's shutter was closed the other half of the time. So that there's another cinema of equal length that could have been made precisely at the same time. And when you play that back, the shutter in the projector is also closed half the time, so that half the time you're in total darkness. You are! OK, you don't have anything particular to do, you're quite comfortable, presumably, there's very little exterior stimulus and you're there for a fiftieth of a second, which is, in terms of energy, an appreciable length of time with nothing to do but think about the frame you've just seen.[25]

> I'm a spectator of mathematics like others are spectators of soccer or pornography.[26]

In May, purchases thirty acres of land in Eaton, Madison County, New York, where he spends the summer. Teaches history of film at School of Visual Arts, New York [through 1971]. Visiting lecturer in history of film at the Cooper Union [through 1973].

Shoots *A Visitation of Insomnia* (1970-1973).

1971	Begins occasional work in video synthesis, image processing and xerography. Makes *Reasonable Facsimiles,* first series of xerographs. Completes first three of seven films in **Hapax Legomena:** **nostalgia** (16mm, 36 min., black and white, sound). An autobiographical film in which the narrator (Michael Snow) reminisces about a series of still photographs (most taken by Frampton) while, out of synchronization, the images are shown being burned on a hot plate:

> 'Nostalgia' is mostly about words and the kind of relationship words can have to images. I began probably as a kind of non-poet, as a kid, and my first interest in images probably had something to do

114

with what clouds of words could rise out of them. Looking back at the words and images that one remembers from a former time, I think there is a kind of shift between what is now memory and what was once conjecture and prophecy and so forth.[27]

Travelling Matte (16mm, 33:30 min., black and white, silent).
Critical Mass (16mm, 25:30 min., black and white, sound).

Participates in New York State Council on the Arts Visiting Artists Program [through 1973].

Early in the year, meets photographer Marion Faller; in fall moves in with her and her son, Will Faller, Jr., to 313 East 9th Street. Spends summer in Eaton, New York. Meets filmmaker Stan Brakhage [during Christmas holidays.] Begins filming for long serial which metamorphoses into the monumental opus [uncompleted], the *Magellan* cycle, an intended total of thirty-six hours of films, organized and meant to be viewed calendrically over the course of 371 days:

> The central conceit of the work derives from the voyage of Ferdinand Magellan, first circumnavigator of the world, as detailed in the diary of his 'passenger' Antonio Pigafetta and elsewhere. During his 5-year voyage, Magellan trespasses (alive and dead) upon every psycho-linguistic 'time zone,' circumambulating the whole of human experience as a kind of somnabulist. He returns home, a carcass pickled in cloves, as an exquisite corpse. The protagonist of my work must be a first person consciousness that bears resemblances to myself (if only as the amalgam H. C. Earwicker/Anna Livia Plurabelle resembles James Joyce) . . . and, even, to Flash Gordon and Fantomas of the filmic vulgate.[28]

1972 Travels to England in summer to research article for *Artforum*. Visits Stonehenge:

> The first time I walked across the Brooklyn Bridge was unquestionably one of the grand aesthetic experiences of my life, and Stonehenge, indeed, was another.[29]

Completes films of **Hapax Legomena**:
Special Effects (16mm, 10:30 min., black and white, sound).
Poetic Justice (16mm, 31:30 min., black and white, silent).
Ordinary Matter (16mm, 36 min., black and white, sound).
Remote Control (16mm, 29 min., black and white, silent).
Apparatus Sum (16mm, 2:30 min., color, silent).
Tiger Balm (16mm, 10 min., color, silent).
Yellow Springs (16mm, 5 min., color, silent).

Retrospective of films at Walker Art Center, November 16–18.

> My own turning away from narrative, or from what is called narrative, really had to do with how suppositious I felt it to be. In fact what the ordinary person thinks of as a slice-of-life-narrative-film, the perfectly conventional narrative film is precisely that—it's conventional. It is riddled with conventions that are precisely as much artifices, they are precisely as much man-made things that are agreed upon, as the notion that c-o-w corresponds to something that weighs 800 pounds and gives milk.[30]

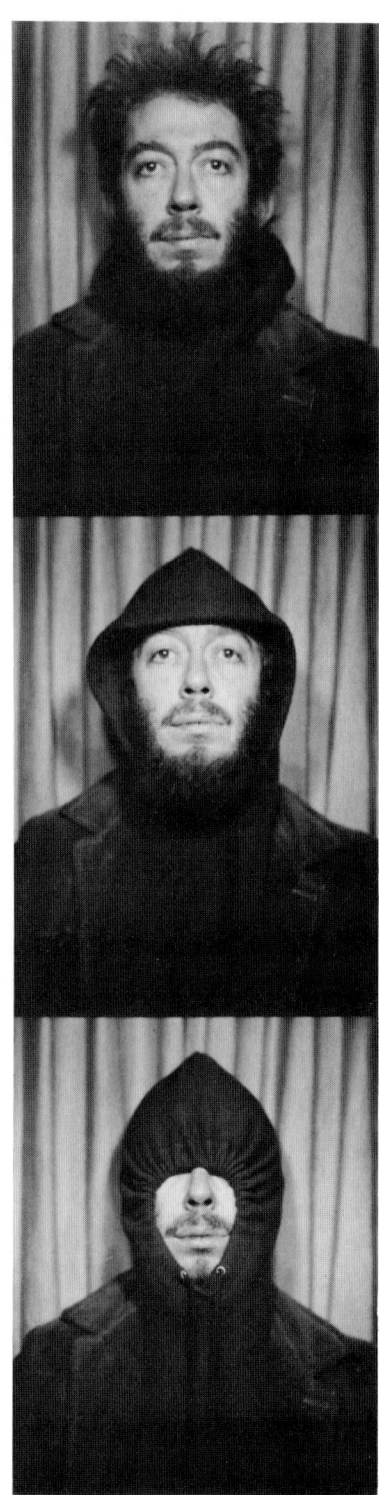

27. *Stopping Down,* 1973, enlargement from copy negative of photo booth picture, 19½ x 5⁵⁄₁₆. [Shot March 11, 1973, enlarged 1984]

1973 Retrospective of films at the Museum of Modern Art, New York, March 8–12. Moves to 803 6th Avenue with Marion and Will.
In spring, teaches seminar at State University of New York at Buffalo. Invited to join staff (beginning fall semester), as associate professor, and to develop Center for Media Study and curriculum. Paul Sharits, Steina and Woody Vasulka, James Blue, Brian Henderson and Tony Conrad subsequently join faculty. [Teaches there through February 1984.]

Public Domain (16mm, 18 min., black and white, silent, unreleased).
Less (16 mm, 1 sec., black and white, silent). For Les Krims.

1974 Moves to farmhouse in Eaton, New York with Marion and Will in summer. Beginning in September, commutes bi-weekly to Buffalo. Continues to travel extensively throughout the seventies as visiting lecturer and artist. Serves on video selection committee, Anthology Film Archives, New York. Participant, American Seminar on Film. Panelist, Coordination Council of Literary Magazines. Major retrospective of films at Fifth International Festival of Experimental Film and Video, Knokke-Heist, Belgium, December 25–January 2, 1975. Continues work on *Magellan* cycle:

> We are taught to read not so that we can be creative, have interesting thoughts, engage with the great minds of the past, but so that we can read signs that say "no right turn." We go to school in order to do that—not even in order to learn to read, but so that we shall be taught to punch in by 8:15 in the morning. By the time we have got out of school, we have learned to punch in by 8:15 in the morning, we have learned to read "no right turn," we have also on our own looked at 15,000 hours of unregulated, ungoverned, undecoded images that constitute our real education. I grew up like that—everyone grows up like that. *Magellan* is a film that, like all things (since I have not had the luxury of perfect alienation, but only the partial luxury of imperfect alienation) comes out of an imperfect understanding of my culture. It is probably easiest to imagine it as a project if it is understood not as a project in drama, or in literature, nor as a project in sculpture, but as one that subsists as a work of sculpture in time rather than space. . . .[31]

Autumnal Equinox (16mm, 27 min., color, silent).
Noctiluca (16mm, 3:30 min., color, silent).
Winter Solstice (16mm, 33 min., color, silent).
Straits of Magellan: Drafts & Fragments (16mm, 52 min., color, silent).
Summer Solstice (16mm, 32 min., color, silent).
Vexilla Regis (16mm, 6:30 min., color, silent, unreleased).
Banner (16mm, 40 sec., color, silent).

1975 Receives National Endowment for the Arts grant to complete *Straits of Magellan*. Retrospective of films at Anthology Film Archives, New York [April]. Receives grant from Creative Artists Program Service Inc., New York State Council on the Arts, for work on *Magellan* cycle.

INGENIVM NOBIS IPSA PVELLA FECIT (16mm, 67 min., color, silent).
SOLARIUMAGELANI, 1974–1975, (16mm, 2 hrs. 39 min., color, silent).
Drum (16mm, 20 sec., color, silent).
Pas de Trois (16mm, 4 min., color, silent).

Shoots *Sixteen Studies for VEGETABLE LOCOMOTION* (with Marion Faller). Spends late December through early January filming in Puerto Rico.

1976 Panelist [through 1978], film program, New York State Council on the Arts. Travels to Edinburgh, London, Paris. Continues *Magellan* cycle:

The *Magellan* cycle purports to be encyclopedic, but it's more like a tour of the possible principles for forming an encyclopedia—all, I hope, dutifully laid out and exemplified, but then to a great extent laid out and exemplified all at the same time. And, of course, since not all modes fit very well together, they begin to generate interferences, and, in fact, it's the interferences between ways of classifying things that begin to generate a form that interests me.[32]

Magellan: At the Gates of Death
  Part I: The Red Gate (16mm, 54 min., color, silent).
  Part II: The Green Gate (16mm, 52 min., color, silent).
Otherwise Unexplained Fires (16mm, 14 min., color, silent).
Cold Walks (16mm, 7:30 min., color, silent, unreleased).
Not the First Time (16mm, 6 min., color, silent).
All in Good Time (16mm, 8 min., color, silent, unreleased).
Time Out of Mind (16mm, 7 min., color, silent, unreleased).
The Test of Time (16mm, 14 min., color, silent, unreleased).
For Georgia O'Keeffe (16mm, 3:30 min., color, silent).
Quaternion (16mm, 4:30 min., color, silent).
Procession (16mm, 4 min., color, silent).
Dreams of Magellan:
  Part I: Ludus Luminus,
  Chromaticus (16mm, 27:30 min., color, silent, unreleased).

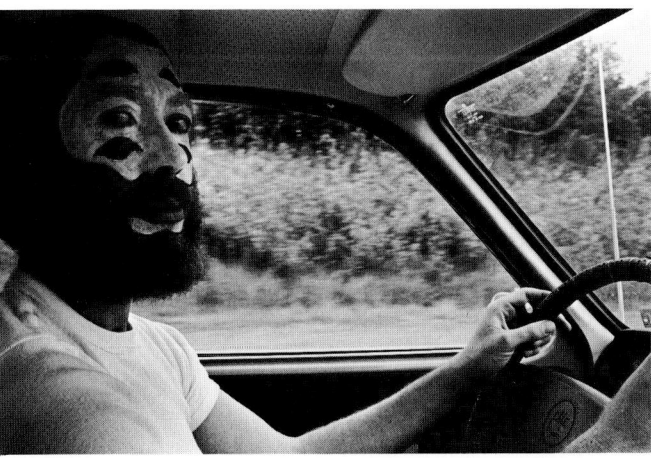

Marion Faller, Portrait of the artist, 1974, black and white photograph, 6¼ x 9½

1977 Designs, with Woody Vasulka, Digital Arts Laboratory at Center for Media Study, SUNY at Buffalo to formulate digital computer hardware and software for graphic, sound and text manipulation.

> Speaking as a working artist, I've never seen a computer-generated image that I found very interesting. But, on the other hand, computers have been used successfully for making music, electronic music. As a musical tool, the computer has matured. As an image tool, however, it is still young. However, we're optimistic . . . Things have their natural time, they come and go. The computer will hopefully only make certain tasks in art obsolete—certain loathsome tasks.[33]

Retrospective of films at Rijksmuseum, Otterlo, The Netherlands [Oct.] Receives grant from American Film Institute for work on *Magellan* cycle. Receives grant from New York State Council on the Arts and Media Study/Buffalo. Again spends Christmas holidays filming in Puerto Rico.

1978 Retrospective of films at Stedelijk van Abbemuseum and Filmuseum, Amsterdam [Sept.].
Continues work on *Magellan:*

> In an interview with James Joyce which took place in the '30s, after *Ulysses* had been in print for several years, Joyce remarked that after all this time, no one has yet noted that the book was funny. I consider the *Magellan* cycle a comedy.
> Comic art resolves itself in favor of the protagonist. In this case the protagonist is the spectator. I would hope he would have some positive experience—like pleasure.[34]

1979 Designs, with colleagues at Digital Arts Lab, DEMON, an interpretive microcomputer language for editing and modifying audio-data and manipulating sound and VOX, a language for voice synthesis. Reviewer for SUNY Research Foundation (through 1983). Resumes work in xerography.
Gloria! (16mm, 10 min., color, sound). First computer generated film.
More Than Meets the Eye (16 mm, 7:30 min., color, silent).

Completes:
The Birth of Magellan: Dreams of Magellan: Parts I–VI, 1977–1979 (16mm, 1 hr. 48 min., color, sound).
Invited as visiting artist by Light Work to use color Xerox machine at Everson Museum of Art, Syracuse, New York, where he makes *False Impressions,* with Marion Faller. Begins printing color xerographs, *By Any Other Name* (six series, 1979–1983).

1980 Work honored in *Ten Years of Independent Film and Video,* Whitney Museum of American Art, New York.
Completes:
The Birth of Magellan: Mindfall, Parts I–VII, 1977–80 (16mm, 2 hrs. 33 min., color, sound).
The Birth of Magellan: Fourteen Cadenzas, 1977–80 (16mm, 1 hr. 17 min., color, sound).

Begins work on *R* (16mm, color, sound, uncompleted). With students at Digital Arts Laboratory, designs IMAGO, computer language for creating high resolution video imagery in sixteen colors:

> I'm sick and tired of the 'two cultures,' of that gulf between what is called science on the one hand, and what is called art on the other. Artists who think there is some great and fundamental gulf between science and art think in terms of a repulsive little cartoon in which the sciences are cold and unfeeling and the arts are warm and emotional. Of course, I get to be typed as an icicle, Frosty the Snowman with his cinematic calculus, which mightily annoys me and hurts my feelings. On the other hand, scientists think of the sciences as straightforward and the arts as abounding in mystery. And none of these things is true. In the sciences in particular, and in the queen of the sciences—mathematics—and, indeed, in the almost celestial, clumsily-named intellectual entity computer science, which has already made mathematics a kind of subset of its own interests, nothing is quite as rampant as a sort of undefined gut aestheticization . . .[35]

1981 Receives grant from New York State Council on the Arts and Light Work, Syracuse, New York, for the production

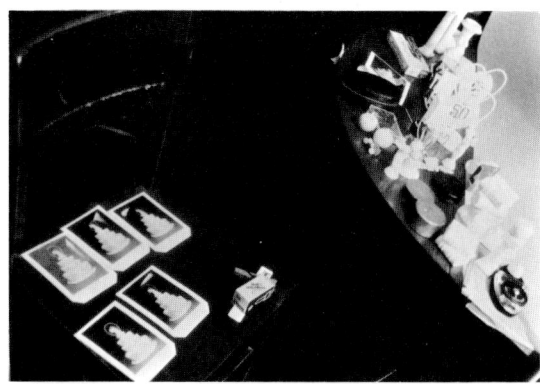

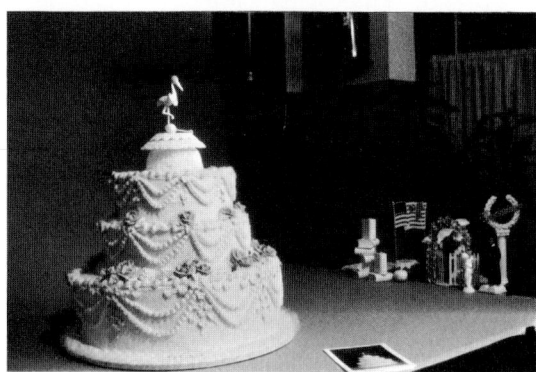

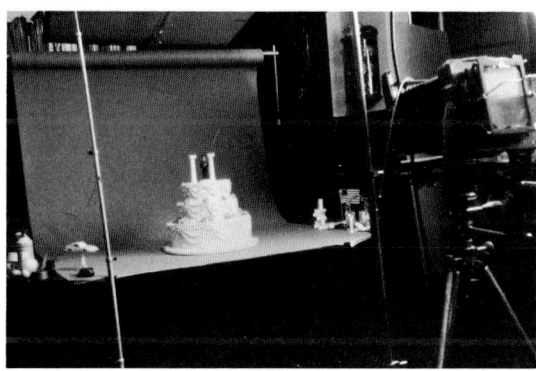

Marion Faller, three production shots of cat. 35. *Rites of Passage*, 1983, black and white photographs from color transparencies, each 4 x 6

of *ADSVMVS ABSVMVS*. In summer, shoots *Protective Coloration*, a project long under consideration. Begins to assemble earlier photographic work and to complete unfinished works.

1982   In August, moves to Buffalo with Marion and Will.

1983   Made full professor, SUNY at Buffalo. In November, shoots *Rites of Passage* with Marion Faller. Receives Service to the Field grant from National Endowment for the Arts and SUNY at Buffalo for the construction of frame buffer for Digital Arts Laboratory and design of software:

> It has never before been possible for an artist to explore the uses of computers in art with the intimacy and flexibility that the painter or writer takes for granted, and finds the necessary condition of creative work . . . [we propose to design] a hospitable computing environment for the arts, emphasizing the notion of the computer as a personal creative tool.[36]

Receives grant from New York State Council on the Arts and Media Study/Buffalo for work on *R*.

1984   Dies at home on March 30, of lung cancer.

> The mind is a labyrinth. Sometimes it's just one of those very dull labyrinths where the rat runs around one way and he gets an electric shock and the other way he gets a grain of corn; and then there are other days when it's a labyrinth that consists of a straight line . . . I have all the time the sense that there are perilous random seas that surround all our discourses. We really are on little rafts, and maybe we make it to the Fiji islands and maybe we don't, but in trying to bring back something of the quality of the journey, we have got to talk about more than the raft . . . If there is not in the tale something of the quality of the random seas as well, then you have essentially falsified it . . . You have, in the phrase of an old friend of mine, snipped off all the necktie ends to make it look as though the suitcase closed neatly. And . . . something I'm more interested in now [as I'm perhaps older or more confident or less reticent or something like that], is getting a sense of that into my work.[37]

NOTES TO CHRONOLOGY

1. Hollis Frampton, transcript entitled "Hollis Frampton on Hollis Frampton," from course at SUNY at Buffalo, *Special Topics: Filmmakers,* session on Sept. 16, 1977, pp. 3-4.
2. Bill Simon, "Talking About Magellan: An Interview with Hollis Frampton," *Millennium Film Journal* (New York), nos. 7-8-9, fall/winter 1980, p. 7.
3. Frampton, "Hollis Frampton on Hollis Frampton," Sept. 16, 1977, p. 11.
4. Michael Snow, "Hollis Frampton Interviewed by Michael Snow," *Film Culture* (New York), nos. 48-49, winter/spring 1970, p. 6.
5. Bruce Jenkins and Susan Krane, interview with the artist, Mar. 7, 1984, Buffalo, New York, p. 6.
6. Jenkins and Krane, interview, p. 5.
7. Frampton, "Hollis Frampton on Hollis Frampton," Sept. 16, 1977, p. 28.
8. Ibid., p. 32.
9. Ibid., p. 33.
10. Ibid., p. 34.
11. Artist's resumé, c. 1975-1976, p. 2.
12. Frampton, "Hollis Frampton on Hollis Frampton," Sept. 16, 1977, pp. 34-35.
13. Ibid., pp. 38-39.
14. Ibid., pp. 40-41.
15. Dorothy C. Miller, ed., *Sixteen Americans* (New York: The Museum of Modern Art, 1959), p. 76.
16. Artist's resumé, c. 1975-1976, p. 2.
17. Scott MacDonald, "Interview with Hollis Frampton: The Early Years," *October* (Cambridge, Massachusetts), no. 12, spring 1980, p. 105.
18. Carl Andre and Hollis Frampton, *Carl Andre/Hollis Frampton: 12 Dialogues, 1962-1963,* Benjamin H. D. Buchloh, ed., (Halifax: The Press of the Nova Scotia College of Art and Design and New York: New York University Press, 1981).
19. Ibid., p. XI.
20. Dorothy C. Miller, ed., *Americans 1963* (New York: The Museum of Modern Art, 1963), p. 87.
21. Scott MacDonald, "Interview with Hollis Frampton," *Film Culture* (New York), nos. 67-68-69, 1979, p. 159.
22. Snow, "Hollis Frampton Interviewed by Michael Snow," p. 8.
23. MacDonald, "Interview with Hollis Frampton: The Early Years," p. 109.
24. Ibid., p. 11.
25. Simon Field and Peter Sainsbury. "Zorns Lemma and Hapax Legomena: Interview with Hollis Frampton." *Afterimage* (London), no. 4, autumn 1972, p. 66.
26. Lucy Fischer, " Frampton and the Magellan Metaphor," *American Film* (Washington, D.C.), vol. 4, no. 7, May 1979, p. 63.
27. Jonas Mekas, "Movie Journal," *The Village Voice* (New York), vol. 18, no. 2, Jan. 11, 1973, p. 67.
28. Artist's statement of intention for [unspecified] grant application, c. 1976, p. 1.
29. MacDonald, "Interview with Hollis Frampton," p. 170.
30. Field and Sainsbury "Zorns Lemma and Hapax Legomena: Interview with Hollis Frampton," p. 50.
31. Hollis Frampton, transcript of untitled lecture, Dec. 1977, The Carpenter Center for the Visual Arts, Harvard University, Cambridge, Massachusetts, pp. 5-6.
32. Mitch Tuchman, "Frampton at the Gates: Interview by Mitch Tuchman," *Film Comment* (New York), vol. 13, no. 5, Sept.-Oct. 1977, p. 58.
33. Charlotte Johnson, "UB Computer Art Course Aims to Create a New Tool for Artists," *The Courier-Express* (Buffalo), Oct. 24, 1980, p. 9.
34. Amy Taubin, "Tilting at Linearity," *The Soho Weekly News* (New York), Jan. 17, 1980, p. 58.
35. Scott MacDonald, transcript of "Interview with Hollis Frampton: *Zorns Lemma,*" fall 1977-spring 1978, Eaton, New York, pp. 10-11.
36. Artist's text for grant proposal to the National Endowment for the Arts, 1983, p. 2.
37. Field and Sainsbury, "Zorns Lemma and Hapax Legomena: Interview with Hollis Frampton," p. 60.

NOTES TO ILLUSTRATIONS

1. Hollis Frampton in Carl Andre and Hollis Frampton, "On Forty Photographs and Consecutive Matters, Part I: January 26, 1963," in *Carl Andre/Hollis Frampton: 12 Dialogues, 1962-1963* (Halifax: The Press of the Nova Scotia College of Art and Design and New York: New York University Press, 1981), p. 57.
2. Hollis Frampton, "Eadweard Muybridge: Fragments of a Tesseract," *Artforum* (New York), vol. 11, no. 7, Mar. 1973, p. 50.
3. Hollis Frampton in Scott MacDonald, "Interview with Hollis Frampton," *Film Culture* (New York), nos. 67-68-69, 1979, p. 159. For artist's further comments on the work, see *Film Culture* (New York), nos. 53-54-55, spring 1972, p. 114.
4. Maurice Tuchman, interview with the artist, Nov. 22, 1971, New York, p. 18.
5. Hollis Frampton, "Eadweard Muybridge: Fragments of a Tesseract," p. 51.
6. Hollis Frampton, transcript entitled "Hollis Frampton on Hollis Frampton," from course at SUNY at Buffalo, *Special Topics: Filmmakers,* session on Sept. 28, 1977, p. 89.

SELECTED EXHIBITIONS

ONE-ARTIST EXHIBITIONS

1965   Goddard College, Plainfield, Vermont. [Nov.]

Peninsula Gallery, Palo Alto, California. [July]

1966   APB Gallery, Tacoma, Washington. [Apr.]

1970   Konrad Fischer Gallery, Dusseldorf. [May]

1975   Visual Studies Workshop Gallery, Rochester, New York. *Sixteen Studies from VEGETABLE LOCOMOTION,* May 2–30. [with Marion Faller]

1982   Light Work/ Community Darkrooms Gallery, Syracuse, New York. *Hollis Frampton,* Apr. 16–May 15.

Visual Studies Workshop Gallery, Rochester, New York. *ADSVMVS ABSVMVS,* Nov. 5–27.

1983   CEPA Gallery, Buffalo. *ADSVMVS ABSVMVS,* Apr. 9–30.

[Included are exhibitions of still photographic work. The numerous exhibitions of Frampton's films have not been listed. Major showings of the films are cited in the chronology.]

GROUP EXHIBITIONS

1969   Goddard College, Plainfield, Vermont. [Mar.]

1970   SVA Gallery, School of Visual Arts, New York. [Jan.]

1973   Yale University Art Gallery, New Haven, Connecticut. *Options and Alternatives: Some Directions in Recent Art,* Apr. 4–May 16. Catalogue, artist's text ["A Stipulation of Terms from Maternal Hopi"], texts by Anne Coffin Hanson, Klaus Kertess, Annette Michelson.

1976   Sidney Janis Gallery, New York. *The Photographer and the Artist,* Feb. 7–Mar. 6. Catalogue.

Carlson Gallery, University of Bridgeport, Connecticut. *A.C. Champagne: Photographic Images from the Collection of A.D. Coleman.* [Nov.–Dec.]

1977   Contemporary Arts Gallery, New York University, New York. *The 1st Postcard Show.* [May]

Experiencenter, Dayton Art Institute, Ohio. *Photo-Images,* Mar. 6–June 10.

International Museum of Photography at George Eastman House, Rochester, New York. *Locations in Time,* Feb. 18–Apr. 10.

1979   The Picker Art Gallery, Colgate University, Hamilton, New York. *Explorations in Color Xerography: The Electrostatic Print as a Creative Medium,* Sept. 14–Oct. 7.

1980   The Picker Art Gallery, Colgate University, Hamilton, New York. *The Gary M. Hoffer '74 Memorial Photography Collection,* May 24–Sept. 28.

1981   International Museum of Photography at George Eastman House, Rochester, New York. *Acquisitions: 1973–80,* June 12–Sept. 13. Catalogue.

Macalester Galleries, Macalester College, St. Paul, Minnesota. *Animated Images/Still Life,* Jan. 8–30.

1982   The Museum of Fine Arts, Houston. *Target III: In Sequence,* July 23–Sept. 19. Catalogue, texts by Anne Wilkes Tucker and Leroy Searle.

1983   The Addison Gallery of American Art, Phillips Academy, Andover, Massachusetts. *Tradition/Transition/New Vision,* May 13–June 19. Catalogue, introduction by Christopher C. Cook.

Henry Art Gallery, University of Washington, Seattle. *Radical Rational/Space Time: Idea Networks in Photography,* Mar. 11–May 15. Catalogue, introduction by Douglas Wadden, text by Paul Berger and Leroy Searle.

SELECTED BIBLIOGRAPHY

BY THE ARTIST

1968   "Phenakistiscope." In *SMS*. New York: The Letter Edged in Black Press, Inc., issue 4, Aug. [Collaborative artists' "book;" other contributions by Arman Fernandez, Paul Bergfold, John Cage, On Kawara, Roy Lichtenstein, Lil Picard, Rotella, Robert Stanley, Robert Watts, Princess Winifred, LaMonte Young, Marian Zazeelá]

1969   "Carl Andre." In *Carl Andre*. The Hague: Haags Gemeentemuseum, pp. 7-13.

Frampton, Hollis, Ken Jacobs and Michael Snow. "Filmmakers Versus the Museum of Modern Art." *Filmmakers' Newsletter* (New York), vol. 2, no. 7, May, pp. 1-2.

1971   "For a Metahistory of Film: Commonplace Notes and Hypotheses." *Artforum* (New York), vol. 10, no. 1, Sept., pp. 32-35. Reprinted in *Circles of Confusion: Film, Photography, Video Texts 1968-1980*. Rochester, New York: Visual Studies Workshop Press, 1983, pp. 107-116.

1972   "A Pentagram for Conjuring the Narrative." In *Form and Structure in Recent Film*. Vancouver: Vancouver Art Gallery. Reprinted in *Circles of Confusion*, pp. 59-68.

"Digressions on the Photographic Agony." *Artforum* (New York), vol. 11, no. 3, Nov., pp. 43-51. Reprinted in *Circles of Confusion*, pp. 177-191.

HAPAX LEGOMENA: Notes for a Screening on 2/16/72. New York: Filmmakers' Cinematheque. [Program notes]

"Meditations Around Paul Strand." *Artforum* (New York), vol. 10, no. 6, Feb., pp. 52-57. Reprinted in *Circles of Confusion*, pp. 127-136.

"(Nostalgia) VOICE-OVER NARRATION FOR A FILM OF THAT NAME, Dated: 1/8/71." *Film Culture* (New York), nos. 53-54-55, spring, pp. 105-111.

"Notes on (Nostalgia)." *Film Culture* (New York), nos. 53-54-55, spring, p. 114.

1973   "Eadweard Muybridge: Fragments of a Tesseract." *Artforum* (New York), vol. 11, no. 7, Mar., pp. 43-52. Reprinted in *Circles of Confusion*, pp. 69-80.

Poetic Justice. Rochester, New York: Visual Studies Workshop Press. [Artist's book]

"Stan and Jane Brakhage, Talking." *Artforum* (New York), vol. 11, no. 5, Jan., pp. 72-79.

"A Stipulation of Terms from Maternal Hopi." In *Options and Alternatives: Some Directions in Recent Art*. New Haven, Connecticut: Yale University Art Gallery. Reprinted in: *Film Dimension*, Apr. 18, 1975, pp. 10ff [supplement to *The Spectrum* (Boston: Boston University)]; *Afterimage* (London) nos. 8-9, spring 1981, pp. 64-69; *Circles of Confusion*, pp. 171-176.

1974   "Incisions in History/Segments of Eternity." *Artforum* (New York), vol. 13, no. 2, Oct., pp. 39-50. Reprinted in *Circles of Confusion*, pp. 87-106.

"The Withering Away of the State of Art." *Artforum* (New York), vol. 13, no. 4, Dec., pp. 50-55. Reprinted in *Circles of Confusion*, pp. 161-170.

1975   Frampton, Hollis and Carl Andre. "Three Dialogues on Photography 1962-1963." In *Interfunktionen No. 12*. Cologne: B. H. D. Buchloh, pp. 1-12.

"Fictcryptokrimsographology." In Les Krims, *Fictcryptokrimsographs*. Buffalo: Humpy Press, Inc.

"Letter to the Editor." *Artforum* (New York), vol. 13, no. 7, Mar., p. 9.

1976   "Letter from Hollis Frampton to Peter Gidal on *Zorns Lemma* [25 August 1972]." In *Structural Film Anthology*. Peter Gidal, ed. London: British Film Institute, pp. 75-77. Reprint 1978.

"Notes on Composing in Film." *October* (Cambridge, Massachusetts), no. 1, spring, pp. 104-110. Reprinted in *Circles of Confusion*, pp. 117-125.

1978   "A Lecture." In *The Avant-Garde Film: A Reader of Theory and Criticism*. P. Adams Sitney, ed. New York: New York University Press, pp. 275-280.

"Impromptus on Edward Weston: Everything in its Place." *October* (Cambridge, Massachusetts), no. 5, summer, pp. 48-69. Reprinted in *Circles of Confusion*, pp. 137-160.

"Mind over Matter." *October* (Cambridge, Massachusetts), no. 6, fall, pp. 81-92.

1979   "CPCON: an ALS-8 to CP/M File Converter." *Dr. Dobb's Journal* (Menlo Park, California), #41, vol. 5, no. 1, Sept., pp. 29-33.

1980   *Inconclusions for Patrick Clancy*. Utica, New York: Utica College of Syracuse University. [In exhibition brochure, *Marginal Works: Atopia—No Man's Land*, Mar. 27-Apr. 11]

"Trio." In *Break Glass in Case of Fire*. Oakland, California: Center for Contemporary Music, Mills College.

1981   "Letters: Krims Critique." *Afterimage* (Rochester, New York), vol. 9, nos. 1-2, summer, p. 2.

Frampton, Hollis and Carl Andre. *Carl Andre/Hollis Frampton: 12 Dialogues, 1962-63.* Benjamin H. D. Buchloh, ed. Halifax: The Press of the Nova Scotia College of Art and Design and New York: New York University Press. [Photographs by Hollis Frampton]

1982 *ADSVMVS ABSVMVS.* Rochester, New York: Visual Studies Workshop Press. [Published in conjunction with photographic portfolio *ADSVMVS ABSVMVS*]

1983 *Circles of Confusion: Film, Photography, Video Texts 1968–1980.* Rochester, New York: Visual Studies Workshop Press. Foreword by Annette Michelson.

INTERVIEWS WITH THE ARTIST

1970 Snow, Michael. "Hollis Frampton Interviewed by Michael Snow." *Film Culture* (New York), nos. 48-49, winter/spring, pp. 6-12.

1972 Field, Simon and Peter Sainsbury. "ZORNS LEMMA AND HAPAX LEGOMENA, Interview with Hollis Frampton." *Afterimage* (London), no. 4, autumn, pp. 44-47.

1973 Mekas, Jonas. "Movie Journal." *The Village Voice* (New York), vol. 18, no. 2, Jan. 11, p. 67.

Mekas, Jonas. "Movie Journal." *The Village Voice* (New York), vol. 18, no. 3, Jan. 18, pp. 70-71.

1976 Gidal, Peter. "Interview with Hollis Frampton." In *Structural Film Anthology.* Peter Gidal, ed. London: British Film Institute, pp. 64-72. Reprint 1978.

1977 Tuchman, Mitch. "Frampton at the Gates: interview with Mitch Tuchman." *Film Comment* (New York), vol. 13, no. 5, Sept.–Oct., pp. 55-59.

1979 MacDonald, Scott. "Interview with Hollis Frampton." *Film Culture* (New York), nos. 67-68-69, pp. 158-180.

MacDonald, Scott. "Interview with Hollis Frampton: ZORNS LEMMA." *Quarterly Review of Film Studies* (Pleasantville, New York), vol. 4, no. 1, winter, pp. 23-37.

1980 MacDonald, Scott. "Interview with Hollis Frampton: The Early Years." *October* (Cambridge, Massachusetts), no. 12, spring, pp. 103-126.

Simon, Bill. "Talking About Magellan: An Interview with Hollis Frampton." *Millennium Film Journal* (New York), nos. 7-8-9, fall/winter, pp. 4-26.

ON THE ARTIST

[A complete bibliography on the artist's films may be obtained through Anthology Film Archives, New York.]

1971 Bershen, Wanda. "Zorns Lemma." *Artforum* (New York), vol. 10, no. 1, Sept., pp. 41-45.

1972 Brakhage, Stan. "Stan Brakhage on Hollis Frampton." In *Form and Structure in Recent Film.* Vancouver: Vancouver Art Gallery.

1974 Mekas, Jonas. "Movie Journal." *The Village Voice* (New York), vol. 19, no. 14, Apr. 4, p. 87.

Mekas, Jonas. "Movie Journal." *The Village Voice* (New York), vol. 19, no. 38, Sept. 19, p. 85.

1976 Gidal, Peter. "Notes on *Zorns Lemma.*" In *Structural Film Anthology.* Peter Gidal, ed. London: British Film Institute, pp. 73-74. Reprint 1978.

1977 Fischer, Lucy. "Magellan: Navigating the Hemispheres." *University Film Study Center Newsletter, Supplement* (Cambridge, Massachusetts), vol. 7, no. 5, June, pp. 5-10.

Jenkins, Bruce. "Hollis Frampton's *Autumnal Equinox:* A Modernist Film and Its Pictorial Past." In *Film Studies Annual: Part Two, Film: Historical–Theoretical Speculations.* Pleasantville, New York: Redgrave Publishing Company, pp. 75-81.

1978 MacDonald, Scott. "Hollis Frampton's *Hapax Legomena.*" *Afterimage* (Rochester, New York), vol. 5, no. 7, Jan., pp. 8-13.

Sitney, P. Adams. "Autobiography in Avant-Garde Film." *Millennium Film Journal* (New York), vol. 1, no. 1, spring, pp. 86-90.

1979 Fischer, Lucy. "Frampton and the Magellan Metaphor." *American Film* (Washington, D.C.), vol. 4, no. 7, May, pp. 58-63.

Sitney, P. Adams, ed. *The Avant-Garde Film: A Reader of Theory and Criticism.* New York: New York University Press, pp. xxxi-xliv, 228-232, and passim.

1980 Taubin, Amy. "Tilting at Linearity." *The Soho Weekly News* (New York), Jan. 17, p. 58.

1983 Bannon, Anthony. "Frampton's Photographic Memories." *The Buffalo News,* Apr. 8, "Gusto" section, p. 22.

Michelson, Annette. "TIME OUT OF MIND: a foreword." In *Circles of Confusion: Film, Photography, Video Texts 1968-1980.* Rochester, New York: Visual Studies Workshop Press, pp. 13-21.

CATALOGUE OF THE EXHIBITION

All works are in private collections unless otherwise noted. Dimensions are given in inches with height preceding width.

The symbol □ indicates catalogue illustration(s); ◇ indicates a recent reprint. The artist's working notations are given in parentheses.

1.
The Secret World of Frank Stella,
1958–1962
eight from a series of fifty-two
black and white photographs
each matted to 17 x 14

◇ □a. *#3*
9½ x 7½
(28 painting Getty Tomb)
b. *#11*
9½ x 7½
(432 Leonardo after Vitruvius)
□c. *#14*
7½ x 9 7/16
(360 "photos")
◇ d. *#26*
7½ x 9 7/16
(485 Franz Kline)
□e. *#33*
7½ x 9 7/16
(440 yogi & rubberplant, 3/17/61)
f. *#42*
9½ x 7½
(163 Cedar Street Tavern)
g. *#50*
9½ x 7½
(084 Mallary)
□h. *#52*
7½ x 9 7/16
(444 Marat, 3/17/61)

2.
Official Portraits, 1959
three of a series of four
black and white photographs
each matted to 24 x 20
◇ □a. *Frank Stella*
16⅝ x 10½
(10/9/59)
◇ □b. *Richard Meier*
16⅝ x 10½
(10/27/59)
◇ □c. *Walter Darby Bannard*
16⅝ x 10½

3.
Ways to Purity, 1959
series of twelve drymounted
black and white photographs
each matted to 17 x 14
□a. *1. 488 Broadway*
9 13/16 x 7¾
(hexagons)
□b. *2. Thompson at Spring Street*
7½ x 9½
(Barnett Newman/hand ball court)
□c. *3. "40" Crosby Street*
9½ x 7½
(Minor White/brick wall)
□d. *4. 154 Spring Street*
9½ x 7 9/16
(A. Burri/screen door)
□e. *5. 400 West Broadway*
9½ x 7 9/16
("axe")
□f. *6. 49 Prince Street*
9½ x 7½
(collage window)
□g. *7. 409 West Broadway*
7½ x 9½
(letter B)
□h. *8. 137 Prince Street*
9 7/16 x 7 9/16
(Motherwell/fish skeleton)
□i. *9. 51 Crosby Street*
9 7/16 x 7 9/16
(Lauterwasser [*sic*]
/aluminum door)
□j. *10. 464 Broome Street*
9 7/16 x 7 9/16
(circles)
□k. *11. 450 Broome Street*
9 7/16 x 7 9/16
(Louise Nevelson/stonework)
□l. *12. 366 West Broadway; 97 Crosby Street*
8 x 7¼
(terminal hoax)

4.
□*Untitled,* 1961–1962
black and white photograph
7½ x 9⅞, mounted to 14 x 18

5.
Untitled, 1961–1962
black and white photograph
7½ x 9⅞, mounted to 14 x 18

6.
◇ *Carl Andre,* 1962
black and white photograph
7⅜ x 7⅜, matted to 17 x 14

7.
□*The Temptation of St. Anthony,* 1962
7a.–7c.: third triad from a series of
four triads of black and white
cameraless photographs from
manipulated negatives
each 24 x 20
[printed 1984]
(7,8,9)

8.
Word Pictures [working title *Words*],
1962–1963
eight from a series of an undetermined number of black and white
photographs
each matted to 14 x 17
◇ a. *Air*
4⅝ x 7
◇ b. *Corn*
4⅝ x 7
◇ c. *No*
4⅝ x 7
◇ d. *Queens*
4½ x 7
◇ □e. *Rock*
3 15/16 x 6
◇ □f. *Sun*
4⅝ x 6 15/16
◇ □g. *Time*
4⅝ x 6½
◇ h. *Waste*
3 15/16 x 6

9.
Lee Bontecou, 1963
black and white photograph
7½ x 9½, matted to 14 x 17
(April 1963)

10.
□*John Chamberlain,* 1963
black and white photograph
7½ x 9½, matted to 14 x 17
(April 1963)

11.
John Chamberlain, 1963
black and white photograph
7½ x 9½, matted to 14 x 17

12.
Friedel Dzubas, 1963
black and white photograph
7½ x 9½, matted to 14 x 17
(April 1963)

13.
Lee Lozano, 1963
black and white photograph
7½ x 9½, matted to 14 x 17

14.
Robert Morris, 1963
black and white photograph
9½ x 7½, matted to 17 x 14
(April 1963)

15.
□*Robert Morris* [studio], 1963
black and white photograph
7½ x 9½, matted to 14 x 17
(April 1963)

16.
□*Larry Poons*, 1963
black and white photograph
7½ x 9½, matted to 14 x 17
(April 1963)

17.
Larry Poons, 1963
black and white photograph
14 x 10⅞, matted to 16 x 20
(L. Poons, T. Poons and Spoons, 10/63)

18.
□*James Rosenquist*, 1963
black and white photograph
9½ x 7½, matted to 17 x 14
(Palm Sunday, 1963)

19.
James Rosenquist, 1963
black and white photograph
9½ x 7½, matted to 17 x 14
(Palm Sunday, 1963)

20.
She Was [a.k.a. *Terry*], 1964
drymark on newspaper, tape
9⅛ x 11⁷⁄₁₆, matted to 16 x 20
[made for Terry Brook in 1964]

21.
◇ □*Spaghetti*, 1964
diptych, Ektachrome photographs
each 11 x 14, assembled and matted to 32 x 24

22.
One Poons Dot, c. 1965
black and white photograph
10 x 8, matted to 17 x 14

23.
A Visitation of Insomnia, 1970–1973
series of twenty-four black and white drymounted photographs
each 10⅝ x 10⅝, assembled and matted in six parts, each 16 x 48
a. nos. 1–4
b. nos. 5–8
c. nos. 9–12
d. nos. 13–16
e. nos. 17–20
f. nos. 21–24
[originally printed 1970, revised 1973]
□nos. 5, 12, 15, 20

24.
The nostalgia *Portfolio*, 1971
series of thirteen black and white photographs with texts
each matted to 17 x 14
[assembled and destroyed in 1971, reprinted and fabricated as portfolio 1984]

□a. *0*, n.d.
7⁵⁄₁₆ x 9⁷⁄₁₆
(Darkroom)
□b. *1*, 1958–1959
7⅜ x 9½
(Andre/Metronome, Dec. 1958–Jan. 1959)
□c. *2*, 1959
9½ x 7½
(Self-portrait, March 1959)
□d. *3*, 1960
8⁹⁄₁₆ x 7½
(Carpenter's Window, Sept. 1960)
□e. *4*, 1961
7½ x 7½
(Cast of Thousands, May 1961)
□f. *5*, 1962
8⁹⁄₁₆ x 7½
(Stella-Smoke Ring, Nov. 1962)
□g. *6*, 1963
9½ x 7½
(Rosenquist, Palm Sunday, 1963)
[vintage print incorporated in portfolio]
□h. *7*, 1963
9½ x 7½
("New Name", June 6, 1963)
□i. *8*, 1964
9½ x 7½
(Toilets, Feb. 1964)
□j. *9*, 1964
7½ x 9½
(Spaghetti, Aug. 1964)
□k. *10*, 1965
7 x 9⁷⁄₁₆
(M. Snow)
□l. *11*, 1965
9½ x 7½
(Poons Reclining, Spring 1965)
[vintage print incorporated in portfolio]
□m. *12*, n.d.
9⅜ x 6¹⁵⁄₁₆
(Grapefruits)
□n. Text
[Jan. 8, 1971]

25.
Reasonable Facsimiles, 1971
series of seven laminated xerographs
original paper size 14 x 8½
each matted to 24 x 20
[© 1982]

□a. *Authentication*
applied color on xerograph
13⅝ x 8⁷⁄₁₆
□b. *Matching Accessories*
applied color on xerograph
13¾ x 8⅜

☐c. *Means and Ends Belong to Different Sets*
applied color on xerograph, collage
13⅝ x 8⁷⁄₁₆
☐d. *Notes for a Project Abandoned in 1963*
applied color on xerograph
13¹¹⁄₁₆ x 8⁷⁄₁₆
☐e. *Rate of Exchange*
applied color on xerograph, collage
8⁷⁄₁₆ x 13¹¹⁄₁₆
☐f. *A Reminder*
applied color on xerograph
13¹¹⁄₁₆ x 8⅞
(5/27/71, cancelled 6/5/71)
☐g. *Terminology*
applied color on xerograph, collage
8⅜ x 13¹¹⁄₁₆

26.
☐Untitled, 1972
black and white photograph
5½ x 8¾, matted to 14 x 17
[made with a wide-angle pinhole camera, paper negative: date questionable]

27.
☐*Stopping Down*, 1973
enlargement from copy negative of photo booth picture
19½ x 5⁵⁄₁₆, matted to 30 x 16
(March 11, 1973)
[shot 1973, enlarged 1984]

28.
Sixteen Studies from VEGETABLE LOCOMOTION, 1975
with Marion Faller
series of sixteen silverprints
each 11 x 14, matted to 16 x 20

☐a. *14. Gourds vanishing* [var. "Mixed Ornamental"]
☐b. *33. Zucchini squash encountering sawhorse* [var. "Dread"]
☐c. *39. Sunflower reclining* [var. "Mammoth Russian"]
☐d. *121. Scallop squash revolving* [var. "Patty Pan"]
☐e. *260. Savoy cabbage flying* [var. "Chieftain"]
☐f. *357. Summer squash undergoing surgery* [var. "Yellow Straightneck"]
☐g. *481. Mature radishes bathing* [var. "Black Spanish"]
☐h. *482. Pumpkin emptying* [var. "Cinderella"]
☐i. *484. Winter squash vacillating* [var. "True Hubbard"]
☐j. *519. Tomatoes descending a ramp* [var. "Roma"]
☐k. *537. Watermelon falling* [var. "New Hampshire Midget"]
☐l. *601. Sweet corn disrobing* [var. "Early Sunglow"]
☐m. *605. Dill bundling* [var. "Rural Splendor"]
☐n. *668. Beets assembling* [var. "Detroit Dark Red"]
☐o. *709. Carrot ejaculating* [var. "Chantenay"]
☐p. *782. Apple advancing* [var. "Northern Spy"]
Collection of the Albright-Knox Art Gallery

29.
By Any Other Name—Series 1, 1979
series of twelve color xerographs, paper size 8½ x 14, each matted to 16 x 20, all 1/14

a. *Grapefruit Juice Brand Florida Bluebird*
6⁹⁄₁₆ x 13³⁄₁₆
☐b. *Tuna Brand Chunk Light Bumblebees*
1½ x 10⅝
☐c. *Chili Bean Brand Blue Boys*
4⅛ x 9⅞
d. *Salmon Brand Kitty With Sauce*
1⁹⁄₁₆ x 10⁹⁄₁₆
☐e. *Peeled Tomato Brand Pine Cones*
4⅛ x 9⁹⁄₁₆
f. *Sweet Pea Brand Green Giants*
4¼ x 9⅞
g. *Clam Brand Whole Baby Geishas*
3¹¹⁄₁₆ x 8⁵⁄₁₆
h. *Bamboo Shoot Brand Globes*
5⁵⁄₁₆ x 7¹¹⁄₁₆
i. *Drum Stick Brand Aeroplanes*
4⁵⁄₁₆ x 9⅜
j. *Rice Vermicelli Brand Egrets*
4⅜ x 10⅞
☐k. *Sake Brand Lotus Flowers*
3⁹⁄₁₆ x 4⁷⁄₁₆
l. *Thick Soy Sauce Brand Pistols*
3¼ x 8⁹⁄₁₆

30.
False Impressions, 1979
with Marion Faller
seven from a series of twenty-one color xerographs, paper size 14 x 8½, all 6/14

a. *From the Virgin Mary's family album*
12⅝ x 8¼, matted to 20 x 16
☐b. *Uncle Rudy at the fourth cervical vertebra*
13¼ x 8⁵⁄₁₆, matted to 20 x 16
c. *Two exemplary applications of applied color*
13⁹⁄₁₆ x 8⁵⁄₁₆, matted to 20 x 16
☐d. *If Muybridge were alive today, he'd turn over in his grave*
14⅝ x 8¼, matted to 20 x 16

☐e. *Which one is the professional golfer? Hint: check the follow-through*
13¾ x 8¼, matted to 20 x 16
☐f. *An Early Practitioner*
13⅛ x 8⅛, matted to 20 x 16
☐g. *The conquest of culture and nature*
8¼ x 13½, matted to 16 x 20

31.
ADSVMVS ABSVMVS, 1982
series of fourteen Ektacolor photographs with texts,
each matted to 24 x 20, 7/14
[© 1982]
☐a. *I. WHITE CLOVER (Melilotus alba)*
20 x 16
☐b. *II. JELLY (Physalia physalis)*
16 x 20
☐c. *III. CUTTLEFISH (Rossia mastigophora)*
16 x 20
☐d. *IV. CHIMAERA (Challorhynchus capensis)*
20 x 16
☐e. *V. LOTUS (Nelumbo nucifera)*
20 x 16
☐f. *VI. MIDSHIPMAN (Porichthys notatus)*
16 x 20
☐g. *VII. OYSTER SHELL (Pleurotus ostreatus)*
20 x 16
☐h. *VIII. COMMON GARTER (Thamnophis certalis) and EASTERN COACHWHIP (Masticophis flagellum)*
16 x 20
☐i. *IX. GARDEN TOAD (Bufo americanus)*
16 x 20
☐j. *X. PEPPER (Capsicum longum)*
20 x 16
☐k. *XI. GRASS FROG (Rana pipiens)*
20 x 16
☐l. *XII. MOURNING DOVE (Zenaidura macroura)*
16 x 20
☐m. *XIII. BROWN RAT (Rattus rattus)*
20 x 16
☐n. *XIV. ROSE (Rosa damascena)*
20 x 16

32.
Milk Chocolate, 1982
Ektacolor photograph from black and white negative
10 x 8, matted to 17 x 14, A.P.
[© 1982]

33.
By Any Other Name–Series 2, 1983
series of twelve color xerographs, paper size 8½ x 14
each matted to 16 x 20, all 2/4
a. *Blue Fruit Brand Pines for Salad*
4 x 10
☐b. *Blue Citrus Brand Goose*
2¾ x 2¾
c. *Tomato Brand Peeled Polly*
4¼ x 11
d. *Swiss Cake Brand Little Debbie Rolls*
6⅝ x 13¹³⁄₁₆
☐e. *Lemon Brand Meteors*
8½ x 12⁷⁄₁₆
f. *Raisin Brand Puffed Seeded Sun-Maids*
7⅞ x 12
g. *Starch Brand Sweet Scented Fairies*
5⁵⁄₁₆ x 9¹⁄₁₆
h. *Genuine Chutney Brand Indian Sun*
4⁷⁄₁₆ x 5½
i. *Tea Brand Night-Owl*
11¹⁄₁₆ x 8
j. *Blood Orange Brand Very Good Moors*
8¹¹⁄₁₆ x 7
k. *Deep Sardine Brand Blue Chunks*
1⁷⁄₁₆ x 10½
l. *Pealand Brand Sweet Dykes*
6⅝ x 8¹⁵⁄₁₆

34.
Industrializacion de la Galina [Industrialization of the Chicken], 1984
color xerograph of poster, contact prints from seven found, glass-plate negatives
five photographs: 7 x 5
two photographs: 5 x 7
poster 9¼ x 13¹⁄₁₆
[conceived 1980–1981; fabricated 1984]

35.
☐*Rites of Passage*, 1983–1984
with Marion Faller
35a.–35t.: series of twenty black and white photographs
each 14 x 11, matted to 20 x 16

36.
Protective Coloration, 1984
series of thirty-six Ektacolor photographs
each 4 x 6, assembled and matted to 44 x 54
[shot summer 1981]
☐two details

ACKNOWLEDGMENTS

The impetus for an exhibition of Hollis Frampton's photographic work initially came in the spring of 1982. Edward Bryant, then director of the University Art Museum at the University of New Mexico, approached us to take a show that he and Hollis were discussing. When their plans subsequently had to be abandoned, the Albright-Knox Art Gallery assumed the organization of an exhibition of Frampton's work, to honor his longstanding importance internationally and within the artistic community of Western New York.

Shortly thereafter we asked Bruce Jenkins, film programmer at Media Study/Buffalo and a scholar of Frampton's films, to write the catalogue essay, consult on the exhibition and organize the accompanying film program. Bruce's essay contains a wealth of information and greatly amplifies our understanding of Frampton's art. I thank him for his contributions to the project and for our many conversations about the work.

From the time that we first undertook this project, and Hollis enthusiastically agreed to unveil an extensive body of work that was largely private, there were given complexities. He was caught midstream in the arduous task of moving: vast accumulations of files, negatives, proof sheets, documentation, photographs and notes for numerous unrealized but long-considered projects needed to be unearthed and pondered, in between an already full teaching schedule. Hollis' insight and foresight have been central to the exhibition since its inception—in discussing the question of showing the unknown, but hardly subordinate, non-filmic work of an artist who was well-known, and often typecast, as a "structuralist" filmmaker; in reconstructing lost or destroyed work; in realizing previous ideas; and in making new prints for the exhibition. This exhibition was shaped by our discussions, both casual and formal. After Hollis' sad and untimely death in March of 1984, in the midst of finalizing the exhibition and the accompanying book, numerous individuals, his friends and fellow artists rallied to support the project and supply information. Without their ready and amiable assistance, an exhibition of this scope would not have been possible.

Carl Andre, Walter Darby Bannard, Peter Feinstein, Lucy Flint, Barry Goldensohn, Robert Huot, Richard Meier, Annette Michelson, Gerald Ordover, Paula Pelosi, Ruth Quattlebaum of the Phillips Academy archives, Michael Snow, Frank Stella, Joyce Wieland, and others too numerous to mention helped with a variety of questions and with documentation. Una McClure and Scott MacDonald graciously gave us access to invaluable unpublished materials. Photographer Biff Henrich made numerous proof and exhibition prints with studied precision, and helped with the reconstruction of several works, as did filmmaker Barbara Lattanzi. Janet Jenkins assisted with verifications and other organizational queries. Beth Mulvaney conducted preliminary bibliographical research and Sarah Jerauld organized archival and exhibition materials. Gail Nicholson and Stephen Gallagher greatly assisted us with various other details.

Our thanks also go to the directors and curators of the participating museums for their cooperation and enthusiasm: Russell J. Moore, director, and Connie Fitzsimons, curator, Long Beach Museum of Art; Trish Knodel, director, Filmforum, Los Angeles; Suzanne Delehanty, director, Neuberger Museum, State University of New York at Purchase; Lawrence Miller, director, Annette D. Carlozzi, curator, and Judith A. Sims, director of the Art School, Laguna Gloria Art Museum.

I thank Douglas G. Schultz, director of the Albright-Knox Art Gallery for his continual support and advice. I am, as always, thankful to the entire staff of the museum for their commitment. I am particularly grateful to Georgette M. Hasiotis, editor of publications, for her professional expertise and amiability; to Laura F. Catalano, assistant to publications/registrar's office, for her assistance with various aspects of the project; to Ida Koch, curatorial secretary, for her tenacious work and overall organizational support; and to Karen Spaulding, freelance editor, for her diligence in checking and proofreading the final galleys. Others on the staff who worked on this exhibition are: Judy C. Beecher, public relations officer; Mary Bell, assistant librarian; Bette Blum, administrator/director's office; Sharon Blume, assistant curator of education for school programs; Christine Daniels, secretary; Zbynek Jonak, installer; David Kempf, engineer; John Kushner, building superintendent; Thomas Loonan, audio-visual specialist; Annette Masling, librarian; Peter Muscato, installer; Alba Priore, assistant registrar; Leta K. Stathacos, coordinator of marketing services; Daisy Stroud, assistant to the building superintendent; and Sarah Ulen, registrar.

Roger Conover of the MIT Press provided advice and facilitated the production of this publication. Our gratitude also goes to Christine Narum-Eberle for her cooperation and sensitive design of the book.

I especially wish to thank Marion Faller, Hollis' longtime companion and colleague, for her invaluable assistance and dedication to the project. She was involved with all aspects of the exhibition and responded with generosity to numerous demands at a very difficult time. In Hollis' absence, Marion, Bruce, and I conferred at every step along the way: this project has truly been a collaborative effort. Marion's steadfast participation and guidance have been crucial to the exhibition and the book, as has her generous loan of artwork.

Above all, we are indebted to the artist for sharing with us his vivid memories, munificence and indescribable wit. We hope that this book in some way reflects the many fascinations of his intelligence and his engaging, provocative presence, which are echoed so clearly in his art.

Susan Krane
Curator

775
F   Frampton, Hollis
    Recollections/Recreations